GeoServer Beginner's Guide

Second Edition

Share geospatial data using Open Source standards

Stefano Iacovella

BIRMINGHAM - MUMBAI

GeoServer Beginner's Guide

Second Edition

First published: February 2013

Second edition: October 2017

Production reference: 1111017

Published by Packt Publishing Ltd.
Livery Place
35 Livery Street
Birmingham
B3 2PB, UK.
ISBN 978-1-78829-737-0

www.packtpub.com

Credits

Author
Stefano Iacovella

Reviewer
Colin Henderson

Commissioning Editor
Merint Mathew

Acquisition Editor
Chaitanya Nair

Content Development Editors
Lawrence Veigas
Akshada Iyer

Technical Editor
Tiksha Sarang

Copy Editor
Zainab Bootwala

Project Coordinator
Prajakta Naik

Proofreader
Safis Editing

Indexer
Aishwarya Gangawane

Graphics
Abhinash Sahu

Production Coordinator
Melwyn Dsa

About the Author

Stefano Iacovella is a long-time GIS developer and consultant living in Rome, Italy. He also works as a GIS courses instructor, and he has a PhD. in Geology. Being a very curious person, he developed a deep knowledge of IT technologies, mainly focused on GIS software and related standards. Starting his career as an ESRI employee, he was exposed to and became confident with proprietary GIS software, mainly the ESRI suite of products. In the last 14 years, he has become more and more involved with Open Source software, also integrating it with proprietary software. He loves the Open Source approach and really trusts in the collaboration and sharing of knowledge. He strongly believes in the Open Source idea and constantly manages to spread it out, not limiting it to the GIS sector. He has been using GeoServer since release 1.5 by configuring, deploying, and hacking it on several projects. Other GFOSS projects he uses and likes are GDAL/OGR, PostGIS, QGIS, and OpenLayers. He is the author of the *GeoServer Cookbook*, which consists of a set of recipes to use GeoServer at an advanced level, by Packt, and he has also authored the first edition of this book. When not playing with maps and geometric shapes, he loves reading about science, mainly Physics and Maths, riding his bike, and having fun with his wife and two daughters, Alice and Luisa.

I would like to thank the many people who helped me make this book a real thing. A special mention for GeoServer's developers; they are the wonderful engine without which the software, and hence this book, would not exist. I would like to thank all the people from Packt working on this book. They helped me a lot and were very patient and encouraging when I was facing difficulties matching the deadlines. Special thanks to my technical reviewer, who constantly checked for my errors and omissions. This book is a better one thanks to all their hard work.

Last but not least, I want to express my gratitude to Alessandra, Alice, and Luisa for their support and patience when I was working on this.

About the Reviewer

Colin Henderson is a spatial solutions architect with 18 years of experience working on solutions to complex spatial problems. He is currently the Geospatial Systems Capability Lead for Atkins, one of the world's leading design, engineering, and project management consultancies. He is the Technical Architect and Lead Developer of Atkins' open source-based spatial integration platform, CIRRUSmaps™, a solution built on the best breed of open source spatial software, including PostGIS and OpenLayers, with GeoServer at its heart, and designed from the ground up for deployment in cloud environments. Colin is the author of *Mastering GeoServer*, also published by Packt.

A self-confessed techie, Colin enjoys digging deeper to understand technology and software, and then applying this learning to create innovative solutions to problems. He is currently working on building automated damage detection algorithms using the structured-light depth sensing equipment on iOS platforms. When possible, he likes to "pay it forward" by helping others with their problems, through contributions on GIS Stack Exchange in particular.

www.PacktPub.com

For support files and downloads related to your book, please visit www.PacktPub.com.

Did you know that Packt offers eBook versions of every book published, with PDF and ePub files available? You can upgrade to the eBook version at www.PacktPub.com and as a print book customer, you are entitled to a discount on the eBook copy. Get in touch with us at service@packtpub.com for more details.

At www.PacktPub.com, you can also read a collection of free technical articles, sign up for a range of free newsletters and receive exclusive discounts and offers on Packt books and eBooks.

www.packtpub.com/mapt

Get the most in-demand software skills with Mapt. Mapt gives you full access to all Packt books and video courses, as well as industry-leading tools to help you plan your personal development and advance your career.

Why subscribe?

- Fully searchable across every book published by Packt
- Copy and paste, print, and bookmark content
- On demand and accessible via a web browser

Customer Feedback

Thanks for purchasing this Packt book. At Packt, quality is at the heart of our editorial process. To help us improve, please leave us an honest review on this book's Amazon page at `https://www.amazon.com/dp/1788297377`.

If you'd like to join our team of regular reviewers, you can e-mail us at `customerreviews@packtpub.com`. We award our regular reviewers with free eBooks and videos in exchange for their valuable feedback. Help us be relentless in improving our products!

Table of Contents

Preface

Nowadays, web mapping is all over the internet. User friendly interfaces and efficiency are mandatory requirements for GIS, as for any other system. If you are going to start a new web mapping application, you will not start from scratch. GeoServer is one of the biggest players in the web mapping field. It has a solid developer community and a high maturity level. Although it's not an easy piece of software to master, the latest releases have greatly improved stability and ease of management. *GeoServer Beginner's Guide* offers you a practical introduction to GeoServer. Beginning with the installation and basic usage, you will learn to use the administration interface for adding data, configuring layers, customizing OGC services, and securing your site. You will find many step-by-step examples covering topics from data store configuration to layer publication and style customization. If all this sounds new and strange to you, don't worry; *GeoServer Beginner's Guide* will introduce you to the fundamentals of GIS and will then clearly explain all the basic tasks performed in order to build maps. This book is meant to expand your knowledge of web mapping from something you have either heard of or have practiced a little into something you can apply at any level to meet your needs in incorporating maps into a site. I hope you will enjoy reading this book as much as I enjoyed writing it.

What this book covers

Chapter 1, *GIS Fundamentals*, introduces you to GIS concepts. It guides you through spatial data types and maps. You will discover how spatial information is stored and how to set up a map. You may want to skip this chapter if you already have a solid background in GIS.

Chapter 2, *Getting Started with GeoServer*, guides you through setting up your first GeoServer instance. It shows you, step by step, how to download the most recent version of the software and its requirements, that is, Java and a servlet container. For each component, a detailed description of how to install it is included.

Chapter 3, *Exploring the Administrative Interface*, covers GeoServer's Web Administration interface. It explains how to log in and access each section. You will familiarize yourself with data configuration following a common workflow that starts by adding data to GeoServer and guides you through to publication. Included in this chapter are screen captures that define the main areas of the program and menu items--all of which is very helpful when accessing the interface for the first time.

Chapter 4, *Adding Your Data,* demonstrates how you can configure data in GeoServer. The examples included will show you how to add and publish shapefiles and PostGIS tables, two of the most common formats, which are also natively supported by GeoServer. The extensions for Oracle is also discussed.

Chapter 5, *Accessing Layers,* guides you through data publication and covers in detail all output types offered by GeoServer for your data. Raster formats such as JPEG and PNG are discussed for maps, while vector formats such as GeoRSS and GEOJSON are explained for vector output. We will also explore OpenLayers, a JavaScript framework that GeoServer includes in its output format when you want to serve your data as an application.

Chapter 6, *Styling Your Layers,* explains how to apply styles to your layers. Styles let you render your data according to attributes, in order to build pretty maps. SLD's syntax, the standard for data rendering, will be explained in detail, with examples for different geometry types such as point, polyline, and polygons. The chapter also illustrates how to build scale-dependent symbology and how to compose different rendering in a group, to mimic a map in WMS.

Chapter 7, *Creating Simple Maps,* describes how to build client applications with the JavaScript framework. JavaScript is a powerful and widespread language and, unsurprisingly, it is one of the best choices when developing a web application. We will build some sample maps using Google Maps API, OpenLayers, and Leaflet.

Chapter 8, *Performance and Caching,* covers the use of integrated GeoWebCache. Caching maps is a common strategy with map servers; it allows you to serve pretty complex maps without running out of resources. The GeoServer 2.X release introduces a great change: you can fully administer the integrated GeoWebCache from the web admin interface. In the examples included, you will configure cache with different strategies, optimizing performance, or disk usage.

Chapter 9, *Automating Tasks - GeoServer REST Interface,* explains how to control the GeoServer configuration from a remote location through the REST interface. This may prove a great help if you have to administer a GeoServer site without the possibility of using the web admin interface, or if you want to automatize, in an external procedure, some admin tasks. The included examples will let you add data, configure styles and layers, and publish them. All the operations are demonstrated with Python and curl syntaxes.

Chapter 10, *Securing GeoServer Before Production,* covers the GeoServer security module. It first discusses general configuration for security, that is, password encryption, and then the security model is explained. A case history shows you how to create a configuration where different users are in charge of administration, editing, and publication tasks.

Chapter 11, *Tuning GeoServer in a Production Environment*, explains the advanced considerations for running a successful GeoServer site. It covers Java Runtime tuning and data and services optimization. Finally, a high availability configuration is detailed, with instructions for configuring a balanced GeoServer installation.

Chapter 12, *Going Further - Getting Help and Troubleshooting*, shows you how to access community tools and help for going further than what you will learn from this book. It also covers a concise introduction to other data publication standards implemented in GeoServer, WCS, and WFS. With WCS and WFS, you can serve vector and raster data to clients that not only need to show a map but have to perform some processing on the data.

What you need for this book

Installation and download instructions are described for all the software packages you will need. You just need to have access to a computer with an online connection for downloading packages. The instructions cover both Linux and Windows operating systems, so you may select the one you prefer. All the software used in this book is freely available, most of the time as an Open Source project. Hardware requirements for development purposes are not very high. A relatively modern laptop or desktop will be enough for running examples. The source code and data used in this book are freely available on the Packt website.

Who this book is for

If you are going to use maps on your site, incorporate spatial data in a desktop application, or you are just curious about web mapping, this book offers you a fast-paced and practical introduction. Particularly if you need to develop a web application supporting maps, you will find that GeoServer is one of the best solutions you can choose. Analysts will discover how GIS works and how it can be integrated into complex systems. System administrators may also find this book useful for planning installation, tuning, and maintenance.

Conventions

In this book, you will find a number of text styles that distinguish between different kinds of information. Here are some examples of these styles and an explanation of their meaning.

Code words in text, database table names, folder names, filenames, file extensions, pathnames, dummy URLs, and user input are shown as follows: "Under the subdirectory structure of `C:\chapter8-benchmark\src\main\java\com\packt` is the `MyBenchmark.java` file."

A block of code is set as follows:

```
http://localhost:8080/geoserver/web/wicket/bookmarkable/
    org.geoserver.wms.web.data.StyleEditPage?
    6&name=PopulatedPlacesBlueLabeled
```

Any command-line input or output is written as follows:

```
<display-name>GeoServer</display-name>
```

New terms and **important words** are shown in bold. Words that you see on the screen, for example, in menus or dialog boxes, appear in the text like this: "The **Encryption** section lets you hide web admin parameters."

Warnings or important notes appear like this.

Tips and tricks appear like this.

Reader feedback

Feedback from our readers is always welcome. Let us know what you think about this book-what you liked or disliked. Reader feedback is important for us as it helps us develop titles that you will really get the most out of. To send us general feedback, simply email feedback@packtpub.com, and mention the book's title in the subject of your message. If there is a topic that you have expertise in and you are interested in either writing or contributing to a book, see our author guide at www.packtpub.com/authors.

Customer support

Now that you are the proud owner of a Packt book, we have a number of things to help you to get the most from your purchase.

Downloading the example code

You can download the example code files for this book from your account at http://www.packtpub.com. If you purchased this book elsewhere, you can visit http://www.packtpub.com/support and register to have the files emailed directly to you. You can download the code files by following these steps:

1. Log in or register to our website using your email address and password.
2. Hover the mouse pointer on the **SUPPORT** tab at the top.
3. Click on **Code Downloads & Errata**.
4. Enter the name of the book in the **Search** box.
5. Select the book for which you're looking to download the code files.
6. Choose from the drop-down menu where you purchased this book from.
7. Click on **Code Download**.

Once the file is downloaded, please make sure that you unzip or extract the folder using the latest version of:

- WinRAR / 7-Zip for Windows
- Zipeg / iZip / UnRarX for Mac
- 7-Zip / PeaZip for Linux

The code bundle for the book is also hosted on GitHub at https://github.com/PacktPublishing/GeoServer-Beginners-Guide-Second-Edition. We also have other code bundles from our rich catalog of books and videos available at https://github.com/PacktPublishing/. Check them out!

Downloading the color images of this book

We also provide you with a PDF file that has color images of the screenshots/diagrams used in this book. The color images will help you better understand the changes in the output. You can download this file from
https://www.packtpub.com/sites/default/files/downloads/GeoServerBeginnersGuideSecondEdition_ColorImages.pdf.

Errata

Although we have taken every care to ensure the accuracy of our content, mistakes do happen. If you find a mistake in one of our books-maybe a mistake in the text or the code-we would be grateful if you could report this to us. By doing so, you can save other readers from frustration and help us improve subsequent versions of this book. If you find any errata, please report them by visiting http://www.packtpub.com/submit-errata, selecting your book, clicking on the **Errata Submission Form** link, and entering the details of your errata. Once your errata are verified, your submission will be accepted and the errata will be uploaded to our website or added to any list of existing errata under the Errata section of that title. To view the previously submitted errata, go to https://www.packtpub.com/books/content/support and enter the name of the book in the search field. The required information will appear under the **Errata** section.

Piracy

Piracy of copyrighted material on the internet is an ongoing problem across all media. At Packt, we take the protection of our copyright and licenses very seriously. If you come across any illegal copies of our works in any form on the internet, please provide us with the location address or website name immediately so that we can pursue a remedy. Please contact us at copyright@packtpub.com with a link to the suspected pirated material. We appreciate your help in protecting our authors and our ability to bring you valuable content.

Questions

If you have a problem with any aspect of this book, you can contact us at questions@packtpub.com, and we will do our best to address the problem.

1
GIS Fundamentals

In this chapter, you will learn the foundation of **Geographic Information System** (GIS) and spatial data. Although you do not need to understand these subjects in great depth to take advantage of the features of GeoServer, we will give you the basic information required to understand what you will be learning in this book. This chapter will introduce you to the magic of spatial data and processing.

In this chapter, we will cover the following topics:

- Why spatial data is special
- Spatial data formats
- The magical world of **Spatial Reference System (SRS)**
- What is a map and why does it matter?
- The art of Cartography.

By the end of this chapter, you will have the basic skills to identify which spatial data format best suits your needs.

What is GIS about?

Since you were a kid at school, you have been exposed to many maps: maps of countries where you spent hours memorizing the boundaries, rivers, and capitals; historical maps, with the rise and fall of ancient empires, where you dreamed of being a great conqueror; economics maps, with the locations and amounts of goods and services. Every day on newspapers, on TV, or, in a far more accurate way, in books and academic papers, you look at data represented on a map. Maps are a spatial representation of data and are often the main output of a GIS.

GIS is an acronym for **Geographic Information System**. Does it sound too complicated to you? Do not be afraid; it is not so different from many other systems to manage the information you probably already know. The main difference is the spatial component of information. All the data contained in a GIS has a spatial dimension or a link to another object with spatial attributes.

So what is GIS? In a nutshell, we can define it as a system to acquire and store, process, and produce data representations, that is, maps. In this book, you will learn that working with GeoServer requires you to prepare your data, process it to render in a beautiful map, and build up a set of functions that enable a user to interact with your data. So, building up a GeoServer instance may be described as GIS-building.

A detailed understanding of GIS is far beyond the scope of this book, and it is not required to start with GeoServer. However, you will need to have some basic skills in spatial data, maps, and spatial reference systems.

 If you want to dig deeper into the topic, there is a lot of online material available. A couple of excellent sources of information are: `https://www.ordnancesurvey.co.uk/support/understanding-gis/` and `http://www.esri.com/what-is-gis`

Let's go; we will turn you into a neo-cartographer!

The foundation of any GIS - spatial data

If you have ever built a simple map to annotate your hiking on mountains or to send driving directions to your girlfriend or boyfriend, you have dealt with spatial data.

Spatial data is the foundation of any GIS. You know that a building is likely to fall down unless it is sitting atop a strong foundation. So, you need to understand spatial data or you will be producing a poor map output.

Then what is spatial data in simple words? Let us start considering, from a general point of view, what a piece of spatial information is. Each description of an object contains a reference to its position on the Earth's surface. Although this is not a rigorous formal definition, it reminds you the mandatory requirements for any spatial data. Any spatial data should contain enough information, irrespective of its format, for determining where it is located on the earth's surface. For now we are fine with this simplistic definition.

Think of some lists of familiar objects:

- A list of bookshops with addresses
- A list of places you visited during your trips
- A list of points of interest, for example, restaurants, museums, and hotels you collected with your mobile phone
- An aerial photo with a view of a city, where you can recognize notable places

You can say where each element is located in a more or less precise way. They are real objects represented with spatial data. As you may have noted, spatial information is represented in quite a heterogeneous way. Most people are able to recognize spatial information in any group from the previous list. Unfortunately, GIS software and GeoServer are an exception to this and tend to prefer a strongly structured piece of information. If you are using your spatial data with GeoServer, you need to organize it more accurately. We will talk specifically about GeoServer's data connectors in `Chapter 4`, *Adding Your Data*, but, for now, it is important that you understand how spatial data is commonly organized and stored. As you keep on making maps, you will deal with lots of different spatial data.

Measuring the world

Spatial data are references for an object's position on the Earth's surface. How can you measure and store them in a numeric format? An elementary model of the Earth could be a sphere. On a sphere's surface, you can measure positions with angular units called **latitude** (ϕ) and **longitude** (λ). Latitude measures the angle between the equatorial plane and a line that passes through that point, and is normal to the surface; whereas, longitude measures the east or west angle from a reference meridian (for example, the one passing through Greenwich observatory) to another meridian that passes through that point. Angular measures can be expressed in decimal degrees or in degrees, minutes, and seconds.

If you want to store the location of the Statue of Liberty, you can express it in the decimal degree form, as shown here:

40.689167, -74.044444

Alternatively, you can use the degrees, minutes, and seconds form as follows:

Lat. 40° 41' 21" N, Long. 74° 2' 40" W

 In the decimal degrees form, you don't need to indicate the North, South, West, or East direction; this is represented from the plus/minus sign (+/-). The positive latitude is for the North direction and the positive longitude is for the East direction.

Consider the image of the model of the Earth given as follows:

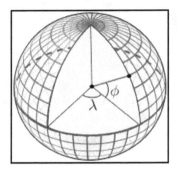

(Image from http://en.wikipedia.org/wiki/Latitude)

We normally think of the Earth as a sphere, but this is not its real shape. Geodesy, the science studying the shape of the Earth, defines the Earth, as represented by a geoid, an ideal surface defined by the level of the sea if oceans were to cover all of Earth. For practical purposes, as in projections, the geoid is too complicated to use, and so the Earth is defined by an **ellipsoid**. The ellipsoid is described by its semi-major axis (equatorial radius) and flattening.

Moving on to the planet with decimal degree coordinates

Does it sound a little bit complicated? Do not be afraid and explore locations on Earth with latitude and longitude coordinates. In the following table, there are a few famous places with coordinates in decimal degrees. Point your browser to http://maps.google.com, insert coordinates in the search textbox, and then press Enter. Your map will shift to the location.

Google Maps enables you to query for coordinates of any place on Earth; find that function and look for some great places.

Latitude	Longitude	Place
41.890	12.492	Rome, Italy
36.055	-112.122	Colorado Grand Canyon, USA
48.858	2.294	Paris, France
-25.688	-54.442	Iguazú National Park, Argentina
-25.345	131.036	Ayers Rock, Australia

Projecting a sphere on a plane

Did you ever play with an orange peel? I did it a lot when I was a child, often pressing them in the hope to flatten it almost perfectly. It's a hopeless challenge, but kids are stubborn and ambitious. Many years later, I found a similar analogy in a geography book. It was about cartographic projection and used an orange as a model of the Earth. If you think of the orange's peel as the Earth's surface, it is suddenly clear why you can't have a planar representation of Earth's surface without a great amount of distortion.

All the maps you will ever find are on a plain paper sheet. Curved digital screens are quite uncommon in GeoGeek's nests. So, how do cartographers represent a curved surface on a plane? This is done by means of a mathematical operation called **projection**. Consider the following image:

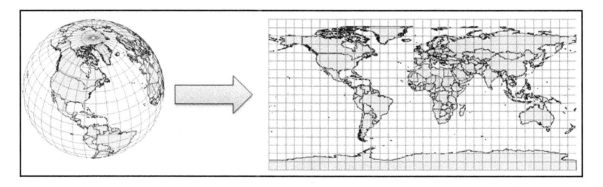

Indeed, there are several different projections developed in the last few centuries by cartographers and mathematicians. There is no mathematical method to transfer a sphere or an ellipsoid to a two-dimensional space without distortion. Hence, projections modify the data and include some deformations about lengths, areas, or shapes you can observe and measure on maps.

We can classify projections according to the geographical features and properties they preserve, as shown here:

- Conformal projections preserve angles locally. Meridian and parallels intersect at 90-degree angles.
- Equal-area projections preserve proportions between areas. In a map with equal-area projections, each part has the same proportional area as the corresponding part of the Earth.
- Equidistant projections maintain a scale along one or more lines, or from one or two points to all other points on the map. Lines along which the scale (distance) is correct are of the same proportional length as the lines they refer to on the globe.

It is important that you understand there is no best projection; choosing one for your map is a trade-off. According to the portion of the earth's surface, the map that you are designing will contain and/or use the projections that suit best. Let's explore some widely-used projections.

Understanding coordinate systems

You learned about Earth's shape and projection. Coordinate systems use these concepts to build a frame of reference to place objects on the Earth's surface. There are two types of coordinate systems: projected coordinate systems and geographic coordinate systems. Let's understand these as follows:

- **Geographic coordinate systems**: These use latitude and longitude as angles measured from the Earth's center, as we saw previously. A geographic coordinate system is substantially defined by the ellipsoid used to model the Earth, and the position of the ellipsoid positioned relative to the center of the Earth called the **datum**.
- **Projected coordinate systems**: These are defined on a flat two-dimensional surface. A projected coordinate system is always based on a geographic coordinate system; hence, it uses an ellipsoid and a datum. Besides, a projected coordinate system includes a projection method to project coordinates from the Earth's spherical surface onto a two-dimensional Cartesian coordinate plane.

Commonly used coordinate systems

Although there are hundreds of different projections, you can limit your knowledge to some that are widely used.

Universal Transverse Mercator system

Commonly known as **UTM**, this is not really a projection. It is a system based on the **Transverse Mercator** projection. This projection uses a cylinder tangent to a meridian to unwrap the Earth's surface. A maximum of 5° of distortion from the central meridian is acceptable. The UTM splits the world into a series of 6° of longitudinal-wide zones. As you may guess, there are 60 zones numbered from Longitude 180W toward the east. Note that you cannot have a map representing more than one UTM zone. Indeed, UTM is well suited for large-scale maps. Consider the following image:

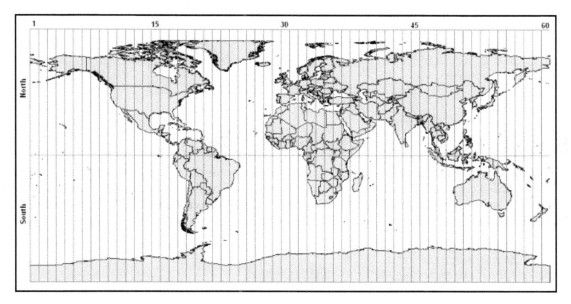

Web Mercator

Web Mercator is a projection derived from Transverse Mercator. It maps ellipsoidal latitude and longitude coordinates onto a plane using Spherical Mercator equations. This projection was popularized by **Google** in **Google Maps**, and it is now widely used in online mapping systems. It stretches areas in a north-south direction and, unlike the Transverse Mercator, it is not conformal. Consider the following image:

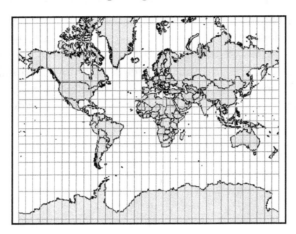

Spatial Reference Identifier (SRID)

A spatial reference system identifier is a code to easily reference a **spatial reference system (SRS)**. An SRS contains parameters about projection, ellipsoid, and datum. It can be defined using the **Open Geospatial Consortium's (OGC) well-known text (WKT)** representation. The SRS for the geographic WGS84 reference system is as follows:

```
GEOGCS["WGS 84",
DATUM["WGS_1984",
SPHEROID["WGS 84",6378137,298.257223563,
        AUTHORITY["EPSG","7030"]],
        AUTHORITY["EPSG","6326"]],
PRIMEM["Greenwich",0,
        AUTHORITY["EPSG","8901"]],
UNIT["degree",0.01745329251994328,
        AUTHORITY["EPSG","9122"]],
        AUTHORITY["EPSG","4326"]]
```

The last line contains the number 4326; this is the SRID uniquely identifying this SRS. The long form should also contain the authority, that is EPSG:4326, but you will often find it indicated only by the number.

 EPSG is the acronym for **European Petroleum Survey Group**. Several European Oil companies founded it in 1986 to collect and maintain geodetic information. In 2005, EPSG was absorbed by OGP (an international forum for Oil and Gas producers) that formed the OGP Geomatics Committee. The committee maintains the registry and publishes it as a public web interface or a downloadable database.

It is very important that you know what SRID your data is in. Without it, you can't represent data on a map without the risk of great errors.

Exploring the EPSG registry

We described a couple of common and widely used SRSs, but there are a lot of them. There are several archives on the internet where you can find detailed information about SRSs and their elements, that is ellipsoids, datums, unit of measurements, projected, or geographic reference systems. One of the most authoritative and complete data sets is the **EPSG Geodetic Parameter Registry**. If you are curious about it, you can open your browser and point it to http://epsg-registry.org. Then, try a simple search by inserting a location name in the **Area** textbox as shown in the following screenshot:

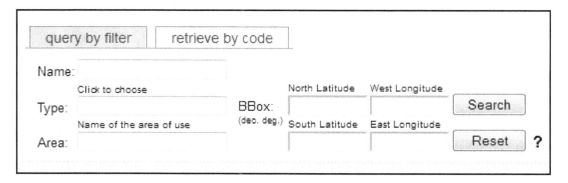

Representing geometrical shapes

You learned how to calculate coordinates on the Earth's surface. However, how can you represent a real object, for example, a river, in a convenient way for a GIS?

There are two main approaches when building a spatial database: modeling **vector data** or **raster data**. Vector data uses a set of discrete locations to build basic geometrical shapes, such as points, polylines, and polygons. This is shown in the following image:

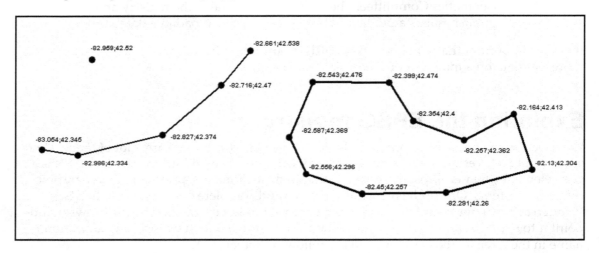

Of course, real objects are neither a point, nor a polyline or a polygon. In your model, you have to decide which basic shape better suits the real object. For example, a town can be represented as a point if you draw a map of the world with the countries' capitals shown. On the other hand, if you publish a countries map, a polygon will enable you to draw the city boundaries to give a more realistic representation.

The simpler geometric object is a point. Points are defined as single coordinate pairs (x,y) when we work in two-dimensional space, or coordinate triplets (x,y,z) if you want to take account of the height coordinates. In the following examples, we use point features to store the location of active volcanoes:

Name of volcano	Latitude	Longitude
Etna	37.751	37.751
Krakatoa	-6.102	105.423
Aconcagua	-32.653	-70.011
Kilimanjaro	-3.065	37.358

Did you guess the units and projections used? The coordinates are in decimal degrees and SRS is WGS84 geographic, that is, EPSG:4326.

Points are simple to understand but do not give you many details about the spatial extent of an object. If you want to store rivers, you need more than a coordinate pair. Indeed, you have to memorize an array of coordinate pairs for each feature in a structure called **polyline** shown as follows:

```
Colorado; (40.472 -105.826, ... , 31.901 -114.951)
Nile; (-2.282 29.331, ... , 30.167 31.101)
Danube; (48.096 8.155, ... ,45.218 29.761)
```

If you need to model an area features such as an island, you can extend the polyline object, adding the constraint that it must be closed; that is, the first and the last coordinate pairs must be coincident. This is the polygon shape:

```
Ellis Island; (-74.043 40.699, -74.041 40.700, -74.040 40.700,
   -74.040 40.701, -74.037 40.699, -74.038 40.699, -74.038 40.698,
   -74.039 40.698, -74.041 40.700,-74.042 40.699, -74.040 40.698,
-74.042 40.696,
   -74.044 40.698, -74.043 40.699)
```

The feature model used in GIS is a little bit more complex than what we have discussed. There are some more constraints regarding vertex ordering, line intersections, and areal shapes with holes. Different GIS specify several different rules, often in proprietary formats. Open Geospatial Consortium (OGC) defined a standard for simple features, and, lately, most systems, open source firstly, are compliant with it. If you are curious about it, you can point your browser at http://www.opengeospatial.org/standards/is and look for **The OpenGIS® Simple Features Interface Standard.**

Modelling the real world with raster data

Raster data uses a regular tessellation, defining cells where one or more values are uniform. Usually, the cells are square; although, this is not a constraint. Raster data is generally used to represent values continuously changing in the space, that is, a field. You can use a regular tessellation to build a digital elevation model of the Earth's surface. In the following figure, each cell has a height and width of 20 meters, and the value stored is the height above sea level in meters:

80	74	62	45	45	34	39	56
80	74	74	62	45	34	39	56
74	74	62	62	45	34	39	39
62	62	45	45	34	34	34	39
45	45	45	34	34	30	34	39

Can you use raster data to model real features, such as a river? Yes, you can, but there are some drawbacks you have to consider. The following figure shows a linear feature represented as vector data (the red line) and as raster data (the black and white cells). If your purpose is drawing the shapes on a map, raster data is not a good choice, as raster graphics are resolution dependent. They cannot scale up to an arbitrary resolution without the apparent loss of quality.

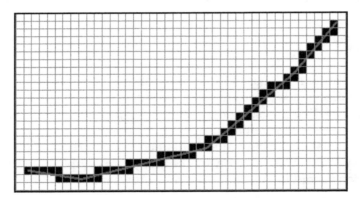

Representing the world

In the previous sections, we explored spatial data and SRS. They are the key elements you need to build your map. Indeed, maps are a planar representation of spatial data. You need to collect the appropriate data to represent the real objects you want to include in your map, and you need to choose an SRS to organize your data onto the map.

Keep in mind that maps are representations, a proposition of yours. They are the way you express your knowledge and your vision of the world. To fully accomplish this, there is a third basic ingredient for your map: symbology.

Symbology enables you to add information to the features shown on a map. For example, colors can be used to indicate a classification of roads. Imagine you need to produce a map of a country with a road network. You have a vector dataset containing road polylines. A simple approach is to render all features with the same symbol, as shown in the following figure. The map is not really informative unless you are a transportation expert. You won't extract any information from the map and it looks ugly too.

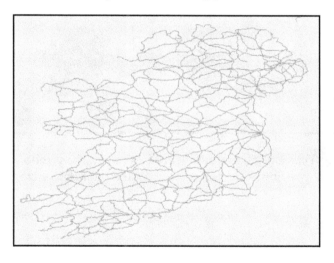

Let's take a look at a similar map produced with **ArcGIS Online** (http://www.esri.com/software/arcgis/arcgisonline).

It contains the road network symbolized with different colors and line widths, labels showing you highway codes, and major towns represented with small circles and labels. Besides, there is a background depicting heights with colors and shading. Does it now look more familiar to you?

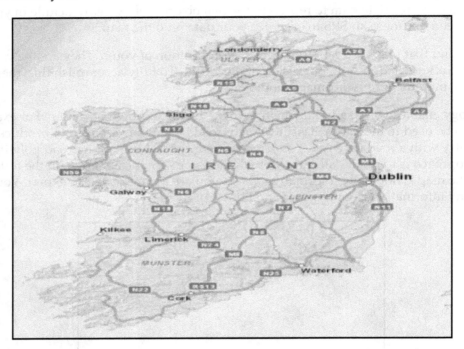

In Chapter 6, *Styling Your Layers*, you will learn how to apply symbols in GeoServer to produce maps like the previous one. For now, you need to familiarize yourself with simple and thematic maps.

Exploring OpenStreetMap

Are you ready to explore some nice maps? We will navigate through a great bunch of spatial data, **OpenStreetMap**. Perform the following steps:

1. Open your browser and go to http://www.openstreetmap.org.

2. The website offers you a small scale map centered on your actual location, as derived from the browser information:

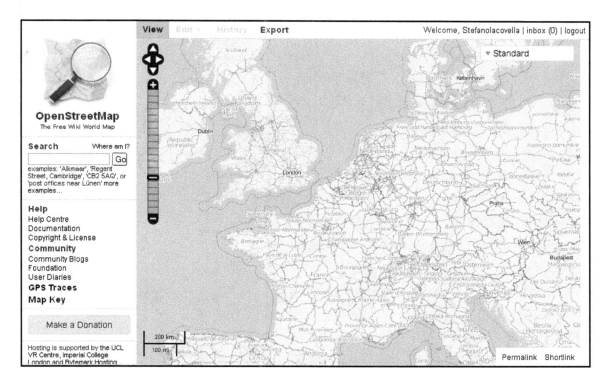

3. Center your map on London, UK, and zoom in with the tool shown on the left-hand side. You can see that many more road types and locations are now shown in this map:

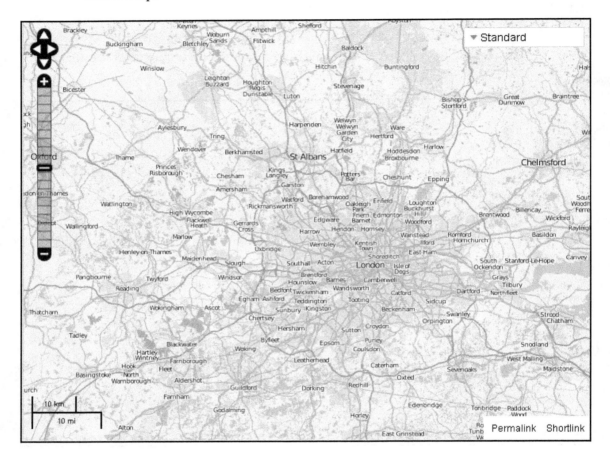

4. Now, enter the `Piccadilly Circus, London, UK` address in the **Search** textbox on the left and click on the **Go** button. A list of results matching your search is presented on the left side of the map. Pick the first item:

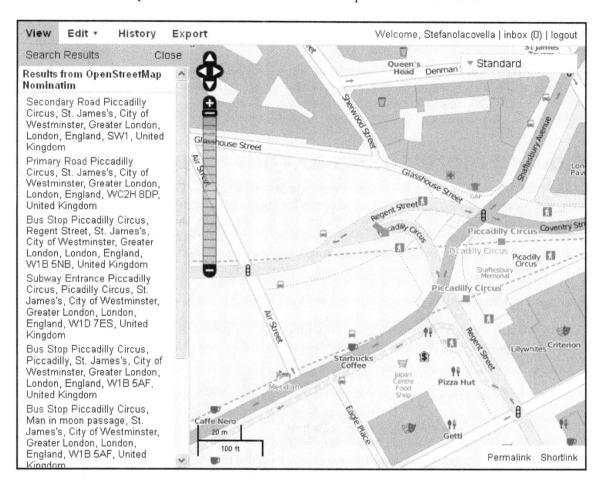

5. The map is now at a great scale (look at the scale bar on the bottom-left of the map panel) and the symbols changed to show you greater detailed information about roads and locations. You can find street names, directions for car traffic, buildings' footprints, and icons for points of interest. The general look and feel resemble a printed city map you can pick up at tourist offices.

OpenStreetMap does not require you to register for browsing or exporting the data. Anyway, if you are interested in maps and open source data, you may consider getting involved in the project. OSM is a collaborative project to create a free editable map of the world, currently involving over half a million users all around the world. You may add data or find errors on locations you know well.

You explored several maps representing the same data set in quite different ways. Different symbols and hiding subsets of data are powerful tools to produce clear and nice looking maps. You are now ready to discover a different kind of map.

Adding more colors to your maps

In the previous paragraphs, we encountered some simple maps. Geographers define these kinds of maps as general maps. General maps focus on the description of the physical, political, and human features on the territory. All this data is portrayed for its own sake. In a nutshell, it can be said that general maps tell you where objects are located on the Earth's surface, while thematic maps talk about things happening on the Earth's surface. Thematic maps focus on displaying a single topic and portray spatial distribution and variation. You have general data, such as administrative boundaries or road networks, but this is represented as a base layer for general reference.

Among thematic maps, those using choropleth or dot representations, are by far the most common type you will be using GeoServer for.

Choropleth maps

Choropleth maps show statistical data aggregated over predefined regions, such as counties or states, by coloring or shading these regions. You can draw states according to their population, gross domestic product, car owners, and the number of national parks. You are not limited to a single variable; indeed, you can merge different values from more than one attribute associated with spatial objects.

The following figure shows a map of European countries colored according to gross domestic product values. **Legend** on the right shows the five classification intervals. Values were normalized to Eu-27 average (EU stands for the European Union, in the period 2007-2013 when it had 27 countries):

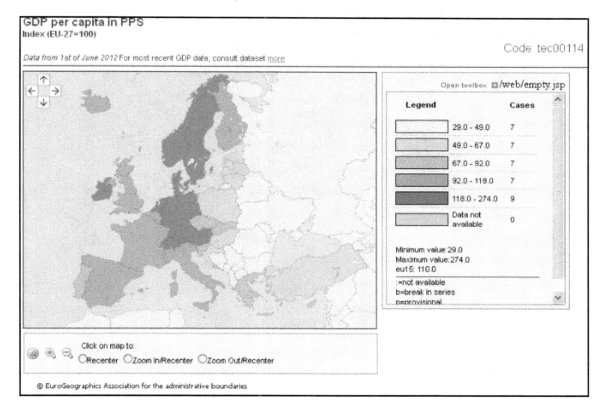

(Image courtesy of http://epp.eurostat.ec.europa.eu)

Proportional maps

In proportional maps, symbols of different sizes represent data associated with different areas or locations within the map. As an example, the countries' capitals can be represented with a circle proportional to their population:

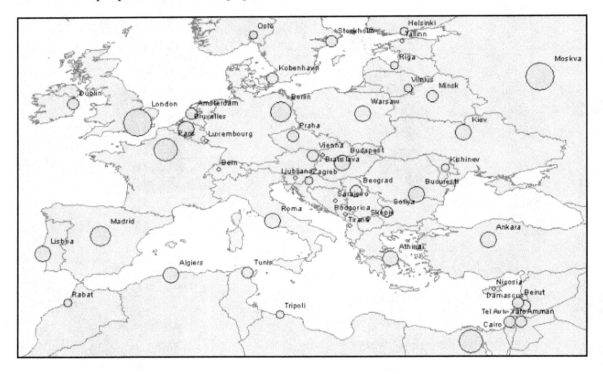

This map contains a representation of European countries. They are drawn all using the same symbology. The information is pointed out by the circles, a nongeographical feature, with a radius proportional to the residents. For the reader convenience there are also some labels, but he may also guess the name of the capital from its position.

Making your thematic map

Are you ready to build some maps? We can do this without the use of GeoServer since we have not yet discussed how to install it; we will cover that in the next chapter. For the moment we will play with an online map engine to assist your understanding of thematic map concepts:

1. First, download the `WorldBank.csv` file from the Packt site. This file contains a set of economic data already prepared for you. The data comes from the World Bank and was preprocessed to let you focus on the thematic map:

    The World Bank is an international financial institution that provides loans to countries of the world for capital programs. It also distributes a lot of social and economic data under an open data license. The data used in this section is available at `http://datacatalog.worldbank.org/`.

2. To build the thematic map, we will use an online engine. Although it's built on open source software, it's a commercial solution. You need to register to use it, but, for the purpose of this section, and for other small maps you may want to create, you can use the free of charge account. Point your browser to `https://carto.com/`:

3. Click on the **Sign up** link from the home page and complete your application for a free of charge account. After signing up, log in to Carto and you will arrive at the front dashboard, the starting point for building your maps:

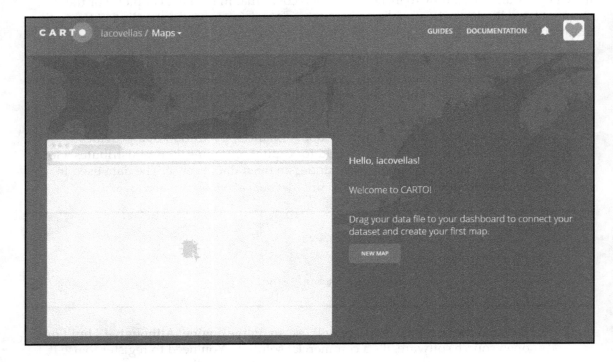

4. Select the `WorldBank.csv` file and drag it on the dashboard to create your first map. The engine will process your data, trying to georeference it, and then a new map will be shown for you:

5. The map you just created does not seem interesting. All the countries use the same orange symbol, what about the economic data from World Bank? Locate the toolbar in the right part of the user interface and press the symbol with a paintbrush; this will show you a custom interface to change the rendering of your data:

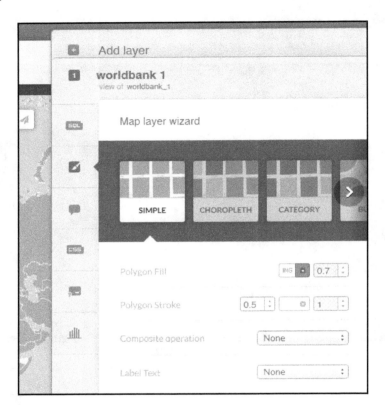

6. Select the choropleth category and leave the other setting at default. Now your map shows the countries with a color ramp, according to the GDP value. You can explore the setting; try to change the classification and the color ramp used:

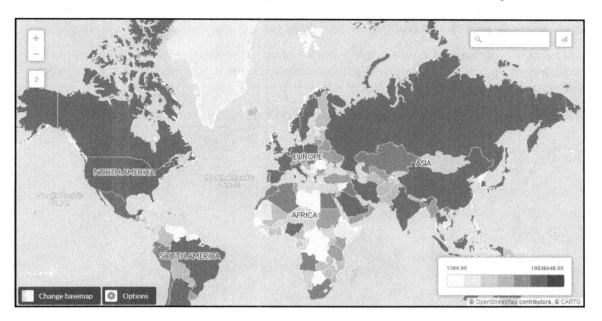

You built a brand new thematic map, selecting data and symbol colors. You will need to set these parameters exactly in GeoServer to produce beautiful maps. This time we did it without exploring the technical details behind feature rendering. In Chapter 6, *Styling Your Layers*, you will learn how to use **SLD (Styled Layer Descriptor)** to make thematic maps.

Summary

We had a brief but complete introduction to spatial data and maps in this chapter. It was somewhat a theoretical chapter, but we promise you it was the first and last of this kind! From now on, we will run real stuff with GeoServer.

Specifically, you learned how an object is referenced to its location and which storage models you can use with spatial data (for example, vector versus raster) and, eventually, you learned to represent spatial features on a map.

You are now ready to pick up GeoServer, unpack, and install it on your computer.

2
Getting Started with GeoServer

Congratulations on your choice to take your data to the world with GeoServer. It can be installed on many different operating systems since it is a Java application, as long as a Java Virtual Machine exists for that operating system. It takes advantage of multithreaded operations and supports 64-bit operating systems.

This chapter will cover, in detail, the steps that will bring you to a successful installation. Although, we will explain the whole process in detail, do not be afraid. As soon as you finish reading it, you will have your running copy of GeoServer. The steps will be illustrated in two scenarios, a Linux Mint 18, and a Windows 7 machine. We chose these two as they cover the majority of users. Because Mint is a Debian derivative, the installation process can easily be reproduced on other similar distributions, for example, Debian or Ubuntu.

We'll talk about the advanced settings most useful in taking your configuration to a production environment in Chapter 10, *Securing GeoServer Before Production*, and Chapter 11, *Tuning GeoServer in a Production Environment*.

In this chapter, we will cover the following topics:

- System requirements
- Obtaining GeoServer (latest 2.10.2)
- Installation on Linux Mint
- Installation on Windows 7
- OS independent installation
- Basic security measures by changing the default username and password

Installing required components

Before you can use GeoServer on your machine, you need to install some required pieces of software. GeoServer is a Java application; therefore, one of the most important things you need to ensure is that a Java virtual machine is working on your machine.

There are two main packages of Java. Depending on what you are planning to do with Java, you may want to install a **JDK** (**Java Development Kit**) or **JRE** (**Java Runtime Environment**).

The former enables you to compile Java code, while the latter has all you need to run most Java applications. Starting from release 2.0, GeoServer does not need a full JDK installation, and you can go safely with JRE. The JDK is only required if you are planning to write and compile Java code. This is the case if you want to modify the GeoServer source code, to fix code, or add functionalities.

 This book will not cover developing Java code, but, in this case, you will need more than a Java JDK. You need to set up a full development environment to properly code and debug the GeoServer source code. You may find a lot of useful information in the developer manual at
http://docs.geoserver.org/latest/en/developer/.

The current version of GeoServer requires Java 8 (see the last paragraph in this chapter for details about the release's schedule). Keep in mind that Java 9 is not supported, it may work on it, but you will not get support for any trouble you will find while using it.

In the 90s, Sun Microsystems started the development of Java. It has developed each new release until it merged into Oracle Corporation. While Oracle did not change the Java license to a commercial one, there are some license issues preventing Oracle Java from being available on Linux repositories, while you can obtain it directly from Oracle online resources.

In the current releases of Linux Mint, you will find OpenJDK already installed in the desktop edition; in the server, you need to choose it during setup. In the past releases, GeoServer was not intensively tested on OpenJDK; today, it has been known to work adequately with no issues, although the Oracle JRE is preferred.

Oracle Java should be your first choice unless you have some specific issues. In this chapter, we will use both. If you are using a Windows machine, then chances are that there is no Java runtime preinstalled. We will check and fix this.

After you have correctly installed the JRE, you can move on and install the servlet container. GeoServer is a web application, and it is built using frameworks such as Java servlet and JavaServer Pages technologies. The servlet container, or web container, is the component server that interacts with the servlets. It is responsible for managing the lifecycle of servlets, mapping a URL to a particular servlet, and ensuring access security.

As for the servlet container, you have a few choices here; a brief list is available at `http://en.wikipedia.org/wiki/Web_container`.

Apache Tomcat, GlassFish, and JBoss are most popular, and they are all available under open source licenses. You may wonder which one is the best choice to run GeoServer. According to the official documentation at `http://docs.geoserver.org/stable/en/user/index.html`:

> *GeoServer has been mostly tested using Tomcat, and so is the recommended application server. GeoServer requires a newer version of Tomcat (7.0.65 or later) that implements Servlet 3 and annotation processing. Other application servers have been known to work, but are not guaranteed.*

In a production environment, usually, several web applications share the same container. In this scenario, you will not choose the container; the architects and system administrators made their choices and you have to conform to them.

As a beginner, you have the opportunity of selecting it! And, in this case, Apache Tomcat should be your first choice as it is widely adopted in the GeoServer developer's community. If you run into any issues, the answer is probably waiting for you in the mailing list archive.

Checking presence of Java on your windows machine

We will verify the presence of a JRE/JDK installation on Windows using the following steps:

1. From the **Start** menu, select **Control Panel**.

2. Then, select **Programs**. If your system has a JRE/JDK installed, you should see an icon with the **Java** logo, as shown in the following screenshot. It is a shortcut to the Java control panel:

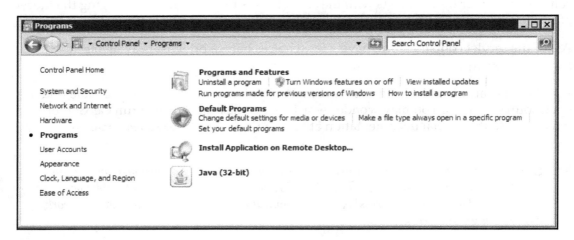

  In case you are using the small or large icons view for the control panel, you will find the Java icon in the main page.

3. Open the **Java Control Panel** and select the **Java** tab. Here, you will find settings for JRE. Click on the **View...** button. A new window shows up as in the following image, here you can visualize the installed release and the installation folder:

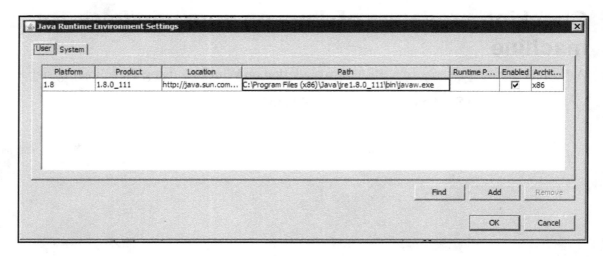

You checked for the presence of Java on your computer. In case you did not find it, we will install it in the next section.

 Did you note the 32-bit string in the Java icon? Indeed, you may download and install Java with two different packages: 32-bit and 64-bit. If you are running a 64-bit operating system, you can select one of them. Using the 64-bit flavor will allow you to use the RAM available on your machine more efficiently and make a larger portion of it available to GeoServer.

Checking the presence of Java on your Linux machine

We will check the JRE/JDK installation from the command line as follows:

1. Log in to your server and run this command:

   ```
   ~ $ sudo update-alternatives --config java
   ```

2. If there is no Java properly configured, you should see the following output:

   ```
   update-alternatives: error: no alternatives for java.
   ```

3. In case there is only one Java installed, the output will be similar to the following command line:

   ```
   There is only one alternative in link group java (providing
       /usr/bin/java):
   /usr/lib/jvm/java-8-openjdk-i386/jre/bin/java
   Nothing to configure.
   ```

4. If you have more than one Java, for example, Oracle JRE and OpenJDK, the output will be similar to this:

   ```
   There are 2 choices for the alternative java (providing /usr/bin/java).
     Selection    Path                                    Priority   Status
   ------------------------------------------------------------
   * 0            /usr/lib/jvm/java-8-openjdk-i386         1081      auto mode
                  /jre/bin/java
     1            /opt/java/jre1.8.0_121/bin/java          1         manual
                                                                     mode
     2            /usr/lib/jvm/java-8-openjdk-i386         1081      maunal
                  /jre/bin/java                                      mode
       Press <enter> to keep the current choice[*], or
       type selection number:
   ```

We determined if a Java installation is already present on your machine. As we mentioned earlier, this is a basic requirement for our installation. We had the opportunity to check if the installed release, in case we found it, is suitable for running GeoServer, which is a version 8.x.

Now we will go through the installation of JRE and the servlet container. You can skip the following steps in case you already found a JRE/JDK installed.

Installing JRE on your server

We will install Oracle JRE 8 on Windows. Although you may find some packages to install OpenJDK on Windows, they are not official distributions and this may lead you to some issues. We will see how to install OpenJDK and Oracle JRE on Linux Mint:

1. Open your browser and go to this URL: `http://www.oracle.com/technetwork/java/javase/downloads/jre8-downloads-2133155.html`. The following screenshot shows the window for installing the environment:

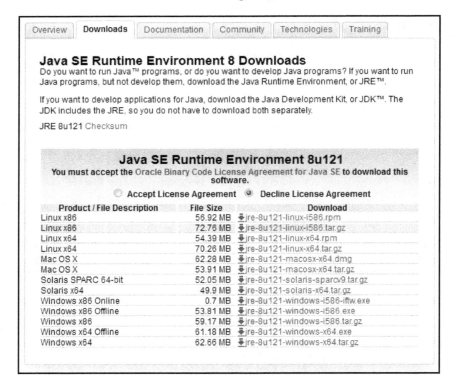

2. The page lists all the available packages for different operating systems and technologies. Select the radio button to accept the license agreement, and then choose the package for your machine. For instance, if you are running a 64-bit Linux Mint machine, select the `jre-8u121-linux-x64.tar.gz` file.

Oracle releases frequent updates for Java, mainly to fix security issues. The minor release number, 121 in the previous example, may be different at the moment you visit the page. Keep in mind that you have to select Java 8 and go with the latest minor update.

3. If you are on a Windows machine, open the location of the downloaded file and run it as an administrator and click on the **Yes** button when asked for the **User Account** control. Go with the default settings and press the **Install** button. After the wizard completes the installation process, you will see a window like the following one:

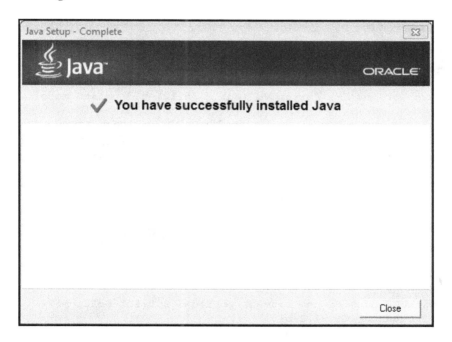

4. If you are running a Linux Mint machine, download the `jre-8u121-linux-x64.tar.gz` or `jre-8u121-linux-i586.tar.gz` file, according to the architecture of your computer.

5. In your terminal, run the command that creates a new subfolder in the directory opt as follows:

```
~ $ sudo mkdir -p -v /opt/java
mkdir: created directory '/opt/java'
```

6. Extract the archive and move it to the new folder you just created:

```
~ $ tar xvfz jre-8u121-linux-i586.tar.gz
~ $ sudo mv jre1.8.0_121 /opt/java/
```

7. Now configure the JRE on your system and make it the default choice:

```
~ $ sudo update-alternatives --install "/usr/bin/java" "java"
"/opt/java/jre1.8.0_121/bin/java" 1
~ $ sudo update-alternatives --set java /opt/java/
jre1.8.0_121/bin/java
```

8. Let's check the installation:

```
~ $ java -version
java version "1.8.0_121"
Java(TM) SE Runtime Environment (build 1.8.0_121-b13)
Java HotSpot(TM) Server VM (build 25.121-b13, mixed mode)
```

9. The previous instructions were for Oracle JRE. In case you prefer using OpenJDK JRE its installation is easy, we are now going to install it, of course, you have to choose among installing one of the two JRE flavors. Open your terminal and execute this command:

```
~ $ sudo apt-get install openjdk-8-jre
```

10. Now check if your installation is working properly using the following commands:

```
~ $ java -version
openjdk version "1.8.0_121"
OpenJDK Runtime Environment (build 1.8.0_121-8u121-b13-
   0ubuntu1.16.04.2-b13)
OpenJDK Server VM (build 25.121-b13, mixed mode)
```

We installed JRE on your computer. This is the core requirement for using GeoServer. It lets you run an instance of a Java virtual machine where you can host the servlet container and GeoServer. In fact, in the next step, you will install and configure the servlet container.

Installing Tomcat on your server

The last component you need to install to run GeoServer is Apache Tomcat. We will download and install the release 8, the latest available at writing time, on Windows and Linux Mint. Consider the following steps:

1. Open your browser and visit the download page for 8.x releases at `http://tomcat.apache.org/download-80.cgi`.

2. For Windows installation, select the `32-bit/64-bit Windows Service Installer (pgp, md5, sha1)` and save the file to a folder on your computer. For Linux Mint, select the `.tar.gz` archive. Consider the following screenshot:

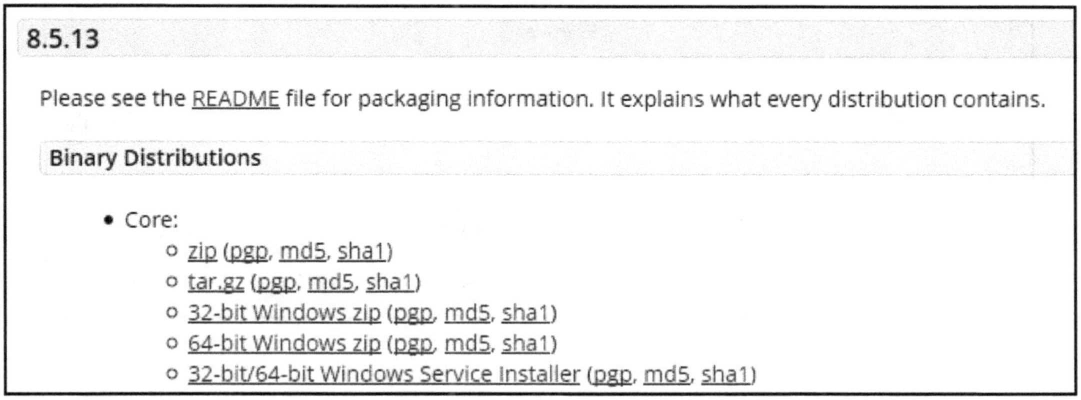

8.5.13

Please see the README file for packaging information. It explains what every distribution contains.

Binary Distributions

- Core:
    - zip (pgp, md5, sha1)
    - tar.gz (pgp, md5, sha1)
    - 32-bit Windows zip (pgp, md5, sha1)
    - 64-bit Windows zip (pgp, md5, sha1)
    - 32-bit/64-bit Windows Service Installer (pgp, md5, sha1)

---

3. For Windows installation, select the downloaded file and run it as administrator, then click on the **Yes** button when asked for the `User Account` control. When requested, agree to the license agreement.

4. You can remove the documentation from the selected options. If you need some information about Tomcat, the documentation is available online:

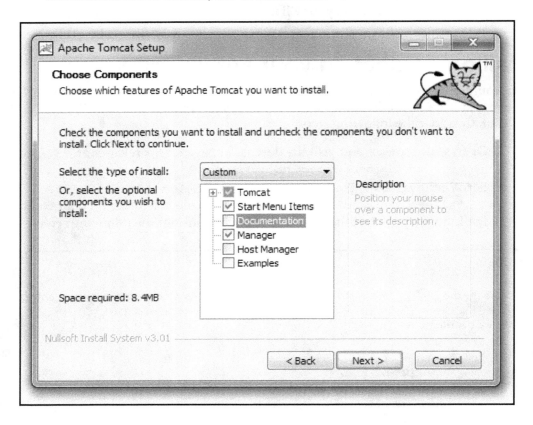

5. You can go with the default port number unless you know there are other services bounded to them. Set **User Name** and **Password** for web administration (for example, Tomcat):

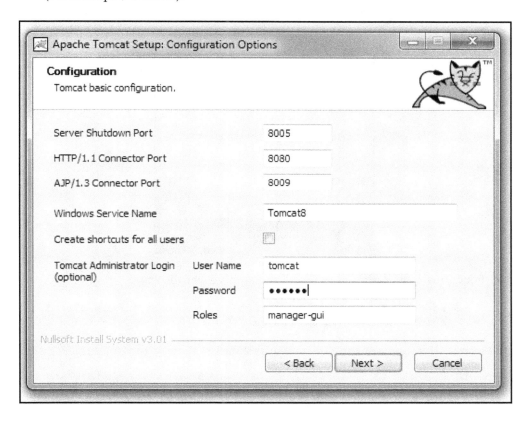

6. If your JRE installation was successful, the installer will prompt you with the right path to it. In case you have more than one JRE/JDK installed, you can choose which one Tomcat will use.

7. Eventually, you have to supply the folder where Tomcat will be installed and then press the **Install** button.

8. The installation process will create a Windows service for you. After the installation, it will try to start the Tomcat 8 service. You will now have a new icon in the system tray. From the pop-up menu, you can control Tomcat, starting and stopping it or accessing the configuration console, as shown in the following screenshot:

9. For Linux installation, download the archive as follows:

```
~$ wget http://it.apache.contactlab.it/tomcat/tomcat-8/v8.5.13/bin/
apache-tomcat-8.5.13.tar.gz
```

10. Extract it in a folder for alternate applications, specific to your server; /opt sounds like a good place:

```
~$ sudo tar xvfz apache-tomcat-8.5.13.tar.gz -C /opt
```

11. You need to configure Tomcat before you can use it. Go inside the main folder created while extracting the archive. The bin and conf folders contain the configuration files, and you can edit the init script in order to adjust settings. In a new Linux box, you shouldn't have any issues with the default configuration.

12. Startup Tomcat as follows:

```
~$ sudo /opt/apache-tomcat-8.5.13/bin/catalina.sh start
Using CATALINA_BASE:   /opt/apache-tomcat-8.5.13
Using CATALINA_HOME:   /opt/apache-tomcat-8.5.13
Using CATALINA_TMPDIR: /opt/apache-tomcat-8.5.13/temp
Using JRE_HOME:        /usr
Using CLASSPATH:       /opt/apache-tomcat-8.5.13/bin/bootstrap.jar
  :/opt/apache-tomcat-8.5.13/bin/tomcat-juli.jar
Tomcat started.
```

13. You can open your browser and check if it's running. Consider the following screenshot:

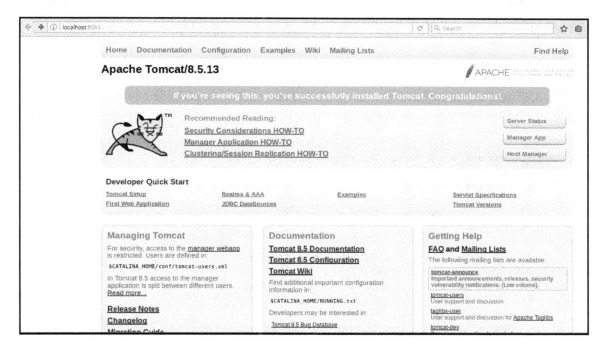

We installed Apache Tomcat on your computer. The basic requirements are now fulfilled, and you can go over with the GeoServer installation.

Configuring Tomcat as a service on Linux Mint

When installing on Windows, the setup configures Tomcat as a system service. This way, it will start when the computer boots without any user action. Are you wondering why do you have to manually start and stop Tomcat on Linux? You do not. As for Windows, the Linux operating system can be configured for an automatic start of programs.

In this section, you will create a script and learn how it works:

1. Download the `tomcat` file from the Packt site for this book and save it on your machine. You have to move it to the `/etc/init.d` folder.

2. Open it with the `vi` editor as follows:

   ```
   ~ $ sudo vi /etc/init.d/tomcat
   ```

3. There are some key settings you need to check in this file. The following lines contain the location of JRE and Tomcat. You can modify them according to your environment:

   ```
   export JAVA_HOME=/opt/java/jre1.8.0_121
   export PATH=$JAVA_HOME/bin:$PATH
   export CATALINA_HOME=/opt/apache-tomcat-8.5.13
   ```

4. Now, set the permissions for your script to make it executable using the following:

   ```
   ~ $ sudo chmod a+x /etc/init.d/tomcat
   ```

5. Let's try to call it and check for any problems:

   ```
   ~ $ sudo service tomcat
   Usage: /etc/init.d/tomcat {start|stop|restart}
   ```

6. Try starting Tomcat by:

   ```
   ~ $ sudo service tomcat start
   ```

7. To check if Tomcat started without errors, you can open the home page with your browser, as you did in a previous example, or you can check for the process to be running. For this second way, you have to use a `ps` shell command that returns the list of all the processes currently running on your machine. Piping the list to `grep` and searching for the Java string, you will find the Tomcat instance:

   ```
   ~ $ ps -ef | grep java
   root      1447     1  4 18:18 ?        00:01:21 /usr/bin/java -
   Djava.util.logging.config.file=/opt/apache-tomcat-8.5.5/conf/
   logging.properties -Djava.util.logging.manager=org.apache.juli.
   ClassLoaderLogManager -Djava.awt.headless=true -Xms1536m
   -Xmx1536m -XX:PermSize=256m -XX:MaxPermSize=256m
   -Djdk.tls.ephemeralDHKeySize=2048 -classpath /opt/apache-
   tomcat-8.5.5/bin/bootstrap.jar:/opt/apache-tomcat-8.5.5/
   bin/tomcat-juli.jar -Dcatalina.base=/opt/apache-
   tomcat-8.5.5 -Dcatalina.home=/opt/apache-tomcat-8.5.5
   ```

```
-Djava.io.tmpdir=/opt/apache-tomcat-8.5.5/temp
org.apache.catalina.startup.Bootstrap start
```

8. We have successfully created a script to start and stop Tomcat, but this still requires you to run it manually from the command shell. For an automatic startup, the last step is adding it to configured services. We will use a system utility, `update-rc`, to do this:

```
~ $ sudo update-rc.d tomcat defaults
```

9. The previous command creates a set of files in some special folders. Each time your operating system changes its run level, for example, when you boot or halt it, the script contained in these folders is executed, so Tomcat will be started or killed. You can take a look at these files:

```
~ $ ls -l /etc/rc?.d/*tomcat
lrwxrwxrwx 1 root root 16 Oct  6 16:18 /etc/rc0.d/K01tomcat
    -> ../init.d/tomcat
lrwxrwxrwx 1 root root 16 Oct  6 16:18 /etc/rc1.d/K01tomcat
    -> ../init.d/tomcat
lrwxrwxrwx 1 root root 16 Oct  6 16:18 /etc/rc2.d/S02tomcat
    -> ../init.d/tomcat
lrwxrwxrwx 1 root root 16 Oct  6 16:18 /etc/rc3.d/S02tomcat
    -> ../init.d/tomcat
lrwxrwxrwx 1 root root 16 Oct  6 16:18 /etc/rc4.d/S02tomcat
    -> ../init.d/tomcat
lrwxrwxrwx 1 root root 16 Oct  6 16:18 /etc/rc5.d/S02tomcat
    -> ../init.d/tomcat
lrwxrwxrwx 1 root root 16 Oct  6 16:18 /etc/rc6.d/K01tomcat
    -> ../init.d/tomcat
```

We created a shell script to start Apache Tomcat. Now, when you boot your Linux machine, Tomcat will automatically start and all the web application content will be available for user requests. If you prefer to manually start and stop Tomcat, the script could yet be useful for you. Just create it as described and avoid the last step. You will use the script to start or stop Tomcat from the command line, that is, sudo tomcat start or sudo tomcat stop.

Installing GeoServer

We are well on our way! Go to the GeoServer download page as shown in the following screenshot (`http://geoserver.org/download/`) and review the installation options available. You will find some different packages for GeoServer. We will use the Web Archive version:

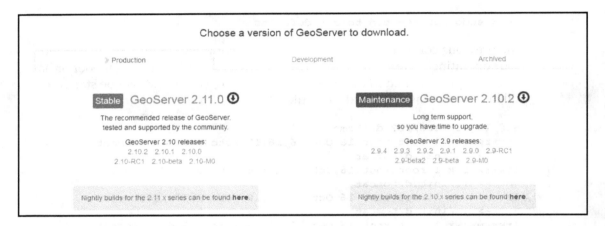

You may select a release from two different branches--**Stable** and **Maintenance**. Both of them are built for production purposes, so you can choose whatever you prefer; also, we suggest you select the latest release as it contains all the new features the developer team has just released.

Apart from the **Production** tab, you may have noted there are two other sections--**Development** and **Archived**. Inside the **Development** section, you will find a nightly build, these releases are not suitable for production as they may be prone to bugs, but it contains all the changes the developers did on the source code, so you can use it to test the fix of a bug you discovered:

Archived contains older releases. These may be useful if you are using an old release of GeoServer and need to upgrade it to a newer one, but you don't want to jump to the last one. Another use case may be if you are deploying GeoServer in an environment where an old JRE version, 7.x or 6.x, is available and you cannot upgrade it.

In the following section, we will deploy the web archive on Apache Tomcat. As you may have guessed, using a Java application server is pretty much the same on any operating system. The next section is common to Linux and Windows, as using Tomcat requires the same steps on both operating systems. As long as you are using GeoServer deployed on Tomcat you will have no difference with examples described in this book, whatever operating system you are using.

Deploying GeoServer on Tomcat

With Java installed and working, let's install GeoServer. When writing this book, the latest version is 2.11.0. Perform the following steps:

1. Download the OS-independent version from GeoServer's download page. You can point your browser to the URL or use a command-line tool like `wget`:

```
~ $ wget
http://sourceforge.net/projects/geoserver/files/GeoServer/
    2.11.0/geoserver-2.11.0-war.zip
```

`wget` is a command-line utility commonly available on Linux systems. If you are using a Windows machine it is probably not available. You can download the items just pasting the URL into your internet browser.

2. Check if Tomcat is not running; if it is, then stop it. Now, unzip the archive you just downloaded in the `webapps` folder:

```
~ $ sudo unzip -d /opt/apache-tomcat-8.5.13/webapps geoserver
  -2.11.0-war.zip geoserver.war
Archive:  geoserver.war.zip
  inflating: ./opt/apache     -tomcat-8.5.13/webapps/geoserver.war
```

 On Windows, you can use the zip GUI, or the uncompressing tools built-in the operating system.

3. Now, you can start Tomcat. You have to wait until GeoServer is properly deployed. This may take a few minutes, then open your browser and point it to the **Web Admin Console** at `http://localhost:8080/geoserver/web`. You should see it like in this screenshot:

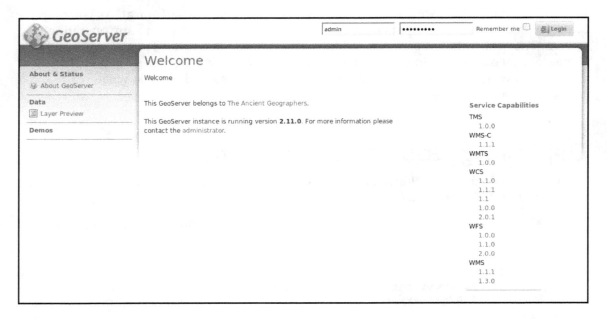

We deployed the GeoServer web archive on Tomcat and it unpacked the archive content. If there were no errors in the package, thanks to the great job of GeoServer developers (chances are that you will not find them), then Tomcat automatically starts GeoServer.

Implementing basic security

The web interface shown at `http://localhost:8080/geoserver/web` requires you to log in. You can use the default values of `admin` as username and `geoserver` as the password. Now you are on the administration console of GeoServer and can change any setting:

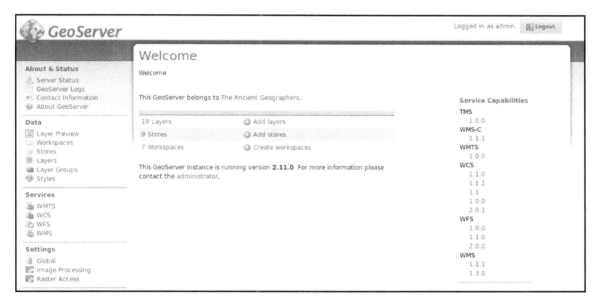

We will explore this interface in the next chapter, but we are sure you are wondering if a default password is a good idea for this console. Indeed it is not, and you should change it as soon as possible. We will cover many other security topics in detail in `Chapter 10`, *Securing GeoServer Before Production*.

Improving security settings

To improve the security settings, perform the following steps:

1. We will start by changing the default password for the administrator. From the **GeoServer Web Interface**, locate the area on the left and go to the **Security** section as shown in the following screenshot:

2. lick on the **Passwords** link and locate the area contained in the following screenshot, then click on the **Change password** link:

3. Insert a new password in the form, at least eight characters are required, and confirm it. Then click on the **Change Password** button:

Although you are setting up a development machine, security is always an issue. GeoServer ships with a default administrative password; you logged onto the web interface and changed the default password, then fixed some other issues. You got just a brief taste of the powerful GeoServer web interface. We will cover it in detail in the next chapter.

Understanding the GeoServer release cycle

In this chapter, we have installed GeoServer and are now ready to use it. However, before starting to explore its features and building maps, we need to consider the release cycle. As any successful software, GeoServer is frequently upgraded, new releases add new features and fix bugs.

GeoServer releases on a 6-month cycle, providing a short turnaround time for new features.

Each GeoServer release is supported with bug fixes for a year, with releases made approximately every 2 months. This allows for an overlap between supported releases, allowing organizations a chance to migrate without undue pressure.

To avoid your server using an old and no longer supported the release of GeoServer, you need to upgrade it frequently, and this is the topic of the next paragraph. The following figure shows the periods of its various releases:

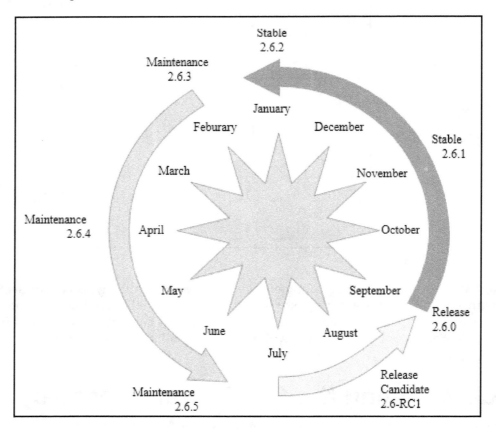

Upgrading your installation

It is a good thing to know that the GeoServer development team is working hard to frequently release new versions. You may be sure that most of the bugs will be fixed in a short time. On the other hand, this means you have to carefully plan an upgrading strategy in order to download and install any new release without having this affect your site too strongly.

Before you get too worried about this, we want to reassure you. Upgrading GeoServer is not a challenging task, and, with some simple steps, you may preserve your configuration when migrating to a new release.

We will explore the interface and the configuration option of GeoServer in the next chapter. For now, keep in mind that all these settings are stored in the file system in a folder called the **GeoServer data directory**. As you may guess from its name, it may also contain the spatial data you want to publish with GeoServer; although, this is not always the case. The most important content for the migration task is the configuration. All the configuration settings are contained in XML files.

We will design a detailed procedure to upgrade in Chapter 11, *Tuning GeoServer in a Production Environment*, but we already want your attention on the fundamental steps required as follows:

1. Select a folder external to the application for the data directory. By default, the GeoServer data directory is inside the application.
2. Backup the data directory frequently and always do a full backup before starting to upgrade GeoServer.
3. Undeploy the old version of GeoServer.
4. Stop the servlet container, for example, Tomcat.
5. Remove any temporary content from the servlet container.
6. Start the servlet container and deploy the new GeoServer release.
7. Point the new GeoServer to the external data directory.

Another important consideration about the data directory is its internal structure. Time after time, a new release of GeoServer applies changes to the structure that makes the migration an irreversible operation. In other words, the data directory is no more usable by a GeoServer release older than the last you deployed. This is the main reason you should always perform a full backup before starting the upgrade.

As a rule of thumb, patch and minor version migrations, for example, from 2.9.0 to 2.9.1, does not modify the internal structure of data directory, while you should expect issues when upgrading to a major release, for example, from 2.8 to 2.10.

Anyway, keep in mind that some minor version migrations may not be reversible since newer versions of GeoServer may make backward-incompatible changes to the data directory.

Summary

We have laid out a basic foundation to get GeoServer up and running.

In this chapter, you learned how to check whether JRE 8 is installed and properly working. You also installed Tomcat on Windows and Linux and configured it to start automatically.

After filling the system requirements, you explored the web archive option to install GeoServer and accessed the administrative interface using a web browser.

The web interface is a very powerful tool and you have to know it well to use all of GeoServer's features. In the next chapter, we will explore all the sections, looking in detail at what you can do to configure it, how to add data and preview maps.

3
Exploring the Administrative Interface

In this hands-on chapter, we'll explore the GeoServer administrative interface. This is the main console where you can control almost all the settings of your GeoServer installation. In the first release, it was a little bit complicated, but since the 2.x series, menu names and icons are consistent across each section. There is also an enhanced interface for the integrated GeoWebCache, where you can perform almost all caching configurations from the GeoServer interface. The good news is that we will use the mouse more here than any other chapter, so the keyboard will get a break.

In this chapter, we will cover all the sections of the Web Administrative Interface. In particular, we will explore the following topics in detail:

- Checking your GeoServer status and log file contents
- Previewing your data
- Tuning settings for **Web Map Service (WMS)**, **Web Feature Service (WFS)**, and **Web Coverage Service (WCS)**
- Tuning global settings
- Performing requests through the demo interface

Let's get right to it. Get logged in.

Understanding the interface

Accessing the interface just requires you to open the browser and point it at `http://localhost:8080/geoserver/web`. If you have read the previous chapter and executed the examples, you should have changed the default password for the admin user.

You can use the new one to log in again on GeoServer; we will now focus our attention on the interface's layout.

Consider the following screenshot. You may recognize three main areas in the GeoServer web interface:

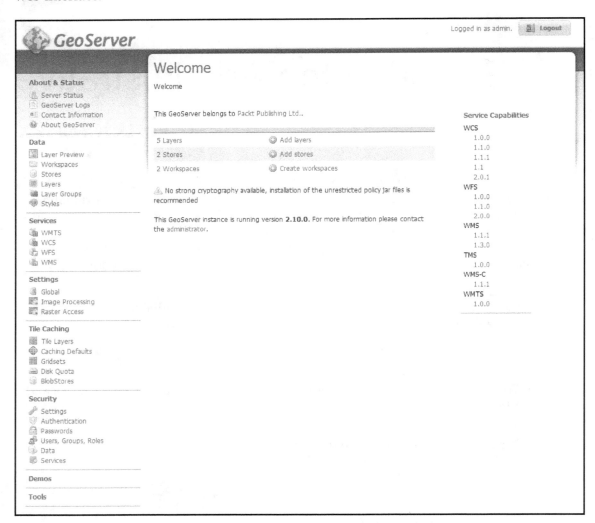

The central area shows you some information about the GeoServer status--the elements inside it change according to the operation you are performing. Just after you log on, it shows you a brief detail of the configured data, and warning or errors that you should correct. The last line shows the release number and there is a link to the administrator mailbox; it defaults to a famous ancient geographer until you insert your data.

 To update information about the administrator and its contact point, you can go on the left panel and select the **Contact Information** link, then insert the proper information about you and your company and press the **save** button.

On the right-hand side, there is a list showing you GeoServer capabilities. The listed acronyms refer to standard OGC protocols; we will talk about some of them in detail in this book, and each of them has at least one release supported. The numbers are links to the XML documents that exactly describe which data and operations each protocol supports. They are very valuable resources for clients willing to use your services.

Try to open the **WMS 1.1.1** link and open the result in a text editor. You can easily understand some sections. Consider the following:

- The first one contains a description of the service exposed:

```
<Service>
<Name>OGC:WMS</Name>
<Title>GeoServer Web Map Service</Title>
```

- Then you can find some information about the administrator:

```
<ContactInformation>
<ContactPersonPrimary>
  <ContactPerson>Stefano Iacovella</ContactPerson>
  <ContactOrganization>Packt Publishing
    Ltd.</ContactOrganization>
</ContactPersonPrimary>
<ContactPosition>Chief geographer</ContactPosition>
```

- The list of the supported operations and the base URL for the requests is as follows:

```
<Request>
<GetCapabilities>
<Format>application/vnd.ogc.wms_xml</Format>
<DCPType>
<HTTP>
  <Get>
    <OnlineResource xmlns:xlink="http://www.w3.org/1999/xlink"
```

```
                  xlink:type="simple"xlink:href="http://localhost:8080
                     /geoserver/wms?SERVICE=WMS&amp;"/>
        </Get>
      <Post>
        <OnlineResource xmlns:xlink="http://www.w3.org/1999/xlink"
           xlink:type="simple" xlink:href="http://localhost:8080
              /geoserver/wms?SERVICE=WMS&amp;"/>
      </Post>
    </HTTP>
    ...
    </GetCapabilities>
    <GetMap>
      ...
    </GetMap>
    <GetFeatureInfo>
      ...
    </GetFeatureInfo>
    <DescribeLayer>
      ...
    </DescribeLayer>
    <GetLegendGraphic>
      ...
    </GetLegendGraphic>
    <GetStyles>
      ...
    </GetStyles>
    </Request>
```

This information helps clients understand what kind of requests they can do and the response format they can expect. We will use this information in the rest of the book:

Operation	Description
GetMap	Retrieves a map image for a specified area and content
GetFeatureInfo	Retrieves the underlying data, including geometry and attribute values, for a pixel location on a map
DescribeLayer	Indicates additional information about the layer
GetLegendGraphic	Retrieves a generated legend for a map
GetStyles	Retrieves SLD styles configured on GeoServer

On the left-hand side, there is a table of contents listing the configuration areas. Each area contains links to administrative operations. When you click on one of them, the central area shows you contextual options. We will explore each area in the rest of this chapter.

The About & Status section

Starting from the top, this is the first section you find. It contains general information about the runtime variables and lets you check the logs to explore errors and warnings thrown by GeoServer when executing a client's request. Consider the following screenshot:

The Server Status link

When you click on the **Server Status** link, it opens a form that gives you a nice overview of the main configuration parameters and information about the current state of GeoServer. A table view organizes the information. Other than being informative, this view lets you perform some maintenance operations.

From top to bottom, you will find several pieces of information:

- The **Data directory** link (first row) shows you the location of the configuration files for GeoServer. If you managed to change the default location, here, you can check that GeoServer is using the new folder you created:

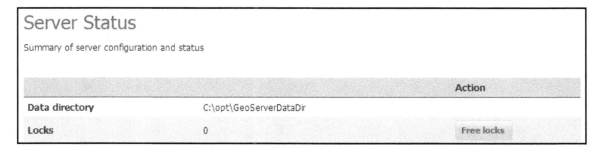

- The **Locks** row shows you useful information for **WFS-T** editing. WFS-T stands for **Transactional Web Feature Service**; and, using this protocol, a client can edit data. To avoid data corruption, GeoServer locks the data on which a transaction is required until it ends. If the number shown is greater than one, then there are some transactions going on with your data.

- The **Free Locks** button lets you reset a hung editing session, removing any orphan processes to free locks that might have been abandoned.
- **Connections** show you the number of vector data store connections. Vector data stores are repositories configured for the persistence of features. You will create them in Chapter 4, *Adding Your Data*. Consider the following screenshot:

Connections	0	
Memory Usage	137 MB / 1 GB	Free memory
JVM Version	Oracle Corporation: 1.8.0_121 (Java HotSpot(TM) 64-Bit Server VM)	
Java Rendering Engine	sun.dc.DuctusRenderingEngine	
Available Fonts	GeoServer can access 571 different fonts. Full list of available fonts	

- **Memory Usage** shows you how much memory GeoServer is using. You can manually run the garbage collector by clicking on the **Free memory** button. This will destroy the Java objects marked for deletion.
- The next three rows show information about the version of the **Java Virtual Machine** (**JVM**) that the GeoServer is using. You configured it in Chapter 2, *Getting Started with GeoServer*, in the installation processes. You will also see a list of the fonts seen by the JVM and GeoServer. Fonts are useful to render labels for spatial features; we will explore this in Chapter 6, *Styling Your Layers*.
- The rows listed in the following screenshot show settings for the **Java Advanced Imaging** (**JAI**). These libraries are used for image rendering and allow for better performance when GeoServer manipulates raster data, as with **Web Coverage Service** (**WCS**) and **Web Map Service** (**WMS**) requests. We will install native JAI support in Chapter 11, *Tuning GeoServer in a Production Environment*:

Native JAI	false
Native JAI ImageIO	false
JAI Maximum Memory	1.007 MB
JAI Memory Usage	0 KB
JAI Memory Threshold	75%
Number of JAI Tile Threads	7
JAI Tile Thread Priority	5
ThreadPoolExecutor Core Pool Size	5
ThreadPoolExecutor Max Pool Size	10
ThreadPoolExecutor Keep Alive Time (ms)	30000
Update Sequence	471

Free memory

- The **Update Sequence** link shows you how many times the server configuration has been updated. It is not that informative as of the time of writing this. The developers seem to have plans to use this to let you know that your configuration file has been updated externally from the application. Possibly from a REST call.
- GeoServer caches connections to stores, feature type definitions, external graphics, font definitions, and CRS definitions as well. Storing all this information increases the amount of memory used by the server. In a developing/debugging scenario, you can press the **Clear** button to force GeoServer to reopen the stores and reread the image and font information. This is shown in the following screenshot:

Resource Cache	Clear
Configuration and catalog	Reload

- The **Configuration and catalog** (last row) allows you to update the configuration without having to restart the service. GeoServer keeps configuration data in memory. If there is an external process updating the files containing the configuration's parameters, you can force GeoServer to reload settings from the XML files.

The GeoServer Logs section

The GeoServer Logs section lets you read the messages, warnings, and errors contained in the log file. According to the current logging settings, we will tune them further in this chapter, where you can find more information about the requests clients send to GeoServer and how it processes them. This is shown in the following screenshot:

You can only read the last 1,000 lines by default from the console. You can change this setting, but if you really need to access the entire log content, we would strongly suggest accessing it with a text editor. You can use the **Download the full log file** link placed just under the text console, or you can access the log file directly. On a Linux machine, you can use the console utility more, as shown in the following example:

```
$ more /opt/geoserver_data_dir/logs/geoserver.log
```

The Contact Information section

In the **Contact Information** panel, you can insert information on the organization and people managing the service. The default configuration pays honor to **Claudius Ptolemaeus**, an ancient cartographer (http://en.wikipedia.org/wiki/Ptolemy). This information is included in the WMS capabilities and is reference information for your users.

The About GeoServer section

Just as it states, this is just a catchall for build information and where to find the GeoServer documentation, bug tracker, and wiki. Consider the following screenshot:

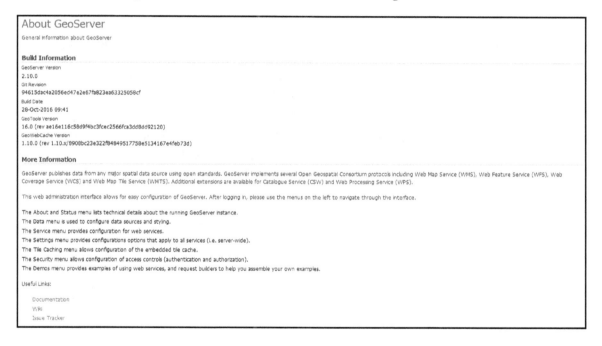

In the preceding screenshot, you can find links to the **Issue Tracker**. We will explore it in detail in Chapter 12, *Going Further - Getting Help and Troubleshooting*, but, here, we want to stress the relevance of contributing to the GeoServer project, reporting any issue you may find in the software at https://osgeoorg.atlassian.net/projects/GEOS/issues.

Manually reloading the configuration

We will now perform a simple change on GeoServer's configuration to demonstrate the reload configuration function. Consider the following steps:

1. To use the reload function, we want to manually edit the setting in the XML files contained in the GeoServer data directory, and, in particular, the `global.xml`, containing information about the administrator. If you didn't change its location, you may find it in the default location at, `{TOMCAT_HOME}/webapps/geoserver/data`, as in the following example:

   ```
   $ sudo vi /opt/apache-tomcat-8.5.13/webapps/geoserver/data/
     global.xml
   ```

    If you are using a Windows machine, point to the folder where you installed Tomcat and open the `webapps/geoserver/data` folder, where you will find the `global.xml` file. You can open it with any text editor, such as Notepad, but we want to suggest a smart and free replacement for it. Notepad++ is a gorgeous editor; you can download it at `https://notepad-plus-plus.org/`.

2. As you scroll down the content of the file, you should find the `contact` tag. Fill it with your details. Note that not all of the following XML tag may be present, but you may insert it, paying attention to the syntax:

   ```xml
   <contact>
     <address>via Roma 115</address>
     <addressCity>Roma</addressCity>
     <addressCountry>Italy</addressCountry>
     <addressType>Work</addressType>
     <contactEmail>stefano.iacovella@gmail.com</contactEmail>
     <contactOrganization>Packt Publishing Ltd.</contactOrganization>
     <contactPerson>Stefano Iacovella</contactPerson>
     <contactPosition>Chief geographer</contactPosition>
   </contact>
   ```

3. Now save the file and close it. Then go to the web interface; in the **About & Status** panel, click on the **Server Status** menu link to display the GeoServer status, scroll down, and click on the **Reload** button.

4. Now, go to the **Contact Information** panel. It shows your updated information.

We explored a simple case to use the reload configuration function. This is very useful in case you have to update a remote server with an automatic procedure, or you configure more GeoServer instances sharing the same configuration. We will explore such deployment options in `Chapter 11`, *Tuning GeoServer in a Production Environment*.

The Data section

This section contains links to the data configuration engine. As you may guess, to publish a map on the internet with GeoServer, you will need to add spatial data to it. Consider the following screenshot:

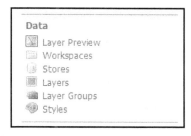

In this area, you can configure the data access and the way it is exposed to clients:

- **Layer Preview** opens a form including every layer published on GeoServer. In addition, if you have not yet added any data to your GeoServer installation, you will find several sample layers already listed. Clicking on the **OpenLayers** link, which is placed on the right side of the layer name, you can open a sample web application to take a look at what your data looks like.

The **Keyhole Markup Language** (**KML**) links let you download the data in a format suitable for preview on Google Earth. There are also several other available formats, listed in the drop-down box on the far right of the line. Consider the following screenshot:

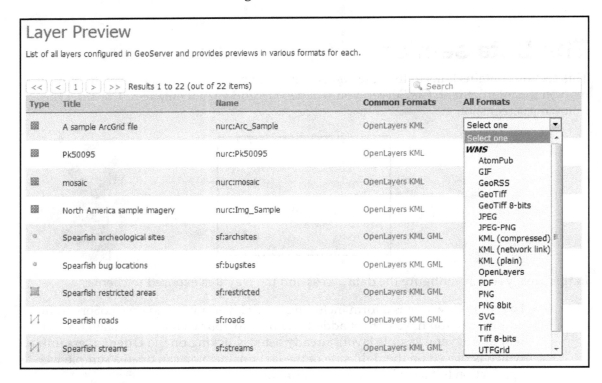

- **Workspaces** are logical entities useful to classify your data into homogenous groups. You may think of a workspace as your own personal namespace. You can associate many layers to one workspace. You are allowed to have several layers with the same name, as long as they are in different workspaces. You may see in the previous screenshot that workspaces and layers referred to each other separated by a colon. For example, when looking at the list of layers in the **Layer Preview**, you'll see a number of layer names, such as **nurc:Img_Sample**. The workspace name is **nurc** and **Img_Sample** is the layer name. Consider the following screenshot:

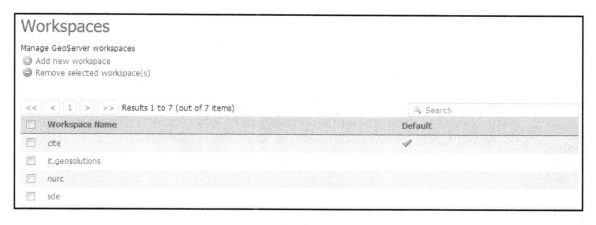

- **Stores** open a list of the configured data connections. Each store connects the GeoServer to repositories where your data is located. It is located inside a workspace, so it is worth setting one up at the beginning instead of sticking stores in one of the defaults. Of course, a set of default stores exist to let GeoServer use the default layers. In the next chapter, you will create stores and use them to add data to GeoServer. Consider the following screenshot:

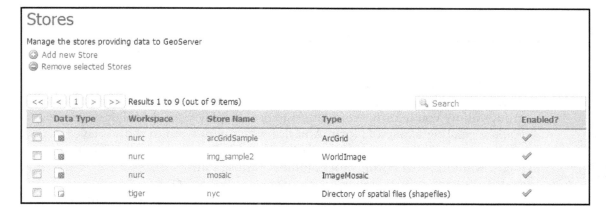

- **Layers** show you the data published from GeoServer with some information. You may see the type of layers in the **Type** column, with a different icon for vector and raster layers, according to the geometry shape. The **Workspace** and **Store** values of each layer are shown. Then, there are the layer **Name** values, which may differ from the file or table name where the data is stored; a tick mark shows if it is enabled, and the last column shows the **Native SRS** values. From this section, you can view and edit an existing layer, add (register) a new layer, or delete (unregister) a layer. Consider the following screenshot:

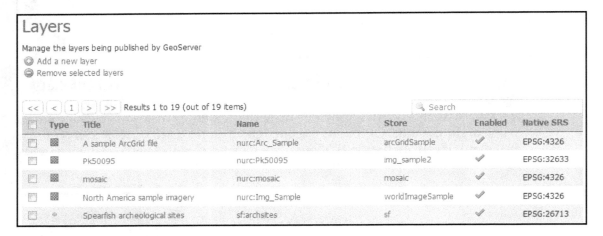

- **Layer Groups** let you logically merge more layers in a single entity. This way, you can publish something more similar to a complex map, where features of different geometry and properties are represented by different symbols. Layer groups allow you to order your layers to best display your data. For example, if you are creating a map of North America, you might want to show a layer of US states on top of North American coastal lines. Then, on top of the US states, you might want to show borders for counties of those states.

- **Styles** are XML files containing a detailed description of how a feature type has to be drawn on a map. In this section, you can access the styles list, edit them, and remove them from the GeoServer configuration. To edit styles, you can use the integrated editor--a simple, user-friendly interface to edit styles. As you may have guessed, building a pretty map is strictly related to styles; we will cover this in detail in Chapter 6, *Styling Your Layers*. Consider the following screenshot:

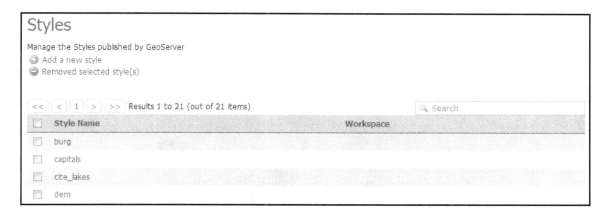

Jump in and look at the layer previews first. We will be visiting the **Layer Preview** section many times as we brew up our own layers.

The OpenLayers preview

We will now explore the features of the **Layer Preview** section. From this section, you can learn to access the data configured in GeoServer in several different ways. One of the most useful is the **OpenLayers** preview. **OpenLayers** is a powerful JavaScript library that is widely used to build web-mapping applications. GeoServer includes a simple template application that lets you look at a map with one layer represented. Consider the following steps:

    1. Open the **Layer Preview** page, and then locate **USA Population** in the layer list:

2. When you click on the **OpenLayers** link, a new browser window is shown. It contains a map of the United States of America colored according to a number of people living in each state:

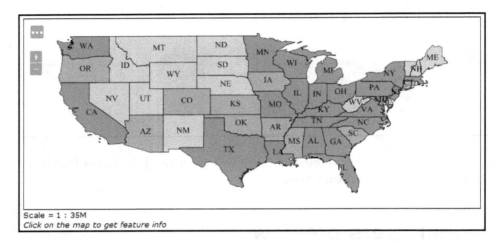

3. Play with the map to explore the capabilities of **OpenLayers**. You can zoom in and out using the plus and minus buttons on the left side or with the scroll wheel of your mouse. Pressing on the map and dragging it in a direction, you can shift the area of view that is panning the map. If you press the **...** button on the top portion of the map, some new options are made available. Consider the following screenshot snippet:

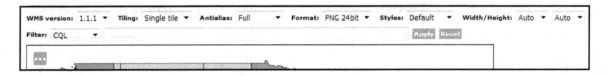

4. Starting from the left, you find a control to change the WMS version used by **OpenLayers** to send GetMap requests to GeoServer. The list contains the **1.1.1** and **1.3.0** versions; this may be useful if you want to be sure that the layer is properly working with both. The **Tiling** control lets you switch between the **Single Tile** mode, that is, a single image is produced each time you request a map, and the **Tiled** mode. The latter splits the map into several requests and may be useful to increase the performance of the map. Let's open the **Styles** control and choose a different one by default. If you choose **pophatch**, the layout of the map suddenly changes. Consider the following screenshot:

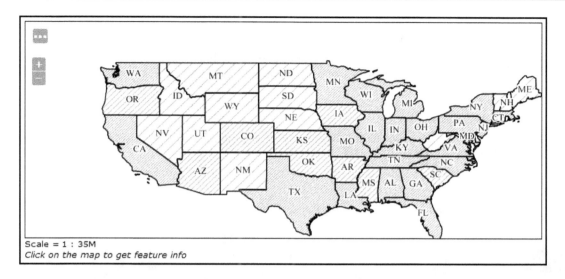

Scale = 1 : 35M
Click on the map to get feature info

5. We will explore styles in detail in Chapter 6, *Styling Your Layers*. The last two controls on the right side are to set the width and height of your map canvas to a specific size.

Did you enjoy this first taste of web mapping? **OpenLayers** is somewhat similar to Google Maps; it allows you to embed maps into a web application and lets users interact with them.

In the previous steps, you had a gentle introduction to the capabilities of **OpenLayers**. It's probably the most used and known JavaScript framework specifically designed to work with spatial data and maps. You can visit the project home page at https://openlayers.org, where you will find a lot of tutorials and information about the project. GeoServer still uses an old version of the framework; you can find information about it at http://openlayers.org/two.

The KML preview

We have seen that other than **OpenLayers**, several preview formats are available. Now we will use another popular format: **Keyhole Markup Language** (**KML**). This time, GeoServer will not open up an application as you select the layer to preview. In fact, KML is a data format and you will need another piece of software to display it on a map. Perform the following steps:

1. If you have not already installed Google Earth, you can download it from http:/ /www.google.com//earth/desktop.

Google also delivers a web version of Google Earth; it does not require you to install anything on your computer. You just need to have a recent release of the Google Chrome browser. Unfortunately, the online version of Google Earth does not allow you to load external KML files.

2. Accept the license agreement and save the installation file. Then, execute it and install Google Earth on your personal computer.
3. Point your browser to the **Layer Preview** page, scroll to the **topp:states** layer, and click on the KML link.
4. You are prompted to save or open the KML output file. Save it on your filesystem.
5. Open the KML file in Google Earth. Consider the following screenshot:

OK, that was pretty cool. We had GeoServer displaying layers on Google Earth. Drop the book and play around with Google Earth. Zoom in and out, and notice how it streams data from GeoServer. In fact, the KML file does not contain any data, just a reference to them. Any operation on the map triggers a request to GeoServer, and its response is a stream of data to the Google Earth client.

The Services section

When you publish your data, GeoServer exposes it through standard services, that is, **WMS** for maps, **WFS** for features, **WCS** for coverages, and **WMTS** for map tiles. Each one of them can be configured from this section, changing the default settings. You can also selectively disable them. This may be useful to increase the GeoServer performance on small servers. By default, all services are enabled:

WMTS

Web Map Tile Service (**WMTS**) is an OGC standard protocol to serve pre-rendered georeferenced map tiles over the internet. On the administration interface, you can change the service metadata, or enable and disable the service. Please note that WMTS is delivered from the integrated GeoWebCache so if GWC is disabled then WMTS would not be available.

WMS

Web Map Server (**WMS**) is an OGC standard to publish data as maps. The GetMap operation, as defined by the standard, lets a client request maps as images; for example, a .png or .jpeg file.

From this section, you can change the service metadata, inserting information that will be published by the capabilities of the service. You can also control the resource allocation, as shown in the following screenshot:

Resource consumption limits

Max rendering memory (KB)

65536

Max rendering time (s)

60

Max rendering errors (count)

1000

Watermark Settings

☐ Enable watermark

Watermark URL

[   ] Browse

Watermark Transparency (0 - 100)

0

Watermark Position

Bottom right ▾

The first value lets you set the maximum amount of memory that GeoServer can use when rendering an image for the client. This may be increased if you know your clients will need huge maps. Be careful when setting a different value from the default to avoid Out of Memory errors.

By increasing the **Max rendering time** value, you can have GeoServer processing more complex requests, but this will reduce the number of requests it can process. When the threshold is reached, GeoServer throws an error to the client.

There is also a maximum value to render errors in a single request before GeoServer throws it and switches to another one.

Watermark Settings lets you add a custom graphic to any map produced by GeoServer; this may be useful if you need to insert information about copyright from data owners.

You can change the compression level of the **PNG** and **JPG** images. Anytime GeoServer responds to a WMS GetMap request, the output is an image file. Changing this setting can help in producing better quality responses, or faster ones:

PNG Options

Compression level (0-100, default 25)

25

JPEG Options

Compression level (0-100, default 25)

25

WFS

Web Feature Server (**WFS**) is an OGC open standard to provide raw vector data. Feature information that is encoded and transported using WFS includes both feature geometry and feature attribute values. GeoServer allows you to share your geospatial data in this standard and lets the client choose among several formats. Output formats include GML2, GML3, ShapeFile, JSON, and CSV.

In this section, you can change, as usual, the service metadata. You can limit the **Maximum number of features** returned by GeoServer for each request. The default value is very high; you may consider reducing it. Consider the following screenshot:

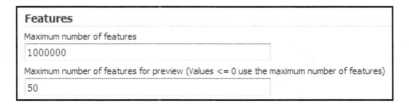

GeoServer is compliant with the full **Transactional Web Feature Server** (**WFS-T**) level of service, as defined by the OGC. Using WFS-T, clients may create transactions to edit data. You can select which level should be exposed by your server. By default the complete level is configured, that is, support for LockFeature is supported by the suite of transactional level operations. If you don't need or want your clients editing the data, set the option to **Basic**. This is shown in the following screenshot:

WCS

Web Coverage Service (**WCS**) publishes raster-based layers. The Geo ArcGrid includes a couple of geospatial example of coverages. It's almost like having both WMS and WFS in one service. It allows clients to get raster data along with geospatial data to make more analysis locally.

 A detailed description of WFS and WCS are out of the book's scope; Chapter 12, *Going Further - Getting Help and Troubleshooting*, will give you a brief view of both. You will learn how to perform basic requests.

Limiting the SRS list from WMS

GeoServer supports many SRSs and can transform on-the-fly spatial features from one SRS to another. Sometimes, this may not be what you want; for example, if you are publishing data only in a few SRSs and want GeoServer to be heavily loaded from transformation requests. You will now learn how to limit the list of supported SRS:

 Do you know that an SRS is a spatial reference system? If you are not reading the book from start to end, and this acronym sounds confusing, take a look at Chapter 1, *GIS Fundamentals*.

1. On your browser, open the WMS capabilities. This is the standard output for the service description. It is an XML file, containing data published, operations supported, and other details. To open it, go to the main page of GeoServer's interface and click on the **1.3.0** link:

2. You should get a huge XML file. Scroll down to **All supported EPSG projections**. The following screenshot shows just a few of them; you now have an idea of how many there are:

```
- <Layer>
    <Title>GeoServer Web Map Service</Title>
  - <Abstract>
      A compliant implementation of WMS plus most of the SLD extension (dynamic styling). Can also generate PDF, SVG, KML, GeoRSS
    </Abstract>
    <!--All supported EPSG projections:-->
    <CRS>AUTO:42001</CRS>
    <CRS>AUTO:42002</CRS>
    <CRS>AUTO:42003</CRS>
    <CRS>AUTO:42004</CRS>
    <CRS>AUTO:97001</CRS>
    <CRS>AUTO:97002</CRS>
    <CRS>EPSG:WGS84(DD)</CRS>
```

3. Now, go to the **Service** section and click on **WMS**. Then scroll down and locate the **Limited SRS list** textbox. Insert the SRS code we will use throughout the book: **4326, 3857, 4269**. Then click on the **Submit** button:

4. Now repeat the capabilities request and search for the CRS section. Is there any difference? Consider the following screenshot:

```
<!--Limited list of EPSG projections:-->
<CRS>EPSG:3857</CRS>
<CRS>EPSG:4269</CRS>
<CRS>EPSG:4326</CRS>
<CRS>CRS:84</CRS>
- <EX_GeographicBoundingBox>
    <westBoundLongitude>-180.0</westBoundLongitude>
    <eastBoundLongitude>180.0</eastBoundLongitude>
    <southBoundLatitude>-90.0</southBoundLatitude>
    <northBoundLatitude>90.0</northBoundLatitude>
  </EX_GeographicBoundingBox>
  <BoundingBox CRS="CRS:84" minx="-180.0" miny="-90.0" maxx="180.0" maxy="90.0"/>
```

We limited the SRS-supported list. This will make the capabilities file clearer, and it will also help some clients to deal with it. You can add or remove SRS from the list at any time, according to the data or maps you have to manage.

Settings

This area contains some configuration parameters that cover general GeoServer behavior. Consider the following screenshot:

Under the **Global** section, as its name states, you can find very general parameters.

Among those included, it is worth discussing the option to enable `Verbose Reporting`, shown as follows:

Turning on this flag, you can enable beautification of XML responses in error messages by adding line returns. Enabling this option consumes a lot of resources, so only enable this option if you need to. Verbose exceptions will give you multiline error messages.

It is also important to get confident with the **Logging Profile**. There are a set of default logging configurations shipped with GeoServer. You can add others in the **Log4J** configuration format.

You may want to keep your log files outside of the data folder in cases where you want to rotate logs. By default, these are in `$GEOSERVER_HOME/data_dir`, and you may want to keep this folder clean.

Changing your logging configuration

When testing client-server interaction or exploring new functions, it may be useful to have more information inside the log file. We will now raise the verbosity of GeoServer:

1. Click on the **Global** link in the **Settings** menu.
2. Scroll down to the **Logging Profile** section.

3. Now change the **Logging Profile** setting to **VERBOSE_LOGGING**:

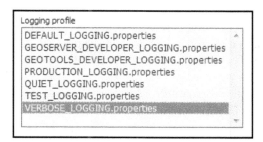

4. Click on **GeoServer Logs** in **About & Status** to review the logs. Optionally, review the log from the filesystem, `/data_dir/logs/geoserver.log`.

You just switched GeoServer to logging in verbose mode. Remember to remove this option when you are no longer testing functionalities since it stresses the server and requires a lot of space on the log file.

Tile Caching

Tile Caching is a way to improve the performance of your server. When a layer is configured in the caching system, maps are split into tiles, and then stored in an ordered structure for later retrieval. Therefore, when a new map request hits an area already calculated, GeoServer can retrieve the tiles without having to retrieve data and render them to produce the map. This requires a smaller time than the process of creating a new map, so, caching can boost the performance of your server.

The caching system of GeoServer uses an integrated package--GeoWebCache. It is a Java-based application that complements GeoServer. Consider the following screenshot:

When creating a new layer, you may choose if it has to be cached or not. Let us explore the available options:

- The **Tile Layers** section lists all cached layers and lets you review and modify parameters. It also contains a link to a layer preview very similar to that listed in the **Data** section. The main difference is that this preview uses cached tiles. GeoWebCache is a companion for GeoServer, and also if it is strictly integrated, there are a set of global parameters to configure it too.
- **Caching Defaults** is your entry point for them.
- The **Gridsets** option lets you create new tiling schemas or modify the existing ones. All the tiles you will create when caching need to be stored on a filesystem.
- The **Disk Quota** and **BlobStores** options let you set predefined amounts of space for each layer.

Caching is a strong ally for your site's performance. In `Chapter 8`, *Performance and Caching*, we will explore in detail how to properly cache data.

The Security panel

GeoServer has a robust security subsystem, modeled on Spring Security. Most of the security features are available through the **Web Administration** interface. In the Security panel, you can find links to set user properties and bind data to security rules, as shown in the following screenshot:

The basic idea is that you create users and roles and combine them with data to enable specific access policies. You can also limit read and write access by role. We will go over these in detail in a later chapter.

The Settings panel

From the **Settings** panel, you can control general settings about security.

You can select a role. Roles are defined in the **Users, Groups, and Roles** section and control security settings for the users.

The **Encryption** settings let you choose how GeoServer will encrypt passwords. As you may note in the following screenshot after you install the software there is a warning about strong cryptography being available. You will learn how to fix this in a later chapter:

Security Settings

Configure security settings

Active role service

default ▼

Encryption

☐ Encrypt web admin URL parameters

Password encryption

Weak PBE ▼   ⚠ No strong cryptography available, installation of the unrestricted policy jar files is recommended

Users, Groups, and Roles

A list of the users, groups, and roles configured on GeoServer are shown here. By default, you have one user called the **admin**, and one role called **role_administrator**. Clicking on the username allows you to edit the account password, assign new roles, and add a role. This is shown in the following screenshot:

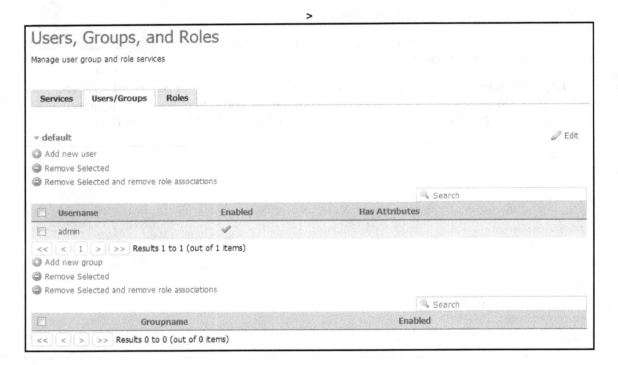

Data

You are able to give access to workspaces and layers in a granular way. Therefore, after you add a number of workspaces, you can assign roles to them here. We will cover security in detail in Chapter 10, *Securing GeoServer Before Production*.

Catalog security

These options are pretty well explained here. In a nutshell, you have three modes when a user is challenged for access. I recommend you to use **HIDE**, which is the default mode. It is better to show users only what they have access to, instead of advertising that other services and layers exist. This is shown in the following screenshot:

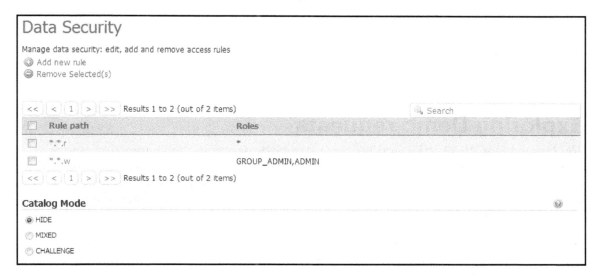

Services security

We went over the various service types (WCS, WFS, WMS) a few pages back. This feature gives you control over read/write access to them. By default, no service-based security is in effect in GeoServer. However, rules can be added, removed, or edited here.

Note that data security and service security cannot be combined; for example, if you disable a user's access to WMS, he will not see any layer even if you grant him access to that layer.

Demos

A few demo applications are included with GeoServer.

The **WCS request builder** application is pretty handy to piece together a **GetCoverage** request. It's not something you'll likely do as a beginner, but it's worth remembering that the tool is available.

The **Demo requests** application has a number of example requests to query WCS, WFS, and WMS. Examples to delete, update, and insert records are also included. Consider the following screenshot:

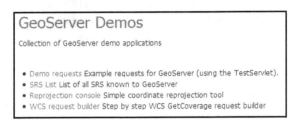

Exploring Demo requests

You learned that WMS, WFS, and WCS are standards describing the interaction among clients and servers. Each standard defines a set of operations that, from a client's point of view, are requests. On the OGC site, you can download detailed documents describing each admitted request. The demo application is a valuable tool to help you practice with requests. Let's explore some basic operations:

1. Open the **Demo requests** application. From the drop-down list, you can select a set of prepared requests. They are listed with a syntax declaring the standard as a prefix and the standard's version as a suffix. Choose **WFS_getCapabilities-1.1.xml**. This is shown in the following screenshot:

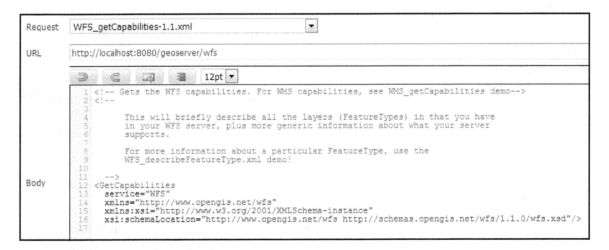

2. Click on the **Submit** button. A new panel is shown, and, after a while, it lists the XML response from GeoServer:

```
- <wfs:WFS_Capabilities version="1.1.0"
  xsi:schemaLocation="http://www.opengis.net/wfs http://localhost:8080/geoserver
  /schemas/wfs/1.1.0/wfs.xsd" updateSequence="153">
  - <ows:ServiceIdentification>
      <ows:Title>GeoServer Web Feature Service</ows:Title>
    - <ows:Abstract>
        This is the reference implementation of WFS 1.0.0 and WFS 1.1.0, supports
        all WFS operations including Transaction.
      </ows:Abstract>
    - <ows:Keywords>
        <ows:Keyword>WFS</ows:Keyword>
        <ows:Keyword>WMS</ows:Keyword>
        <ows:Keyword>GEOSERVER</ows:Keyword>
      </ows:Keywords>
      <ows:ServiceType>WFS</ows:ServiceType>
      <ows:ServiceTypeVersion>1.1.0</ows:ServiceTypeVersion>
      <ows:Fees>NONE</ows:Fees>
      <ows:AccessConstraints>NONE</ows:AccessConstraints>
    </ows:ServiceIdentification>
```

3. Another basic WFS operation is `getFeature`, which will retrieve a feature for you. Select **WFS_getFeature-2.0.xml**. If you look at the XML code, you can see a clear reference to the **sf:bugsites** layer, which is included in the sample set. Change it to **topp:states**, as shown in the following screenshot:

[87]

4. Click on the **Submit** button. A new panel is shown, and, after a while, it lists the XML response from GeoServer. The code is a GML representation of the features with `fid = 11`, as requested in the filter:

```
- <wfs:FeatureCollection numberMatched="1" numberReturned="1" timeStamp="2017-06-09T15:49:41.266Z" xsi:schemaLocation="http://www.opengis.net/wfs/2.0 http://localhost:8080/geoserver/schemas/wfs/2.0
/wfs.xsd http://www.openplans.org/topp http://localhost:8080/geoserver/wfs?service=WFS&version=2.0.0&request=DescribeFeatureType&typeName=topp%3Astates http://www.opengis.net/gml/3.2 http://localhost:8080
/geoserver/schemas/gml/3.2.1/gml.xsd">
 - <wfs:member>
  - <topp:states gml:id="states.11">
   - <topp:the_geom>
    - <gml:MultiSurface srsName="urn:ogc:def:crs:EPSG::4326" srsDimension="2">
     - <gml:surfaceMember>
      - <gml:Polygon>
       - <gml:exterior>
        - <gml:LinearRing>
         - <gml:posList>
           33.027668 -114.519844 33.036743 -114.558304 33.026962 -114.609138 33.033527 -114.633179 33.044373 -114.644371 33.038883 -114.663162 33.095345 -114.710564 33.122337 -114.708672
           33.167213 -114.67733 33.22456 -114.67926 33.239223 -114.68692 33.267982 -114.676903 33.305676 -114.734634 33.352386 -114.702812 33.41103 -114.724144 33.419086 -114.644302 33.439396
           -114.629784 33.468571 -114.6203 33.486099 -114.597298 33.509418 -114.586273 33.560047 -114.528633 33.580482 -114.539459 33.622112 -114.526382 33.665482 -114.524475 33.682713
           -114.535645 33.708347 -114.494888 33.743179 -114.509499 33.771694 -114.503769 33.826012 -114.520332 33.841946 -114.510933 33.862907 -114.520172 33.925018 -114.497398 33.952396
           -114.524841 33.965046 -114.517418 34.029827 -114.428192 34.078316 -114.423241 34.102638 -114.409378 34.141281 -114.322014 34.171215 -114.284584 34.186207 -114.234993 34.266964
           -114.149132 34.272606 -114.124451 34.314533 -114.133347 34.336433 -114.152634 34.365192 -114.181297 34.405476 -114.257057 34.412056 -114.282608 34.435741 -114.302078 34.454861
           -114.331848 34.459667 -114.375717 34.477074 -114.383072 34.536552 -114.376038 34.583714 -114.408951 34.598953 -114.43351 34.610886 -114.421478 34.709866 -114.464844 34.744751
           -114.497009 34.748905 -114.524757 34.759953 -114.541245 34.831856 -114.56942 34.87553 -114.626465 34.919498 -114.629677 34.943607 -114.620209 34.99765 -114.631477 34.998913
           -114.62027 35.041862 -114.63298 35.076057 -114.594833 35.118656 -114.635109 35.133907 -114.625641 35.132561 -114.581818 35.140068 -114.571457 35.174347 -114.560242 35.220184
           -114.558784 35.304771 -114.58709 35.358383 -114.588783 35.450768 -114.644592 35.515762 -114.67141 35.546646 -114.648987 35.584843 -114.652328 35.611359 -114.639061 35.646595
           -114.653259 35.65641 -114.667679 35.693111 -114.664284 35.732609 -114.688011 35.764717 -114.681931 35.847458 -114.689056 35.870975 -114.661652 35.880489 -114.660789 35.911629
           -114.698463 35.987667 -114.735397 36.036777 -114.716858 36.058773 -114.728149 36.085983 -114.727333 36.105202 -114.711945 36.141987 -114.620796 36.138355 -114.598122 36.155109
           -114.529762 36.124729 -114.465805 36.121071 -114.443138 36.151009 -114.379997 36.137497 -114.34343 36.111454 -114.315292 36.087124 -114.303055 36.062248 -114.306786 36.018345
           -114.232674 36.017269 -114.205971 36.041744 -114.128227 36.121105 -114.106979 36.193993 -114.044312 36.216038 -114.036598 36.841873 -114.042915 36.996563 -114.043137 36.996243
           -112.899216 36.998009 -112.541763 36.995506 -112.236511 37.00172 -111.355453 37.002491 -110.739372 37.003929 -110.483398 36.991749 -110.451546 36.992065 -109.996399 36.996643
           -109.047821 35.996655 -109.047195 34.954613 -109.045998 34.59174 -109.048012 33.783249 -109.049721 33.205101 -109.049904 32.77948 -109.050728 32.441967 -109.048882 31.343348
           -109.045006 31.337559 -110.451942 31.335555 -111.07132 31.431438 -111.368866 32.04356 -113.328377 32.487114 -114.820969 32.615993 -114.808601 32.72081 -114.72126 32.734966
           -114.711906 32.741379 -114.693253 32.726238 -114.603157 32.73584 -114.602737 32.737392 -114.571175 32.748783 -114.571426 32.74889 -114.559967 32.760708 -114.560799 32.760704
```

5. Modify the following lines of code by inserting the `states.23` value:

```
<fes:Filter>
  < fes:ResourceId rid="states.23"/>
</fes:Filter>
```

6. Click on the **Submit** button again; when the panel shows the GML code, scroll down until you see the **STATE_NAME** field. Which state did you select?

```
        </gml:LinearRing>
      </gml:exterior>
    </gml:Polygon>
  </gml:surfaceMember>
</gml:MultiSurface>
</topp:the_geom>
<topp:STATE_NAME>Florida</topp:STATE_NAME>
<topp:STATE_FIPS>12</topp:STATE_FIPS>
<topp:SUB_REGION>S Atl</topp:SUB_REGION>
<topp:STATE_ABBR>FL</topp:STATE_ABBR>
<topp:LAND_KM>139852.123</topp:LAND_KM>
<topp:WATER_KM>30456.797</topp:WATER_KM>
<topp:PERSONS>1.2937926E7</topp:PERSONS>
<topp:FAMILIES>3511825.0</topp:FAMILIES>
<topp:HOUSHOLD>5134869.0</topp:HOUSHOLD>
<topp:MALE>6261719.0</topp:MALE>
<topp:FEMALE>6676207.0</topp:FEMALE>
<topp:WORKERS>4943568.0</topp:WORKERS>
<topp:DRVALONE>4468021.0</topp:DRVALONE>
<topp:CARPOOL>818546.0</topp:CARPOOL>
<topp:PUBTRANS>116352.0</topp:PUBTRANS>
<topp:EMPLOYED>5810467.0</topp:EMPLOYED>
<topp:UNEMPLOY>356769.0</topp:UNEMPLOY>
<topp:SERVICE>1683987.0</topp:SERVICE>
<topp:MANUAL>675050.0</topp:MANUAL>
<topp:P_MALE>0.484</topp:P_MALE>
```

The **Demo requests** interface lets you select sample requests and modify them to perform testing on GeoServer. When in doubt with a specific operation, this application should be the first point where you go to debug. From here, you can concentrate on the request's syntax, avoiding network issues or other problems that you may have experienced on an external client.

Filtering the projection list

In a previous **Time for Action** section, in this chapter, you learned how to filter the SRS list for WMS. Are you wondering what you will find inside this demo? Let's see:

1. Open the **SRS List** demo application. Wow, there are 5,846 items in the list! Yes, you just filtered items for WMS; however, all supported SRSs are still there. This is shown in the following screenshot:

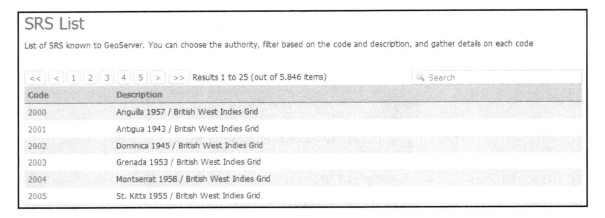

2. In the Search textbox, type in the project code for the basic projection, 4326; then click on Enter. Consider the following screenshot:

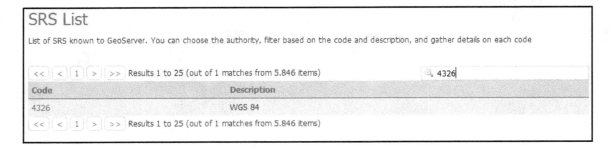

3. Click on the projection code to show the projection detail. Along with the Well Known Text description of the SRS, there is also a map showing you the area of validity. For 4326, it is the planet's surface:

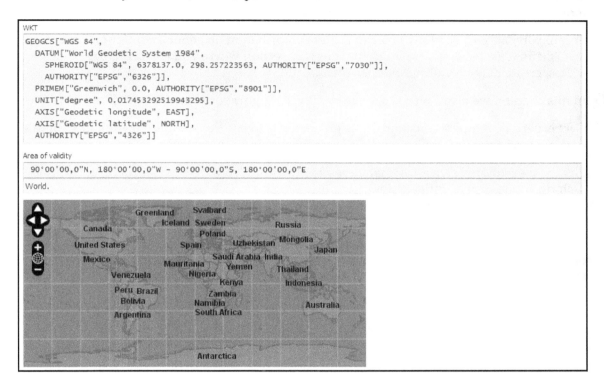

```
WKT
GEOGCS["WGS 84",
  DATUM["World Geodetic System 1984",
    SPHEROID["WGS 84", 6378137.0, 298.257223563, AUTHORITY["EPSG","7030"]],
    AUTHORITY["EPSG","6326"]],
  PRIMEM["Greenwich", 0.0, AUTHORITY["EPSG","8901"]],
  UNIT["degree", 0.017453292519943295],
  AXIS["Geodetic longitude", EAST],
  AXIS["Geodetic latitude", NORTH],
  AUTHORITY["EPSG","4326"]]
```

Area of validity

90°00'00,0"N, 180°00'00,0"W - 90°00'00,0"S, 180°00'00,0"E

World.

4. Repeat these steps to review 3857, which is the Google Mercator projection.

This gives you an idea of how each projection (4326 and 3857, in this example) is defined. Each projection is defined by several parameters formatted in the WKT format.

If you have custom projections, they will be included in this list. You can also check your data_dir/user_projections folder for an epsg.properties file. Any custom projection configured will be here, along with those that are overridden.

Summary

We had a concise introduction to the GeoServer web interface. Hopefully, you are now more confident with every section, and you have a good idea of how they work.

Specifically, we covered how you can retrieve information on general configuration, server status, and logs. Next, we explored the interface section where you can configure data access, create new layers, and publish them.

In this chapter, we also covered service-specific configurations for WFS, WMS, and WCS.

GeoServer's developers constantly take great efforts to enforce standard compliance. In this area, you can tune the services and discover the vendor options that GeoServer offers you.

Finally, we explored two areas that were greatly improved in recent GeoServer releases-- caching and security configuration.

All of these topics will be further explored in the following chapters.

In the next chapter, we will explore data stores. You will add new data to GeoServer. Not only will you use the shapefile and PostGIS built-in data formats, you will also download and configure a data extension to add data stored in an Oracle database.

With all these formats, you will be ready to publish 90 percent of the existing vector data.

4
Adding Your Data

In this chapter, you will learn which types of data you can use with GeoServer. We will take a quick overview of the formats supported, both built-in and via extensions, and how to add them to your configuration. More specifically, we will load data from a shapefile, a PostGIS table, and an Oracle table using US census data.

In this chapter, we will cover the following topics:

- Vector data sources
- Connecting to a PostGIS database
- Connecting to an Oracle database
- Raster data sources
- Data source extensions

We will add data now. Buckle up!

Configuring your data

In Chapter 3, *Exploring the Administrative Interface*, we covered the administration interface. Specific to data configuration, we explored workspaces, data sources, and layers. In this chapter, you will use them to publish new data sets.

You learned how to explore the default data, bundled with GeoServer, with the layer preview function. However, where is this data stored? How can you add your own data and use them to build your maps?

In Chapter 1, *GIS Fundamentals*, we explored different spatial data formats, learning the differences among vector and raster data. GeoServer can use both, and in many different binary formats. It can access some data formats by default, while others require optional extension and libraries. Go to the **Web administration interface**, select the **Stores** item from the **Data** section and click on the **Add new Store** link.

GeoServer lists the data formats available by default. For the vector formats, you can use the properties file, shapefile, and PostGIS tables, and cascade WFS from another server. Supported Raster data formats include ASCII Grid by ESRI, GeoTiff, Raster Mosaic, and World Image. You can also use WMS services from another server and cascade them to your users.

Are you wondering, what is the meaning of cascading WMS and WFS? GeoServer has the ability to load data from a remote **Web Feature Server** (**WFS**) or **Web Map Server** (**WMS**). This may be useful in several scenarios, most notably if you want to integrate the data from the remote server with other data configured on GeoServer.

The following image shows you all available formats in a default GeoServer installation:

Vector Data Sources

- Directory of spatial files (shapefiles) - Takes a directory of shapefiles and exposes it as a data store
- PostGIS - PostGIS Database
- PostGIS (JNDI) - PostGIS Database (JNDI)
- Properties - Allows access to Java Property files containing Feature information
- Shapefile - ESRI(tm) Shapefiles (*.shp)
- Web Feature Server (NG) - Provides access to the Features published a Web Feature Service, and the ability to perform transactions on the server (when supported / allowed).

Raster Data Sources

- ArcGrid - ARC/INFO ASCII GRID Coverage Format
- GeoTIFF - Tagged Image File Format with Geographic information
- Gtopo30 - Gtopo30 Coverage Format
- ImageMosaic - Image mosaicking plugin
- WorldImage - A raster file accompanied by a spatial data file

Other Data Sources

- WMS - Cascades a remote Web Map Service

Configuring vector data sources

The default vector data formats are among the most used in both proprietary and open source GIS packages. Chances are that the data you need to publish is in one of these formats. So, let's learn how to add them to the GeoServer configuration and publish them on a map.

Java properties files

You can store your data in the Java properties files. They are plain text files where you insert all the information about your objects; both the spatial description and all the alphanumerical attributes.

Properties files are easy to manage; you can update the content adding or deleting features, for instance without needing to recreate or reconfigure the data store. On the other hand, the performance of this format is not good. This format uses plain file text without any indexing mechanism, hence retrieving features takes a lot of time. Using the properties file is a viable option if you only have a handful of features (few tens for any datasets), and creating a real data store would be overkill.

A properties file always contains a header, describing the name and data type for each field, and a row for each record with *KEY=VALUE* pairs.

Adding properties files

Thus, creating the properties files seems an easy task. So, now we will add a few features to your GeoServer installation:

1. Before adding data, we may want to create a workspace for them. Do you remember what a workspace is? Similar to a namespace, it is a logical area for grouping homogenous data. We will now create a workspace and it will be the default workspace for any other procedure in this book. Go to the list of workspaces and click on the **Add new workspace** link.

Insert values as shown in the following figure, and then click on the **Submit** button:

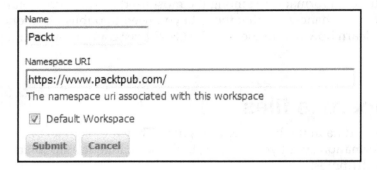

2. We will start with a few point features. Do you remember the places list in Chapter 1, *GIS Fundamentals*? You can use the `places.properties` file, bundled with the book, or you can create a new text file and insert the information as follows:

```
_=id:Integer,name:String,country:String,shape:Geometry:srid=4326
places.1=1|Rome|Italy|POINT(12.492 41.890)
places.2=2|Grand Canyon|Usa|POINT(-112.122 36.055)
places.3=3|Paris|France|POINT(2.294 48.858)
places.4=4|Iguazu National Park|Argentina|POINT(-54.442 -25.688)
places.5=5|Ayers Rock|Australia|POINT(131.036 -25.345)
```

 When creating a properties file, there are some constraints. The first field must have this form: `_=id`, and the values should be unique. It is the primary key of the dataset. The geometry field can have an extra suffix, `srid=XXXX`, which defines the Spatial Reference System by its numeric EPSG code.

3. Save the previous file to a folder on your server. Open the **Stores** list and click on the **Add new Store** link, then, from the list of vector formats, choose the **Properties** format. Insert a name, a description, and the full path to your file, then click on **Save**:

4. GeoServer browses the folder and lists the files contained. Click on **Publish** to create a layer for the `places.properties` file, as shown here:

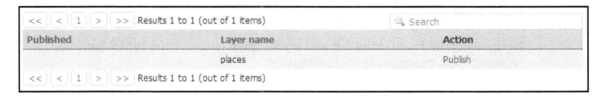

5. There are many parameters that you can customize when creating a new layer. For the moment, you can leave default values for most of them; we will explore them in detail in the following chapters. Scroll down to the **Coordinate Reference Systems** section and check that **Native** and **Declared SRS** are **EPSG:4326**, the same value you inserted in the file. In the **Bounding Boxes** section, showed in the following image, click on **Compute from data** and **Compute from native bounds**:

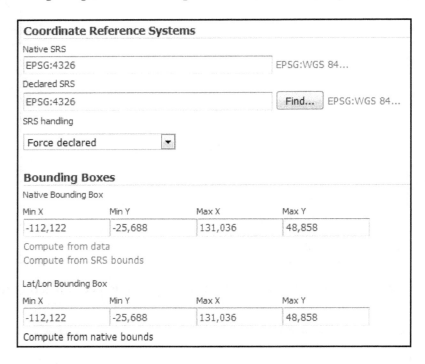

6. Now, select the **Publishing** tab and scroll down to locate the **WMS Settings** section. Select **point** as the **Default Style**:

7. Scroll down to the end of the page and click on the **Save** button.

8. Open the **Layer Preview** page. The new layer is now present in the list:

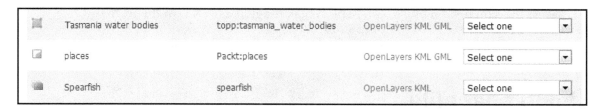

9. Click on the **OpenLayers** link and you will see a new map with the points contained in the `places.properties` file:

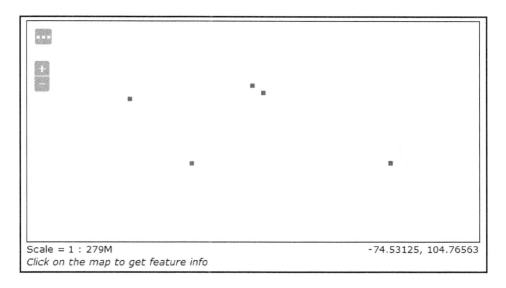

You just created your first layer. It was really simple and straightforward, wasn't it? Now you can try something more complex and publish a properties file containing polylines. Pick up the `rivers.properties` bundle file and repeat the previous procedure. Mind step 6. You are now publishing polylines so you have to select line as the default style.

If you open the `rivers.properties` file, you may note that the content is quite larger than in the `places.properties` file. A polyline is an ordered sequence of points, and, to have an acceptable representation of a river, you need many points. The syntax is again as WKT, in the form of `LINESTRING(8.2197880387794 48.0468091904552,8.55335940922345 47.9808183864184, ...)`.

Using shapefile

Shapefile is one of the most popular spatial data formats. It is widely supported by almost any GIS package and this makes it great for interoperability purposes. It is also easy to create, edit, and manage.

You can publish shapefiles in GeoServer with two different options. Choosing the first, you can configure a folder containing a set of shapefiles, and you can also add new ones after the data source is created. The other option works the same way as the shapefile directory store, except you provide a path to just one shapefile.

Adding shapefiles

There are sources of open data available in the shapefile format. We will use the freely available Natural Earth dataset.

Natural Earth provides several datasets about cultural and physical features, packaged in three different reference scales. For more information, visit `http://www.naturalearthdata.com`.

Now follow the steps to learn how to configure shapefiles on GeoServer:

1. Download the Administrative data as a shapefile and place it in an appropriate folder as follows:

```
~/shapes$ wget http://www.naturalearthdata.com/
http//www.naturalearthdata.com/download/50m/cultural/
ne_50m_admin_0_countries.zip
```

2. Unzip the archive:

```
~/shapes$ unzip ne_50m_admin_0_countries.zip
Archive:  ne_50m_admin_0_countries.zip
inflating: ne_50m_admin_0_countries.dbf
inflating: ne_50m_admin_0_countries.prj
inflating: ne_50m_admin_0_countries.shp
inflating: ne_50m_admin_0_countries.README.html
inflating: ne_50m_admin_0_countries.shx
inflating: ne_50m_admin_0_countries.VERSION.txt
```

In fact, a shapefile is not a single file. According to specifications (http://www.esri.com/library/whitepapers/pdfs/shapefile.pdf), you need at least three files with shp, dbf, and shx extensions. Although not strictly required, it is really worthwhile to also have the .prj file. It contains the SRS definition for the data contained in the shapefile.

3. If you are unsure about the SRS of data, take a look at the .prj file. The administrative boundaries data are in geographic coordinates and the EPSG code is 4326:

```
~/shapes$ cat ne_50m_admin_0_countries.prj
GEOGCS["GCS_WGS_1984",DATUM["D_WGS_1984",SPHEROID[
"WGS_1984",6378137.0,298.257223563]],
PRIMEM["Greenwich",0.0],UNIT["Degree",0.0174532925199433]]
```

Do you feel confused with this syntax? If you didn't go through Chapter 1, *GIS Fundamentals*, it could be the right moment to take a look at http://epsg-registry.org and http://www.spatialreference.org.

4. Now open the administration interface, go to the **Data | Stores** section, and click on **Add new Store | Directory of spatial files (shapefiles)**.

5. We will use the Packt Workspace. Fill the required and optional fields, as shown in the following figure. For **Connection Parameters**, click on **Browse** and select the directory where you downloaded and unzipped the shapefile:

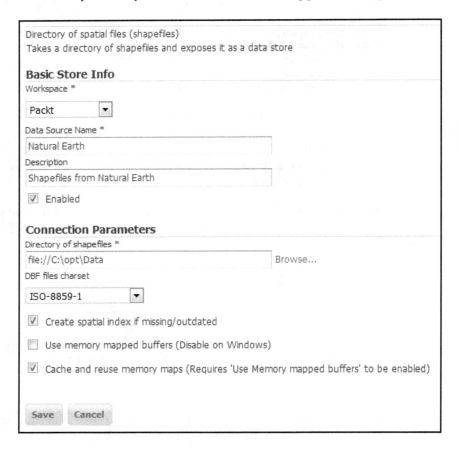

6. Click on **Save**. GeoServer browses the folder and lists the files contained. Click on **Publish** to create a layer for the ne_50m_admin_0_countries shapefile:

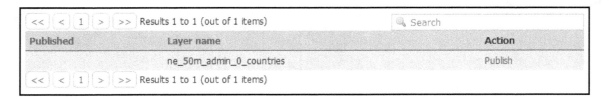

7. As you did to create a layer for the properties file, you need to customize some settings. Scroll down to the **Coordinate Reference Systems** and check the **Native SRS** and **Declared SRS**. You see that GeoServer didn't recognize the SRS, so, insert the `EPSG:4326` value in the **Declared** textbox:

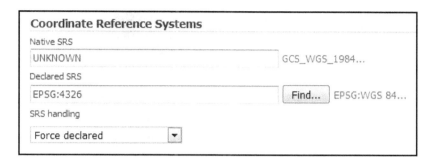

 Are you wondering why GeoServer did not recognize the SRS code properly? This is because the `prj` accompanying the shapefile uses a WKT string, but it is described with an ESRI dialect and it is not properly formatted.

8. Scroll down to the **Bounding Boxes** section. Click on **Compute from data** and **Compute from native bounds**:

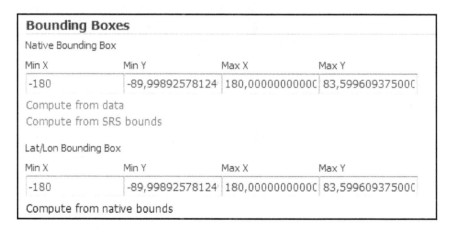

9. With shapefiles, GeoServer can properly identify the shape type and select an appropriate style. Therefore, you do not need to open the publish tab. Click on the **Save** button.

10. Go to **Layer Preview** and click on **OpenLayers** on the row of the newly created layer. You will see a map of countries with the default polygon symbol:

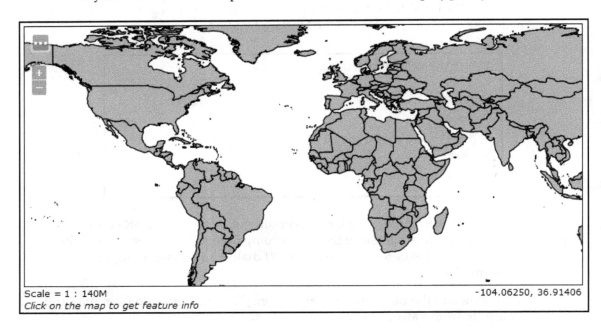

Scale = 1 : 140M   -104.06250, 36.91406
Click on the map to get feature info

We downloaded countries borders from the US census and unzipped it into the folder called shapes. We then walked through the steps to create a new vector data store for shapefile and publish it. With a little effort, the data is now available from a client making a WMS or WFS request. Publishing data in GeoServer is really straightforward, isn't it?

Using PostGIS

This is the most popular and most capable of all open source relational databases with spatial capabilities, and its features are constantly increasing. It leverages on PostgreSQL, a well-known and powerful RDBMS challenging top commercial products such as Oracle. At the time of writing release for PostGIS is 2.3.2 and for PostgreSQL is 9.6.3.

Both have an equally bad reputation of being a hard horse to ride. While fully understanding all possibilities or dealing with fine-tuning may be complicated, using PostGIS as a repository for your data is not rocket science. Are you wondering where PostGIS is located in the GeoServer installation? It is not there, but we will be making sure you install it in a few steps, and loading some data to play with in GeoServer.

If you are eager to learn more than the simple steps we will perform, then there are two wonderful references to read. Project sites for PostgreSQL and PostGIS contain a lot of pages ranging from basic to complex topics. These can be found at `http://postgis.net/docs/manual-2.3` and `https://www.postgresql.org/docs/9.6/static/index.html`.

Installing PostgreSQL and PostGIS

We will transform the census data from a shapefile to a PostGIS table. Unless you already have a PostGIS installation, we will first need to build it up. You can install PostGIS in several ways, and official and user documentation on customized installation is widely available. In order to get you started, we will use nice packages freely distributed from EnterpriseDB™. Apart from choosing the proper binary package, the installation runs the same way on Linux or Windows:

1. Open your browser and point it to `https://www.enterprisedb.com/advanced-downloads`; the page lists all available packages, both free and commercial. Scroll down to the **Option B - POSTGRESQL** section. Here, we can find the interactive installer for the latest release of PostgreSQL:

OPTION B - POSTGRESQL

Component Version	Operating System	Type	How to Access
v9.6	Linux x86-64	Interactive Installer	Download
v9.6	Linux x86-32	Interactive Installer	Download
v9.6	Windows-64	Interactive Installer	Download
v9.6	Windows-32	Interactive Installer	Download

2. Select the proper download according to your operating system and its architecture (32-bit or 64-bit operating system), and save it to a local folder on your computer.

3. Run the installer.

4. The installer wizard will guide you through the installation options. You may go with the default options; the only option needing your input is the password for the `postgres` user. At the end of the installation process, let the wizard launch StackBuilder on your computer:

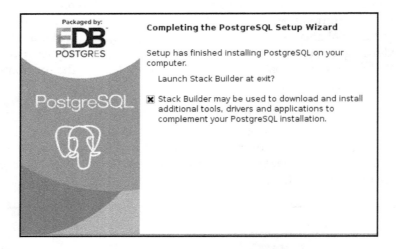

5. Select the only installation of PostgreSQL in the list and click on the **Next** button:

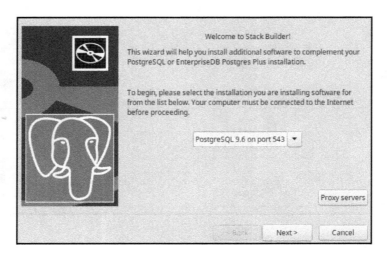

6. Locate the PostGIS spatial extension among those listed and flag it, then click on the **Next** button:

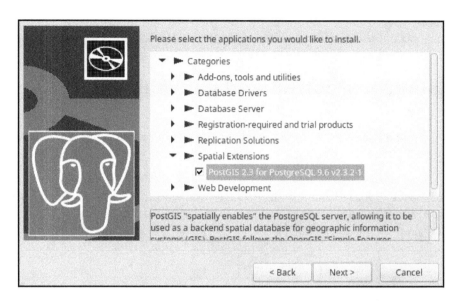

7. You can proceed with the installation of PostGIS, accepting default options. Wait for the wizard to terminate installation, then click on the **Finish** button:

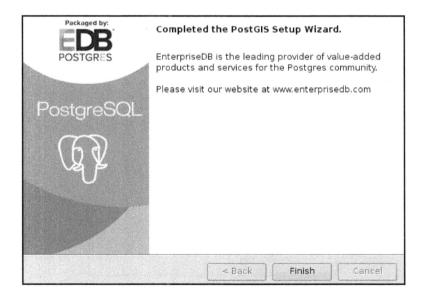

We have installed PostgreSQL and PostGIS. Indeed, PostGIS is just an extension of the RDBMS and you first need to have a running installation of PostgreSQL.

With these tools, you can build a full repository for your spatial data. We will lay the first brick of your geodatabase in the next section. Let's use PostGIS!

Loading data in PostGIS and publishing them in GeoServer

Now that you have a functioning instance of PostGIS, it is time to load some data. We will import the same Natural Earth data configured as shapefiles and turn them into a PostGIS spatial table:

1. Before we can load the data in PostGIS, we want to create a repository for them. From the following programs list, select the **pgAdmin 4** item:

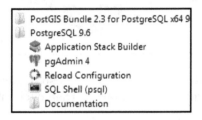

2. The utility called pgAdmin is the standard administration console for PostgreSQL. In the left panel, select your server--there should only be one item in the tree--and double-click on it to connect. Input the password for the postgres user and you will see the content of the PostgreSQL installation:

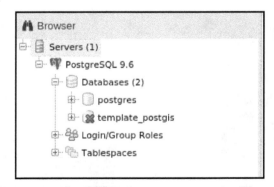

3. The first step is creating a new database. Right-click on the databases item and select create a database from the context menu. Call it `gisdata` and leave all other parameters with a default value. Click on the **Save** button to create it:

4. Select the new database from the list, right-click on it, and choose the **create | extension** item from the context menu. Select `postgis` from the list and click on the **Save** button. Your spatial data repository is now ready for loading:

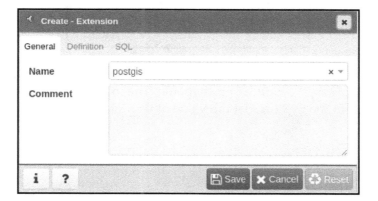

5. Start the PostGIS Shapefile Import/Export Manager, an easy tool installed along with PostGIS:

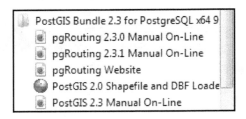

6. Click on the **View Connection details** button and insert the parameters needed to connect to PostGIS, as shown in the following screenshot:

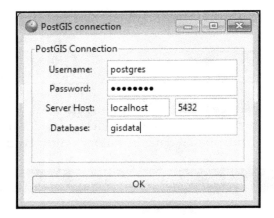

7. Now, click on the **Add File** button and browse to the folder containing the ne_50m_admin_0_countries shapefile. The tool does not recognize the SRS contained in the prj file. Set the value of the field to 4326, as shown here:

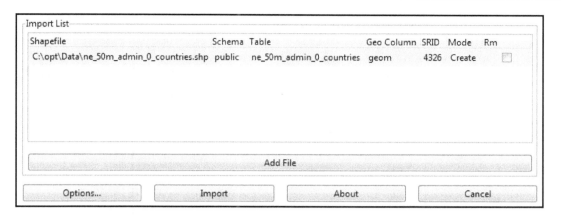

8. Click on the **Import** button and wait while the loader transforms your data and inserts them into a new PostGIS table. Eventually, you should see a success message in the log textbox. Click on **Cancel** to dismiss the loader utility:

```
================================
Importing with configuration: ne_50m_admin_0_countries, public, geom, C:\opt\Data\ne_50m_admin_0_countries.shp,
mode=c, dump=1, simple=0, geography=0, index=1, shape=1, srid=4326
Shapefile type: Polygon
PostGIS type: MULTIPOLYGON[2]
Shapefile import completed.
```

9. Now open the GeoServer administration interface, go to the **Data** | **Stores** section, and click on **Add new store** | **PostGIS**.

10. You need to insert connection parameters for the database in PostGIS. Select **Packt** for **Workspace**. Set **Data Source Name** and **Description** as `gisdata`. For **Connection Parameters**, you need to insert the same values you used with the loader. For your simple database, you don't need to play with the other settings; go with default values and click on **Save**:

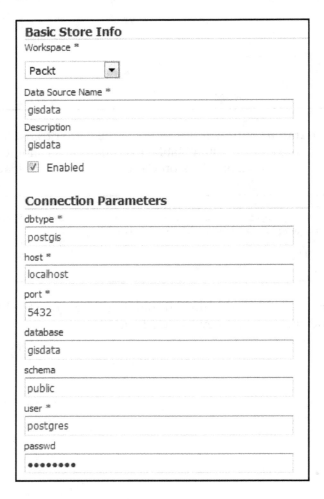

11. GeoServer will connect to PostGIS and present you a list of all tables containing spatial features. Click on the **Publish** link to the right of the `ne_50m_admin_0_countries` table:

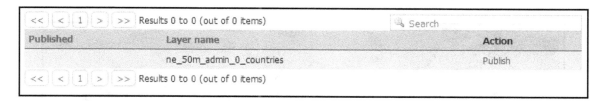

12. GeoServer shows the same publishing form we used for the properties file and shapefile. As we already published a shapefile with the same name, you have to insert a different one--`NaturalEarthCountries`. Scroll down and note that this time, GeoServer recognizes the native SRID for data. Click on **Compute from data** and **Compute from native bounds** in the **Bounding Boxes** section:

13. Click on the **Save** button and your data is published. With PostGIS tables, as with shapefiles, you do not need to select a style, as GeoServer recognizes the geometry type and chooses a proper one. You can now see a preview of **Layer Preview | OpenLayers**, next to **Packt:NaturalEarthCountries**:

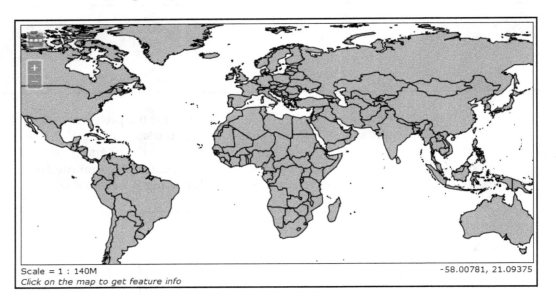

Scale = 1 : 140M   -58.00781, 21.09375
Click on the map to get feature info

We installed PostgreSQL/PostGIS, then loaded the countries dataset and published it in GeoServer. Did you notice that the layer's publishing runs almost the same, whatever the format of the data is? GeoServer architecture relieves you from the details of different data sources; as long as you have a driver for a specific RDBMS or binary format you can add data in GeoServer, simply ignoring the actual format.

The GUI loader is a great tool, but you may need to load shapefiles on a remote server, probably with only a remote shell session. Do not be afraid! The shp2pgsql is there to help you. It is a command-line tool, available on both the Windows and Linux editions of PostGIS. In fact, shapefiles are not really loaded by shp2pgsql, but they are translated in a form that psql can keep and load for you. Therefore, you just have to pipe the output to psql:

```
$ shp2pgsql -s 4326 -g geom -I
~/shapes/ne_50m_admin_0_countries.shp
public.ne_50m_admin_0_countries | psql -h localhost -p
5432 -d gisdata -U postgres
```

These are the basic sets of parameters required:

-s to set the spatial reference system

-g to name the geometric column (useful when appending data)

-I to create a spatial index

There are quite a few of the other parameters that make it a flexible tool; as usual, -? is your friend if you need to execute a less trivial data loading. Apart from creating a new table--default option--you can append data to an existing table, drop it, and recreate or just create an empty table modeling its structure according to the shapefile data.

Configuring raster data sources

Raster data sources are commonly used to read satellite imagery, scanned maps, and **digital elevation model** (DEM). You can add this data as a base layer for your maps.

ArcGrid

ArcGrid is a proprietary binary format created by ESRI and used with ArcGIS. A sample is included with GeoServer. Check out the arcGridSample data store and the nurc:Arc_Sample layer.

GeoTiff

A TIFF file is commonly used as the storage format for an aerial picture. A GeoTiff (http://trac.osgeo.org/geotiff) is an extension of the TIFF format. It includes Geospatial reference data in the header, an SRS, and the bounding box. Check out the sample data store called sf:sfdem.

Gtopo30

Gtopo30 is a format for DEM developed by the **United States Geological Survey** (**USGS**). The 30 in the name stands for 30 arc seconds, which is the fixed cell size for this format.

ImageMosaic

This data store allows the creation of a mosaic from a set of georeferenced images, for example, a folder of geotiff files. It is commonly used when you want to combine several images together to create continuous flowing coverage. This is a pretty advanced topic.

> Check out the GeoServer online reference to learn more:
> `http://docs.geoserver.org/stable/en/user/data/raster/imagemosaic`
> `/index.html`.

WorldImage

WorldImage is another format originally developed by ESRI. It's a plain ASCII-formatted file coupled with a raster image. The text file describes how the image is to be used. You can easily recognize them by the tfw (tiff) or jpw (jpeg) file extensions. Some samples are included with GeoServer. You will see a data store called `worldImageSample` and a layer called `nurc:Img_Sample`.

Adding a raster

After discussing the different raster formats, you may wonder if configuring them is as easy as with vector data. In fact, it is a really simple operation. In the following steps, we will guide you through obtaining a raster file and adding it to the GeoServer configuration:

1. First of all, we need a raster dataset. As with vector data an excellent source is the Natural Earth data web site. Open your browser and point it to `http://www.naturalearthdata.com/downloads/10m-raster-data/10m-cross-bl end-hypso`. Here you can find a few raster dataset, scroll down the page until you locate the datasets; as in the following screenshot:

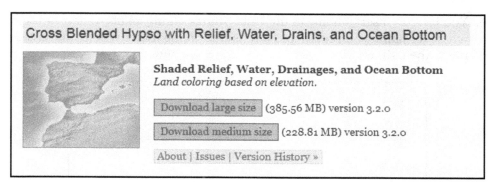

2. Download the medium size dataset by clicking on the corresponding link.

3. Extract the zip archive using the command line tool, as in this example, or the zip GUI:

```
$ unzip HYP_LR_SR_OB_DR.zip
```

4. From the GeoServer administration interface select the **Stores** section and click on the **Add new Store** link:

5. In the **Raster Data Sources** section, click on the **GeoTIFF** link:

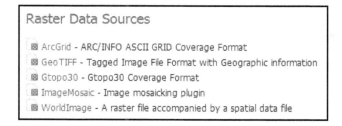

6. You have to insert a name in the **Data Source Name** text box, you can select whatever name you prefer, and a reference to the folder where you saved the tiff file in the URL textbox. Then click on the **Save** button:

7. GeoServer presents you the list of raster datasets, only one, in this case. Click on the **Publish** link:

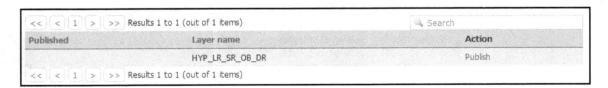

8. In the publishing page, scroll down to locate the **Coordinate Reference System** section. Here you have to insert the code EPSG:4326 in the **Declared SRS** textbox:

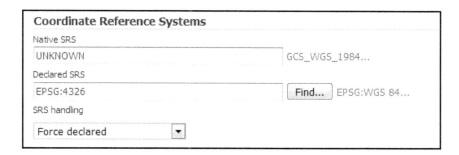

9. Scroll down to the bottom of the page and click on the **Save** button. Your layer is now published. Open the **Layer Preview** section and select the new layer. The resulting map should look like the following image:

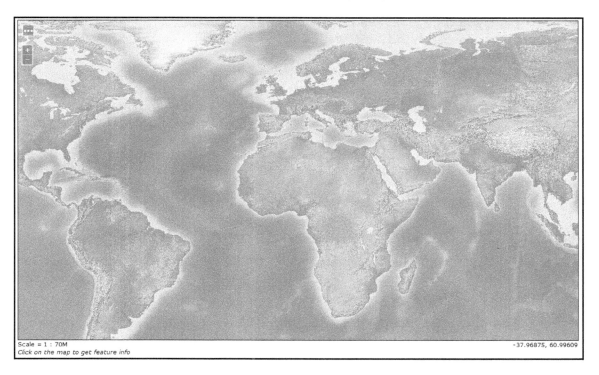

Exploring additional data sources

GeoServer supports several optional formats beyond the built-in data sources. In the remaining part of this chapter, we will explore a quite popular RDBMS that supports spatial data--Oracle.

Using Oracle

Oracle is probably the most widely used commercial RDBMS. It has support for spatial data since release 7, back in the 1980s. The current release, 12, comes with two flavors of spatial data extensions--Oracle Spatial and Oracle Locator. They share the same geometry type and a basic set of operators and functions. Oracle Spatial incorporates a richer set of functions for spatial analysis. Oracle is not free open source software, such as GeoServer or PostGIS, and it has a quite complicated and expensive license model. We will not cover installation here; as long as you are using Oracle, you should have the expertise and/or a proper budget to have it up and running.

If you want to try Oracle, and you don't have a commercial license available, you may consider using the Oracle Express Edition (`http://www.oracle.com/technetwork/database/database-technologie s/express-edition/downloads/index.html`).

Oracle Database 11g Express Edition (Oracle Database XE) is an entry-level, small-footprint database based on the Oracle Database 11g Release 2 code base. It is free to develop, deploy, and distribute; fast to download; and simple to administer. It does not include the Spatial functions, but the simpler locator is available and it is all you need to store the spatial data into it.

Adding Oracle support in GeoServer

We are assuming that you have an Oracle service with spatial data loaded here. If this is the case, you are now just two steps away from victory. We will add the Oracle data source and configure it properly:

1. To add Oracle support, we need to download an extension. Point your browser to `http://geoserver.org/release/stable`, locate the **Extensions** section, and click on the **Oracle** link to download the ZIP file:

Vector Formats

- App Schema
- ArcSDE
- DB2
- H2
- MySQL
- Oracle
- Pregeneralized Features
- SQL Server
- Teradata

When adding extensions to GeoServer, pay attention to the release number. You should always match GeoServer and an extension's releases.

2. Stop the Tomcat service. Extract the content of the ZIP file. It contains three files: two text files with instructions about installation and a `gt-jdbc-oracle-xx.y.jar` file. Select the jar file and move it to the `webapps/geoserver/WEB-INF/lib` folder under the Tomcat installation folder.

3. You also need to get the Oracle JDBC driver to complete the installation. Open your browser and point it to `http://www.oracle.com/technetwork/database/features/jdbc/index-091264.html`. You have to select the JDBC driver according to your Oracle Server release; the last three major releases are on the page. After you click on a release, you will access a page listing a JAR files. Accept the license agreement and select `ojdbc6.jar`, if using Oracle 11g, or `ojdbc7.jar`, if using Oracle 12c. Save this file in the same path you saved the previous one.

4. Start the Tomcat service and then log in to the GeoServer administration interface. Go to the **Data | Stores** section and click on **Add new store**. You can now see some new options. Select **Oracle NG**:

Vector Data Sources

- Directory of spatial files (shapefiles) - Takes a directory of shapefiles and exposes it as a data store
- Oracle NG - Oracle Database
- Oracle NG (JNDI) - Oracle Database (JNDI)
- Oracle NG (OCI) - Oracle Database (OCI)
- PostGIS - PostGIS Database

5. You have to insert the hostname for the Oracle server, the port on which the Oracle listener is waiting for connection requests (this is 1521 by default but ask your DBA for an exact value). The value to insert into the **database** textbox is the Oracle instance name. Finally, insert a username and password. The **schema** textbox is an optional parameter; it tells GeoServer where it should look for spatial data. Click on **Save**:

Basic Store Info

Workspace *

| Packt ▼ |

Data Source Name *

| Oracle11G |

Description

| Oracle Spatial |

☑ Enabled

Connection Parameters

dbtype *

| oracle |

host

| vmOra11Gsrv |

port

| 1521 |

database *

| GISDATA |

schema

| GISUSER |

user *

| gisuser |

passwd

| •••••••• |

6. GeoServer will connect to Oracle and present you a list of all tables containing spatial features. Clicking on the **Publish** link to the right of a table will bring you to the same publication form you used for shapefiles and PostGIS tables.

You have added Oracle support to GeoServer. To do this, you copied a couple of JAR files in to the GeoServer installation. The `ojdbc14.jar` file contains base classes for Oracle communication and usage and `gt-jdbc-oracle-2.7.5.jar` is the GeoTools library for spatial data management.

 GeoTools is a free software (LGPL) GIS toolkit for developing standards compliant solutions. It provides an implementation of **Open Geospatial Consortium** (**OGC**) specifications as they are developed. GeoTools is written in Java and is currently under active development. It is the core library in GeoServer. It can be found at `http://geotools.org/`.

Loading data in Oracle

Are you wondering how to load data in an Oracle database?

When we installed PostGIS, you learned it is shipped with a simple tool to load shapefiles in the database. Unfortunately, Oracle has no such a beautiful tool. However, you may use several packages to complete the task. One of the best choices is the GDAL/OGR suite.

It is an open source project and it contains a set of libraries and tools to manipulate several raster and vector formats. To install it, there are several different options. If you are on Windows, one of the best binary packages is the OSGeo4W suite; you can download it at `https://trac.osgeo.org/osgeo4w` and find useful information about its installation.

If you are using a Linux distribution, you should find the GDAL/OGR package in the repositories of your distribution. On Mint, you can install them using the command tool; for instance, consider the following:

```
~ $ sudo apt-get install gdal-bin
```

After you have a working installation of the GDAL/OGR package, you may use the `ogr2ogr` utility to convert vector data from a lot of formats to others. In our case, you may want to use it to load the Natural Earth shapefile in an Oracle database:

```
$ ogr2ogr -f "OCI" -nln NE_50M_ADMIN_0_COUNTRIES -progress -lco
GEOMETRY_NAME=GEOM -lco SRID=4326 -lco DIM=2 OCI:GISUSER/GISUSER@GISDATA
ne_50m_admin_0_countries.shp
```

The examples create a new table called NE_50M_ADMIN_0_COUNTRIES and load the geometries in a field called GEOM, assigning the EPSG:4326 code to the table. The ogr2ogr tool has many parameters; you may read the documentation at http://www.gdal.org/ogr2ogr.html.

 If you are curious about the GDAL/OGR project, you may read the dedicated site. It contains a lot of introductory and detailed information about how to use the tools and integrate libraries in your code. This can be found at http://www.gdal.org.

Summary

In this chapter, we added some datasets to GeoServer. We used different formats for vector data. It should be now clear to you that as long as there is a data source available, you can manage different binary formats in GeoServer and mix them together in a map.

Specifically, we covered how to publish shapefiles and PostGIS tables. We then explored additional extensions and added Oracle support to GeoServer.

In the next chapter, we will go forward with the data publication. We will cover in detail how you can use the data you publish from the clients, exploring different ways to create a web application showing maps to users, and letting them interact with data.

5
Accessing Layers

One of the main aims of this book is to help you learn how to publish your data. GeoServer lets you create layers, items containing configuration for your data, and the way they are represented on a map. In this chapter, we'll go over different vector and raster layer output types and explore ways to use them. We will discover a hidden gem called the **Reflector**. For good measure, we will toss in some other output extensions.

In this chapter, we will cover the following points in detail:

- Vector output types including GeoRSS and GeoJSON
- Raster output types such as JPEG and PNG
- OpenLayers single tile and tiled output
- Freemarker templates
- Using the WMS Reflector
- Output extensions

Web services

In the previous chapter, you learned how to add data to GeoServer. All this data is available through standard interfaces, **Web Map Service (WMS)**, **Web Feature Service (WFS)**, and **Web Coverage Service (WCS)**.

WMS lets you publish data in the form of maps, your data is represented in a graphical form with symbols and colors; all the map preparation work is done by the server. The client just needs to present the graphical file to the user.

WFS lets your clients receive a geometrical representation of the features, the server does not add any symbolization or graphical decoration; the clients get the raw data.

WCS is the standard method to get raster data in a raw mode; analogous to WFS for vector data, the server does not transform the data and sends it to the clients as it is.

Whatever mode you choose to create a request, you will insert a layer in it. As you have seen in the previous chapters, all the data in GeoServer is organized in layers.

From the **Layer Preview** window, you can find a list of available formats to request a layer. The following screenshot illustrates the WMS formats:

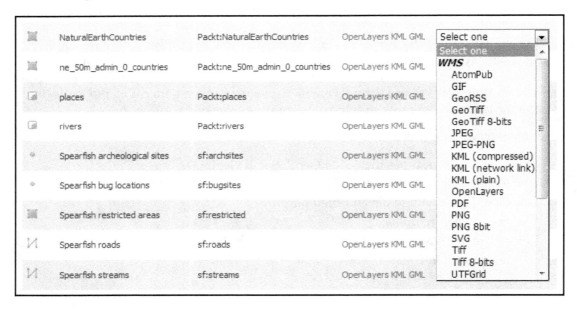

Working with standard web services is essential to create web applications with GeoServer. In this book, you will learn the basics to create requests and retrieve maps and data. Many parameters and details exist beyond the basic. In order to completely master WMS, WFS, and WCS, the best documents to study are the official standard papers from OGC. You can find them here:

Service	Document
WMS	http://portal.opengeospatial.org/files/?artifact_id=14416
WFS	http://docs.opengeospatial.org/is/09-025r2/09-025r2.html
WCS	https://portal.opengeospatial.org/files/09-110r4

WMS formats

Do you remember what happens when you click on the **OpenLayers** link from the **Layer Preview** page? A small web application opens, and it shows you a map with the data contained in the layer you selected. It is an application based on the **OpenLayers** framework, and this is also a specific format of output for your layers.

 OpenLayers is an open source JavaScript library to display web-based maps, similar to the mapping client from Google Maps and a growing number of others. OpenLayers is also a project of the **Open Source Geospatial Foundation** (**OSGeo**). LeafLet (`http://leafletjs.com`) is a promising mapping client with ties to OpenLayers. Be on the lookout for examples using LeafLet in future chapters.

OpenLayers

Let's look at the URL, and carefully, at all parameters, and analyze the request sent to GeoServer. Consider this output request for the **OpenLayers** demo:

```
http://localhost:8080/geoserver/Packt/wms?service=WMS&version=1.1.0
&request=GetMap&layers=Packt:NaturalEarthCountries&
styles=&bbox=-181.800003051758,-90.8669281005859,181.800018310547,
84.4676132202148&width=768&height=370&srs=EPSG:4326
&format=application/openlayers
```

This URL contains a few parameters, let us look at them:

Parameter	Description
service	Explains to GeoServer what kind of request you are sending. The value is WMS as we want to retrieve a map.
version	Indicates the specific version of WMS you want to use.
request	Defines what operation you are requesting, among those supported by the service, GetMap in this case.
layers	Lets you select what data has to be represented on the map. We can insert a comma-separated list of layers, but, in this case, we are happy with just `Packt:NaturalEarthCountries`.
style	This is the parameter to specify a different rendering from the default one. You can use one of those configured on GeoServer or insert a URI of an external style.

bbox	This is the bounding box or area of the map we want to display. The format of `bbox` is `minx, miny, maxx, maxy`.
width and height	Specify the size in pixels of the picture to be produced.
srs	Defines the SRS of the map. Mind that the coordinate you input as values for `bbox` should be compliant with the SRS.
format	This is the key parameter to this chapter. It lets you select the format of the map that you are requesting. Most of the possible values are image binary formats, such as JPEG, TIFF, and PNG. In the previous request, the value in application/OpenLayers is application

All the previous parameters are defined in the WMS standard, and GeoServer extends it with some vendor parameters for extra functionality. You can find a detailed description at `http://docs.geoserver.org/stable/en/user/services/wms/vendor.html`.

Exploring the OpenLayers options

As the OpenLayers map opens, you will see three icons on the map. Clicking on the top-left one shows several options to interact with the GeoServer WMS. We will now explore some of these options:

1. If you haven't already, select the **OpenLayers** output option for `Packt:NaturalEarthCountries` or use the following URL to open the demo:

   ```
   http://localhost:8080/geoserver/Packt/wms?
   service=WMS&version=1.1.0&request=GetMap&layers=
   Packt:NaturalEarthCountries&styles=&
   bbox=-181.800003051758,-90.8669281005859,
   181.800018310547,84.4676132202148&width=768
   &height=370&srs=EPSG:4326&format=application/openlayers
   ```

2. Click on the ... button to display options. Change the height to `400` and width to `600`:

3. Did you notice that the map area was resized? If you inspect the URL in the address bar of the browser, you can see that the `bbox` values changed accordingly. Try other sizes to see what happens.

4. Now insert a **CQL** filter. You need to press the **...** icon to access the optional parameters, then in the text box, you can insert the CQL `where` condition and click on the **Apply** button; your map should change as shown in the following image:

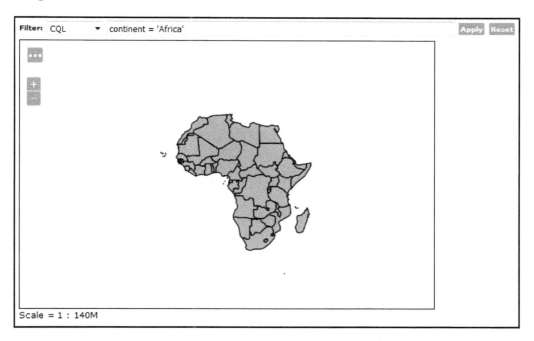

5. If you inspect the request sent to GeoServer, you can see that a new parameter is attached:

```
CQL_FILTER=continent%20%3D%20%27Africa%27
```

CQL (Common Query Language) is a plain text language created for the OGC Catalog specification. GeoServer has adapted it to be an easy-to-use filtering mechanism. GeoServer actually implements a more powerful extension called **ECQL (Extended CQL)**, which allows expressing the full range of filters that OGC Filter 1.1 can encode. Its syntax is very similar to SQL. You can find a reference and tutorial at `http://docs.geoserver.org/stable/en/user/filter/ecql_reference.html#filter-ecql-reference` and `http://docs.geoserver.org/stable/en/user/tutorials/cql/cql_tutorial.html#cql-tutorial`.

6. Add a second condition to your filter and look at how your map reflects the change, as shown here:

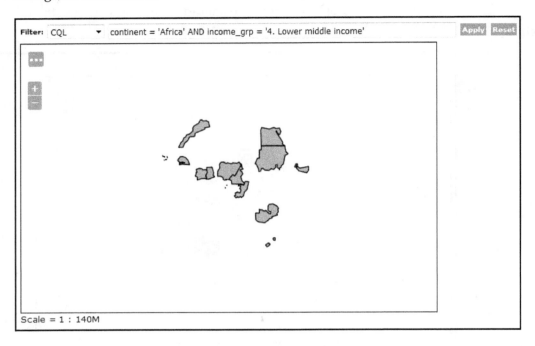

7. CQL lets you use not only the simple attribute query, but you can also add the spatial operator to select features that satisfy some spatial relationship. In the following example, we want to select all the features inside an area:

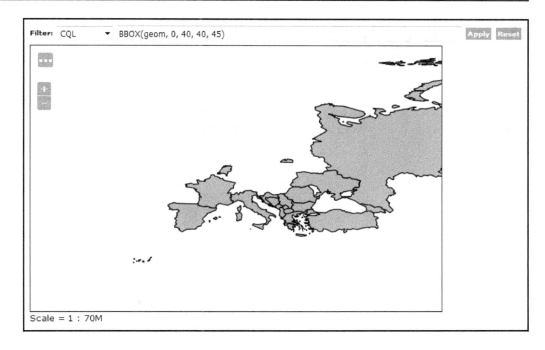

8. In the tiling drop-down list, toggle between **Single tile** and **Tiled** as you pan and zoom the map. Notice how the map refreshes for each option.

Single tile loads an image that fills the entire viewable area, and the **Tiled** version gets 256x256 square images and combines them. If you use Firebug for Firefox, you can see the request sent to GeoServer as `width=256&height=256` for the tiled version, and one request as `width=600&height=400` for the single tile:

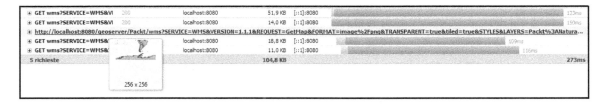

Working with tiles

In the previous section, you used an **OpenLayers** map of width 600 and height 400. The server sent you a single image of that size when you used the Single tile option. Switching to the tiled mode, **OpenLayers** split the map in tiles of 256x256 pixels. So, it sends 9 GetMap requests to GeoServer. In the following image, you can see the blue rectangle covering the 600x400 area of the map, while the 9 256x256 squares are the tiles:

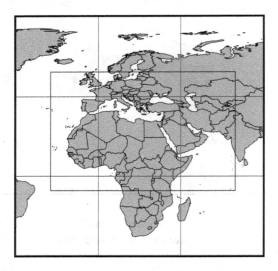

Each request to the server is the same for any single tile, except the bbox parameter specifying the area.

 The bounding box parameter is called bbox. The value for bbox is the latitude and longitude of the area you're calling from GeoServer. The format for this parameter is bbox=minx,miny,maxx,maxy.

If your map's height and width are fairly small, using a single tile will likely take less time to render. This depends on your data filter and number of features too, but it is a good rule of thumb. Using a single tile will also be useful if you need to output, JPEG or PNG larger than 256x256 for larger display needs. It is the same display but as a single tile.

Most of your web-based maps (using **OpenLayers**, for example) will use tiled images. Splitting images into smaller chunks helps them load faster.

Exploring further Web Map Service output formats

The **OpenLayers** format is a special case. Indeed, when you ask for it, GeoServer is not answering with a single object, but with a full web application. As you learned, the application then issues other WMS requests to get a representation of the map.

In the following sections, we will discover what formats you can use and which are best suited for your applications.

The AtomPub format

The **Atom Publishing Protocol** (**AtomPub**) format is a XML-based output. Also known as a **Vector output type**, it is comparable to RSS feeds, which are more common. It allows others to subscribe to features published by GeoServer. The output format is specified by `application/atom+xml` as the format parameter value.

The GIF format

The **Graphics Interchange Format** (**GIF**) output format is well-known. It has been around for a long time on the Web. This format only supports 256 colors, so it is rarely used for high-quality images. In some cases, it is useful when simple shape outputs are produced. It's not the best for completeness, and you will most likely favor PNG, TIFF, or JPEG instead.

The output format is specified by `image/gif` as the format parameter value.

The GeoRSS format

This output format is similar to your RSS feeds you would use to syndicate other content. The noticeable difference is the `georss` tag. Take a look at the `georss` output for the `Packt:places` layer; you'll see that the first item has the location using `<georss:point>41.89 12.492</georss:point>` to specify the location of the site. Google and other search engines are indexing this content. Google accepts this output format as a Geo sitemap.

The following output format is specified by `application/rss+xml` as the format parameter value:

```
<?xml version=""1.0"" encoding=""UTF-8""?>
<rss xmlns:georss=""http://www.georss.org/georss""
  xmlns:atom=""http://www.w3.org/2005/Atom"" version=""2.0"">
<channel>
<title>Packt:places</title>
<description>null</description>
  ...
<item>
  <title>places.1</title>
  <link>
    <![CDATA[http://localhost:8080/geoserver/Packt/wms/reflect?
        format=application%2Fatom%2Bxml&layers=Packt%3Aplaces
        &featureid=places.1]]>
  </link>
  <guid>
    <![CDATA[http://localhost:8080/geoserver/Packt/wms/reflect?
        format=application%2Fatom%2Bxml&layers=Packt%3Aplaces
        &featureid=places.1]]>
  </guid>
  <description>
    <![CDATA[<h4>places</h4><ul class="
        "textattributes""><li><strong><span
        class=""atr-name"">id</span>:</strong> <span
        class=""atr-value"">1</span></li><li><strong><span
        class=""atr-name"">name</span>:</strong> <span
        class=""atr-value"">Rome</span></li><li><strong><span
        class=""atr-name"">country</span>:</strong> <span
        class=""atr-value"">Italy</span></li></ul>]]>
  </description>
  <georss:point>41.89 12.492</georss:point>
</item>
```

For more resources, take a look at the following links:
`http://en.wikipedia.org/wiki/GeoRSS`, `http://www.georss.org`, `http://docs.geoserver.org/stable/en/user/tutorials/georss/georss.html`.

The JPEG format

There is not much to say about the JPEG output format. Since PNG is more widely used these days, it seems that this output is not often called from GeoServer. You may want to use this format when static images of areas of maps are needed though. You can call these URLs with wget or CURL to manually cache the output.

You can do this with GeoWebCache, but this method is quick and easy.

The output format is specified by image/jpeg as the format parameter value.

The KML (Plain) format

We talked about KML a little bit in Chapter 3, *Exploring the Administrative Interface*. The **Time for Action** section installed Google Earth and viewed the `topp:state` layer. You can also use this format directly with Google Maps. You can type the URL directly into the Google Map search field. Obviously, your GeoServer needs to be accessible from the internet.

Google accepts this output format as a Geo sitemap. Google is sensitive to the mime-type for KMZ and KML outputs for Sitemaps. GeoServer meets these requirements.

The output format is specified by `application/vnd.google-earth.kml.xml` as the format parameter value.

The KMZ (Compressed) format

KMZ is a Keyhole compressed formatted file. In a nutshell, it's a ZIP file of KML. Google accepts this output format as a Geo sitemap as well.

The output format is specified by `application/vnd.google-earth.kmz+xml` as the format parameter value.

 If you're proxying a request to/from GeoServer, you'll want to ensure that its setting is the mime-type. For Apache, use `AddType` in your `httpd.conf` using the following command: `AddType application/vnd.google-earth.kmz .kmz`

The PDF format

The PDF output format is ideal to share maps. For example, you may want to display a map using **OpenLayers** and provide a link to export the visible map to PDF.

The output format is specified by `application/pdf` as the format parameter value.

The PNG format

PNG is the format you will be using more often for your maps; it is widely supported by browsers and it is the format usually used by tiles. We will go over that further in `Chapter 8`, *Performance and Caching*.

The output format is specified by `image/png` as the format parameter value.

The SVG format

Using the SVG format, you can save the map as a vector graphical object. You can use it with a graphics editor, such as Adobe Illustrator or Inkscape. This may be useful when you need to include your map in a graphical document.

Open the **Layer Preview** section and export the SVG format for the `Packt:rivers` layer. The browser will render it and you will see a map; however, if you switch to see the source code of the page, you will see that there is an XML code with a vector representation of the features:

```
<?xml version="1.0" encoding="UTF-8"?>
<!DOCTYPE svg PUBLIC '-//W3C//DTD SVG 1.0//EN'
    'http://www.w3.org/TR/2001/REC-SVG-20010904/DTD/svg10.dtd'>
<svg color-interpolation="auto" color-rendering="auto" fill="black" fill-opacity="1" font-family="&apos;Dia
><!--Generated by the Batik Graphics2D SVG Generator--><defs id="genericDefs"
  /></g
  ><defs id="defs1"
    ><clipPath clipPathUnits="userSpaceOnUse" id="clipPath1"
      ><path d="M0 0 L768 0 L768 437 L0 437 L0 0 Z"
      /></clipPath
    ></defs
    ><g fill="blue" stroke="blue" stroke-linecap="butt" stroke-miterlimit="1" stroke-width="1.5" text-rende
      ><path clip-path="url(#clipPath1)" d="M632.6951 5.1621 L634.4517 5.5094 L638.9845 4.6802 L645.8612 1.99
      /><path clip-path="url(#clipPath1)" d="M299.3682 333.4405 L297.4872 333.6404 L293.8634 335.3867 L292.
      /><path clip-path="url(#clipPath1)" d="M727.6427 319.8786 L726.0049 319.408 L724.4319 316.946 L724.80
      /><path clip-path="url(#clipPath1)" d="M764.2831 256.6906 L764.1797 255.8133 L762.6307 251.1641 L761.
      /><path clip-path="url(#clipPath1)" d="M211.9831 338.7936 L212.8656 335.9299 L212.5687 333.2694 L212.
      /><path clip-path="url(#clipPath1)" d="M6.2051 22.6381 L5.2271 22.8897 L4.3304 22.4813 L3.227 21.8921
    /></g
  ></g
></svg
>
```

If you save the code in a file, calling it `rivers.svg` for instance, you can open it in a graphical editor and see what it looks like. The following image shows you the file inside Inkscape. Can you see any features, for example, a river, as a graphical object? You can transform it or change its properties using the tools provided by the editor. This is shown as follows:

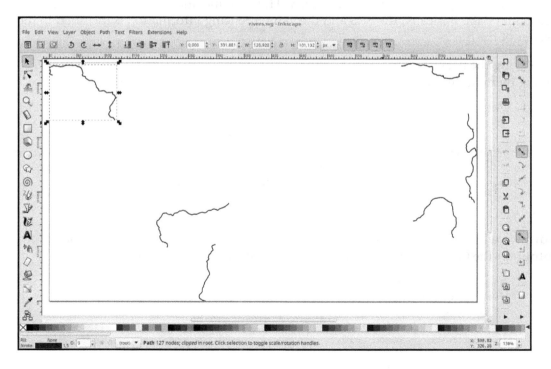

The output format is specified by `image/svg+xml` as the format parameter value.

From the Inkscape FAQ:

> *Inkscape is an open-source vector graphics editor similar to Adobe Illustrator, Corel Draw, Freehand, or Xara X. What sets Inkscape apart is its use of Scalable Vector Graphics (SVG), an open XML-based W3C standard, as the native format.*

Check out their website:

`http://inkscape.org`

The TIFF format

As many other image formats, TIFF is a family of formats with many options and different flavors. GeoServer offers you two options available by default--TIFF and TIFF-8. The difference is the palette used and the number of colors supported by the image.

The GeoTIFF output is the same as a normal TIFF, but includes metadata to describe geospatial data. Basically, the SRS and the georeferencing information is included in the header of the file.

Try saving the preview from `Packt:NaturalEarthCountries` as TIFF and GeoTIFF, saving them in different files:

```
~$ curl ""http://localhost:8080/geoserver/Packt/wms?service=WMSversion=1.1.
0request=GetMaplayers=Packt:NaturalEarthCountriesstyles=bbox=-181.
800003051758,-90.8669281005859,181.800018310547,84.4676132202148width=768
height=370srs=EPSG:4326format=image%2Fgeotiff"" -o countries_g.tiff~$ curl
""http://localhost:8080/geoserver/Packt/wms?service=WMSversion=1.1.0
request=GetMaplayers=Packt:NaturalEarthCountriesstyles=bbox=-181.
800003051758,-90.8669281005859,181.800018310547,84.4676132202148width=768
height=370srs=EPSG:4326format=image%2Ftiff"" -o countries.tiff
```

Now, we will run the `gdalinfo` tool to check the properties of the two files. The following output for the GeoTIFF file includes information about SRS and coordinates:

```
~$ gdalinfo countries_g.tiff
Driver: GTiff/GeoTIFF
Files: countries.tiff
Size is 768, 370
Coordinate System is:
GEOGCS[""WGS 84"",
DATUM[""WGS_1984"",
    SPHEROID[""WGS 84"",6378137,298.257223563,
```

```
            AUTHORITY[""EPSG"",""7030""]],
            AUTHORITY[""EPSG"",""6326""]],
            PRIMEM[""Greenwich"",0],
            UNIT[""degree"",0.0174532925199433],
            AUTHORITY[""EPSG"",""4326""]]
    Origin = (-181.800003051758011,84.467613220214801)
    Pixel Size = (0.473437527815501,-0.473877138704867)
    Metadata:
      AREA_OR_POINT=Area
      TIFFTAG_RESOLUTIONUNIT=1 (unitless)
      TIFFTAG_XRESOLUTION=1
      TIFFTAG_YRESOLUTION=1
      Image Structure Metadata:
      INTERLEAVE=PIXEL
    Corner Coordinates:
      Upper Left  (    -181.800,       84.468)
                  (181d48'' 0.01""W, 84d28'' 3.41""N)
      Lower Left  (    -181.800,      -90.867)
                  (181d48'' 0.01""W, 90d52'' 0.94""S)
      Upper Right (     181.800,       84.468)
                  (181d48'' 0.07""E, 84d28'' 3.41""N)
      Lower Right (     181.800,      -90.867)
                  (181d48'' 0.07""E, 90d52'' 0.94""S)
      Center      (   0.0000076,   -3.1996574)
                  ( 0d 0'' 0.03""E,  3d11''58.77""S)
```

When you run the same command on the TIFF file, you can see that all spatial information is lost and the boundaries of the image are in pixels:

```
~$ gdalinfo countries.tiff
Driver: GTiff/GeoTIFF
Files: countries.tif
Size is 768, 370
Coordinate System is `''
Metadata:
  TIFFTAG_RESOLUTIONUNIT=1 (unitless)
  TIFFTAG_XRESOLUTION=1
  TIFFTAG_YRESOLUTION=1
  Image Structure Metadata:
  INTERLEAVE=PIXEL
Corner Coordinates:
  Upper Left  (     0.0,      0.0)
  Lower Left  (     0.0,    370.0)
  Upper Right (   768.0,      0.0)
  Lower Right (   768.0,    370.0)
  Center      (   384.0,    185.0)
```

The output format is specified by `image/tiff`, `image/tiff8`, or `image/geotiff8` as the format parameter value.

 If you want to read further information about the GeoTiff format, these are excellent starting points: `https://en.wikipedia.org/wiki/GeoTIFF`, `http://trac.osgeo.org/geotiff`, and `http://www.gdal.org/frmt_gtiff.html`

Web Feature service

Creating a request to access a layer through WFS is not so different from WMS. However, the output is very different; with WFS, you get a vector representation of the data in a textual or binary format. The following code snippet is a request for the `Packt:places` layer:

```
http://localhost:8080/geoserver/Packt/ows?
service=WFS&
version=1.0.0&
request=GetFeature&
typeName=Packt:places&
maxFeatures=50&
outputFormat=text/xml; subtype=gml/2.1.2
```

As we did previously with WMS, we are now going to discuss each parameter:

Parameter	Description
service	Explains to GeoServer what kind of request you are sending. The value is WFS as we want to retrieve a vector representation of the data.
version	Indicates the specific version of WFS you want to use.
request	Defines what operation you are requesting, among those supported by the service, GetFeature is the basic request to obtain data.
typeName	Specifies what layer should be used to extract the data.
MaxFeatures	Lets you retrieve a subset of all features contained in the layer.
outputFormat	This is the parameter to select the format of the data that you are requesting.

In this request, we are asking for the GML format. It is a XML-based format that contains the spatial features and their properties. The following code snippet shows the first element of the result set:

```
<?xml version=""1.0"" encoding=""UTF-8""?>
<wfs:FeatureCollection xmlns=""http://www.opengis.net/wfs""
    xmlns:wfs=""http://www.opengis.net/wfs""xmlns:gml=
    ""http://www.opengis.net/gml""
    xmlns:Packt=""https://www.packtpub.com/""
    xmlns:xsi=""http://www.w3.org/2001/XMLSchema-instance""
    xsi:schemaLocation=""https://www.packtpub.com/
    http://localhost:8080/geoserver/Packt/wfs?
    service=WFS&amp;version=1.0.0&amp;request=
        DescribeFeatureType&amp;
    typeName=Packt%3Aplaces http://www.opengis.
    net/wfshttp://localhost:8080/geoserver/
     schemas/wfs/
      1.0.0/WFS-basic.xsd"">
  <gml:boundedBy>
  <gml:null>unknown</gml:null>
  </gml:boundedBy>
  <gml:featureMember>
  <Packt:places fid=""places.1"">
    <Packt:id>1</Packt:id>
    <Packt:name>Rome</Packt:name>
    <Packt:country>Italy</Packt:country>
    <Packt:shape>
    <gml:Point srsName=""http://www.opengis.net/gml/srs
        /epsg.xml#4326"">
    <gml:coordinates xmlns:gml=""http://www.opengis.net/gml""
        decimal="".""  cs="","" ts="" "">12.492,41.89</gml:coordinates>
    </gml:Point>
    </Packt:shape>
    </Packt:places>
  </gml:featureMember>
```

GML serves as a modeling language for geographic systems as well as an open interchange format for geographic transactions on the internet. There are several versions supported by GeoServer, you can select one of them using the subtype option in the request, as shown in the previous example.

Wikipedia has a good overall history of GML and its usage at http://en.wikipedia.org/wiki/Geography_Markup_Language.

The CSV format

The plain CSV text format is often used for data exchange.

It can be read from many packages, for example, Microsoft Excel. Or, it is a good format to use as input to import into an external database where other layer output formats don't apply. You can easily process CSV files with scripting languages or command tool.

The following code snippet contains the features from the `Packt:places` layer:

```
FID,id,name,country,shape
places.1,1,Rome,Italy,POINT (12.492 41.89)
places.2,2,Grand Canyon,Usa,POINT (-112.122 36.055)
places.3,3,Paris,France,POINT (2.294 48.858)
places.4,4,Iguazu National Park,Argentina,POINT (-54.442 -25.688)
places.5,5,Ayers Rock,Australia,POINT (131.036 -25.345)
```

The output format is specified by `csv` as the `outputFormat` parameter value.

The GeoJSON format

GeoJSON is another plain text format. It is a specialization of the JSON format.

JSON is a language-independent data format. It was derived from JavaScript, but, as of 2017, many programming languages include code to generate and parse JSON-format data. For example, Python has a module to parse JSON and GeoJSON strings. GeoJSON adds support for spatial objects, including information about SRS and geometry. Let's take a look at that next.

The output format is specified by `json` as the `outputFormat` parameter value.

Parsing GeoJSON

You may want to query GeoServer and parse features in Python. We're just parsing a JSON string as follows:

1. Go to the **Layer Preview** screen and click on the drop-down for **All Formats** for the `Packt:places` layer.

2. Select the **GeoJSON** option; your browser should open a new tab showing the output of the request. Take a note of the URL, or take the following:

```
http://localhost:8080/geoserver/Packt/ows?
   service=WFS&version=1.0.0&request=GetFeature&typeName=Packt:
   places&outputFormat=application/json
```

3. Now open your preferred text editor and create a new text file. Copy the following code and paste it, then save it as `parser.py`:

```
import urllib2, json
if __name__ == ''__main__'':
url = ''http://localhost:8080/geoserver/Packt/ows?
   service=WFS&version=1.0.0&request=GetFeature&typeName=Packt:
   places&outputFormat=application%2Fjson''
uh = urllib2.urlopen(url)
datastring = uh.read()
data = json.loads(datastring)
for feature in data[''features'']:
print, feature[''geometry''][''coordinates''])
```

4. Open a console and execute the file, the output should list the coordinates of the features contained in the layer, as shown here:

```
[12.492, 41.89]
[-112.122, 36.055]
[2.294, 48.858]
[-54.442, -25.688]
[131.036, -25.345]
```

5. The first line of the Python script imports two standard modules, adding support for URL requests and JSON parsing. The following lines send a WFS `GetFeature` request to GeoServer, read the response, and extract some information from it.

6. Now modify the last line of the Python script, as shown in the following snippet:

```
print(''{0} -- {1}'').format(feature[''properties'']
   [''name''], feature[''geometry''][''coordinates''])
```

7. Run the script again and you should get a list containing the feature's name and coordinates:

```
Rome -- [12.492, 41.89]
Grand Canyon -- [-112.122, 36.055]
Paris -- [2.294, 48.858]
Iguazu National Park -- [-54.442, -25.688]
Ayers Rock -- [131.036, -25.345]
```

You learned how to use GeoJSON in your procedures. We used Python, as it is a very easy-to-understand language, but a similar approach is easy to reproduce in almost any modern programming language.

Shapefile

Shapefile seems to be the most common output format for GIS data exchange, but it is not so useful for building web-based maps. If you need to exchange large static data sets with someone else, then this might be a good option. The output file is a ZIP file containing the details for the layer. For example, consider this unzipped file for the topp:states layer:

states.cst	07/07/2017 15:34	File CST	1 KB
states.dbf	07/07/2017 15:34	File DBF	19 KB
states.prj	07/07/2017 15:34	File PRJ	1 KB
states.shp	07/07/2017 15:34	File SHP	183 KB
states.shx	07/07/2017 15:34	File SHX	1 KB

The output format is specified by SHAPE-ZIP as the outputFormat parameter value. This is the URL for it:

```
http://localhost:8080/geoserver/topp/ows?
service=WFS&version=1.0.0&request=GetFeature&typeName=topp:
states&maxFeatures=50&outputFormat=SHAPE-ZIP
```

Extra output options

GeoServer gives you the ability to extend the output options for your data using extensions. Most of those extensions require additional setup outside of dropping some additional libraries, that is, JAR files, into the WEB-INF/LIB folder. The following image shows the available options:

Output Formats
- DXF
- Excel
- Image Map
- JPEG Turbo
- NetCDF
- OGR (WFS, WPS)
- XSLT

The TEXT/HTML format

One of the ways you can get information from GeoServer about features you click on is by querying WMS with a point and getting a list of surrounding features.

The output format can be anything. The INFO_FORMAT should be text/HTML.

Using the GetFeatureInfo freemarker template

We are going to customize the template for freemarker output. With the following steps, you can have a different layout for information:

1. Go to the **OpenLayers** demo for topp:states.
2. After the map loads, click on a state. The layer information about that state loads under the map. Consider the following example for clicking on **Alabama**:

states									
fid	**STATE_NAME**	**STATE_FIPS**	**SUB_REGION**	**STATE_ABBR**	**LAND_KM**	**WATER_KM**	**PERSONS**	**FAMILIES**	**HOUSHOL**
states.17	Alabama	01	E S Cen	AL	131443.119	4332.268	4040587.0	1103835.0	1506790.0

3. Now, examine the URL that was called. The INFO_FORMAT=text/html outputs the feature as an HTML string by default:

```
http://localhost:8080/geoserver/topp/wms?
 REQUEST=GetFeatureInfo&EXCEPTIONS=application/vnd.ogc.
 se_xml&BBOX=-139.848709,18.549282,-51.852562,55.77842&SERVICE=
 WMS&INFO_FORMAT=text/html&QUERY_LAYERS=topp:states&FEATURE_COUNT=
 50&Layers=topp:states&WIDTH=780&HEIGHT=330&format=image/png&
 styles=&srs=EPSG:4326&version=1.1.1&x=471&y=201
```

4. Create new files in $GEOSERVER_DATA/workspaces/topp/states_shapefile/states called content.ftl, footer.ftl and header.ftl. We are working in this particular folder to have the changes applied just to this single layer and not to all GeoServer configuration.
5. Place the following text in the header.ftl file:

```
<?xml version=''1.0'' encoding=''utf-8''?>
<states>
```

6. In the `content.ftl` file, place the following text:

```
<#list features as feature>
<state>
<STATE_ABBR>${feature.STATE_ABBR.value}</STATE_ABBR>
<STATE_NAME>${feature.STATE_NAME.value}</STATE_NAME>
<SUB_REGION>${feature.SUB_REGION.value}</SUB_REGION>
</state>
</#list>
```

7. For the `footer.flt` file, the text will be simpler:

```
</states>
```

8. Go to **Server Status | Configuration and catalog** and click on the **Reload** button shown as follows:

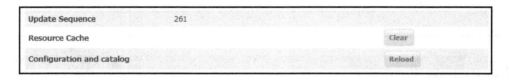

9. Click on a state, for example, **Alabama**. The new state information will be shown on the map.

We changed the default template for the `topp:states` layer by creating three new files and adding them to `workspaces/topp/state_shapefiles/states`. We then reloaded the GeoServer configuration using the Reload feature in Server Status, or, optionally, by restarting GeoServer.

Since GeoServer is setting the output as text/HTML, you will need to treat the returned string as text, and then parse to XML before using it in JavaScript.

ImageMap

Everyone remembers the days when ImageMap was commonly used. The idea of using an image map to describe POIs on your maps seems like a good one.

One of the extensions you can install by just dropping a JAR into `$GEOSERVER_HOME/WEBINF/lib` is ImageMap. The only challenge with this output option is that `PointSymbolizer` is represented as circles only, and, in most cases, you will have icons for features that aren't circles. The image maps don't always match.

For more information, take a look at
`http://docs.geoserver.org/latest/en/user/extensions/imagemap.htm`
`l`.

Using the WMS Reflector

This is a great way to preview options in GeoServer without coding a long URL. The reflector will output PNG (the default), JPEG, PNG 8, and GIF. Also, in cases where you don't want to use GeoWebCache, this is quite useful.

The URL passes a number of parameters to specify what output you want. Most of these will not be changed. Reflector uses default values for missing parameters. The only parameter you need to provide is the layers parameter by default. Check out the GeoServer documentation for more information on these values. There's no need to rehash them here.

For more information, take a look at
`http://docs.geoserver.org/stable/en/user/tutorials/wmsreflector.`
`html`.

1. Let's use the `topp:states` layer preview for this example. Enter the following URL into your browser or select the JPEG output option from the **All Formats** drop-down list on the **Layer Preview** page. The **Layer Preview** URL is quite long:

```
http://localhost:8080/geoserver/topp/wms?
    service=WMS&version=1.1.0&request=GetMap&layers=topp:states&
    styles=&bbox=-124.73142200000001,24.955967,-66.969849,49.371735
    &width=780&height=330&srs=EPSG:4326&format=image/png
```

2. Open a new window or browser tab and use the Reflector to get the same results. Just type the following URL in the address bar and then press *Enter*:

```
http://localhost:8080/geoserver/wms/reflect?layers=topp:states
```

3. Now add a new projection from the native `EPSG: 4326` to Google Mercator. `EPSG:900913`. You will see the image flatten out as follows:

```
http://localhost:8080/geoserver/wms/reflect?layers=topp:states&
srs=EPSG:900913
```

4. Consider the following image:

We just saved some considerable time for sure. All we needed to do was provide the layers parameter, since that is the minimum, and the Reflector would default to a PNG for its output.

Then, we changed the projection to Google Mercator `EPSG: 900913`. The Reflector does some heavy lifting for you.

To output PDF, you will want to add the format parameter application/PDF, as shown in the following URL. Want to reproject? Add the `srs` parameter, most commonly `Google Mercator EPSG:900913`:

```
http://localhost:8080/geoserver/wms/reflect?
layers=topp:states&format=application/pdf&srs=EPSG:900913
```

Summary

That was a quick overview of the output options GeoServer offers you.

We talked about the vector outputs, such as GeoRSS and GeoJSON. We also talked about raster output formats, such as JPEG and PNG. One of the coolest things we talked a little about was the Reflector.

In the next chapter, we will explore the styling of data. You will discover how to ask GeoServer to create beautiful maps using symbols, colors, and graphical effects.

6
Styling Your Layers

In the previous chapters, you learned how to add data to GeoServer and include it in maps. Any map, including the really simple ones that you explored in **Layer Preview**, requires a fundamental process--rendering of features. GeoServer performs the rendering, applying a symbology to features. This involves assigning a symbol to each feature and applying a set of rules about how features have to be drawn. Choosing a symbol and its properties is called the styling process. Styling is really important in web mapping. A map cannot be rendered without a style associated to the data. When you configured layers, you were using styles bundled with the GeoServer. In this chapter, we will explore what the style documents are and how you can create custom styles to produce beautiful maps.

In this chapter, we will cover the following topics:

- What is the content of a style?
- What symbols can be used in GeoServer?
- How can you set rendering rules?
- How to edit your styles with the GeoServer web interface and external tools?
- How to use the concise CSS syntax to create styles

By the end of this chapter, you'll be able to style layers and also use style rules.

Understanding Styled Layer Descriptor (SLD)

Any map contains a set of layers, for example, a graphical representation of spatial features. Each layer contains features of a determined geometry type. When you ask GeoServer for a map, for instance, by issuing a WMS `GetMap` request, it extracts features from the repository (a PostGIS database or a shapefile) and draws them according to some rules. Of course, it needs a repository to store those rules; therefore, GeoServer developers needed to decide a format for the storage medium containing rules.

Map rendering is not just a GeoServer problem; unsurprisingly, it is common to all software-producing maps. Hence, it is not surprising that someone has defined a standard approach to styling layers. Indeed, GeoServer does not use a custom format for styles; instead, it leverages on an OGC standard.

The standard describes the structure of the documents and what kind of rules can be used and mixed inside the style. A document containing symbols' definitions and drawing rules is called a **Styled Layer Descriptor** (**SLD**) style, and it is a text/XML file (its extension in GeoServer is .sld). Hence, SLD is an XML-based markup language; attached to the standard, there is an XSD schema defining SLD syntax.

In this chapter, we will explore several basic and intermediate topics about SLD. for further information and a detailed reference; you can use the official papers at `http://portal.opengeospatial.org/files/?artifact_id=22364` and XSD schemas at `http://schemas.opengis.net/sld/`.

Editing styles

We have seen that styles are XML files, and hence are plain text files. We can use different editing tools to edit a style. A simple and effective choice could be your preferred text editor, for example, vi, emacs, or Notepad++. Using a text editor lets you concentrate on the content and avoid the learning curve of a new tool. On the other hand, you need to consider that as long as you add rules and symbols, things may become fairly complicated and the final style can be a huge file. A tool that has highlighted syntax for XML may greatly help you in debugging your styles. Of course, if you are already familiar with a specialized XML editor, you can also appreciate its support for XSD validation; however, usually, I find it overkill.

If you are using Windows as an operating system, I really suggest you consider using Notepad++ as your default text editor. Notepad++ is a text editor and source code editor. It supports tabbed editing, which allows working with multiple open files in a single window. Its already rich core of tools and functions can be extended with plugins. Currently, over 140 compatible plugins are developed for Notepad++. You can download the program and find a lot of useful information about it at `https://notepad-plus-plus.org/`.

Another option to edit styles is the web editor included in the GeoServer administration interface. Indeed, GeoServer includes a simple GUI editor to view and edit XML files containing style rules. It contains basic editing tools and an SLD validator; you got the first look at it in `Chapter 3`, *Exploring the Administrative Interface*.

A different approach to styling is to use GIS desktop software to create styles; some open source Desktop GIS may produce SLD files. One of the most used and easy to understand is QGIS. It may translate a layer legend in an XML file. QGIS supports data in different formats as shapefiles, Oracle, and PostGIS layers. After you add them to a map, you can use its GUI to set color, line width, and other drawing properties. You can then export your layer symbology in an SLD file.

Take a look at the QGIS project site at `https://www.qgis.org/en/site/`.

Before we start studying the styles' syntax, we need an optional module on GeoServer. Let's install it.

Installing the CSS module

To add support for CSS to GeoServer, you need to install some optional files. The CSS module started as a community module, that is, an unofficial set of features that are not fully supported by the official releases and may or may not work. It is an example of a successful community module that grew fast and has recently graduated as a formal extension.

Let us install it:

1. Stop the GeoServer service. Open the page at
   `http://geoserver.org/release/stable/` and look for the CSS Styling extension
   link:

   ```
   Miscellaneous

     • Chart Symbolizer
     • Control Flow
     • Cross Layer Filtering
     • CSS Styling
     • CAS
     • Monitor (Core, Hibernate)
     • Importer (Core, BDB Backend)
     • INSPIRE
     • Printing
     • YSLD Styling
   ```

2. Download the archive and extract and copy the `.jar` files into the `/WEB-INF/lib/` directory in the GeoServer web app.
3. Start the GeoServer service again.

Enabling the CSS module is an easy task. The developer team packed it into a couple of JAR files that contain all the code for the logic and the user interface. The older version of the module used a separate interface to edit SLD using XML or CSS code. Now the interface is fully integrated, and this is the reason we installed it at the start of this chapter. However, we will use it only at the end of it.

Exploring the standard structure of a style

Regardless of the tool, you are using to create your style, it is worthwhile that you understand the basic syntax and structure of your documents. You may need to modify the styles after creation, and the features you need to add may not be supported by the program, or you may be simply on a server where the only way to edit is using a text editor. Besides, you will write XML code in the examples in this chapter.

A style always starts with a section, as shown in the following code fragment:

```
<?xml version="1.0" encoding="UTF-8"?>
<StyledLayerDescriptor version="1.0.0"
xmlns="http://www.opengis.net/sld"
xmlns:ogc="http://www.opengis.net/ogc"
    xmlns:xlink="http://www.w3.org/1999/xlink"
xmlns:xsi="http://www.w3.org/2001/XMLSchema-instance"
    xsi:schemaLocation="http://www.opengis.net/sld
http://schemas.opengis.net/sld/1.0.0/StyledLayerDescriptor.xsd">
```

The first line is the XML declaration, common to any XML document and not only to styles. Then, we have the root element for the SLD file, the `<StyledLayerDescriptor/>`. It contains an attribute declaring the version of the standard it is using (GeoServer can use 1.0 and 1.1.0 SLD documents), followed by the namespaces and schema declarations. In the remainder of the chapter, we will omit this part from our example, for the sake of brevity; however, keep in mind that it is absolutely mandatory for the files you are writing.

The `<StyledLayerDescriptor/>` tag contains a collection of the `<NamedLayer/>` or `<UserLayer/>` elements. Each defines drawing rules for a single layer. Indeed, they contain a collection of the `<UserStyle/>` elements.

A `<UserStyle/>` element contains `<FeatureTypeStyle/>` if the layer is a vector one, or `<CoverageStyle/>` if we are writing rules for a raster.

Both `<FeatureTypeStyle/>` and `<CoverageStyle/>` contain a collection of the `<rule/>` element. This is the element where we will define how to draw features, and we will look at its syntax in detail.

Exploring GeoServer bundled styles

We will start to write rules specific to feature types in the next section; however, before doing it, just take a look at the styles bundled with GeoServer. You already used them when you added data in the previous chapters.

Let's take a look at those documents and look for the elements we described in the previous paragraph:

1. Open your GeoServer administration interface and log in. Then select the **Data |
   Styles** item from the left menu. You can now see the list of styles configured in
   GeoServer; at the moment, only the default styles bundled with the installation
   package are available, as in the following image:

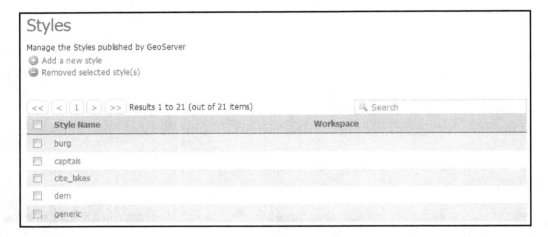

2. Select the **capitals** style. The content of the file shows up inside the **Style Editor**
   window:

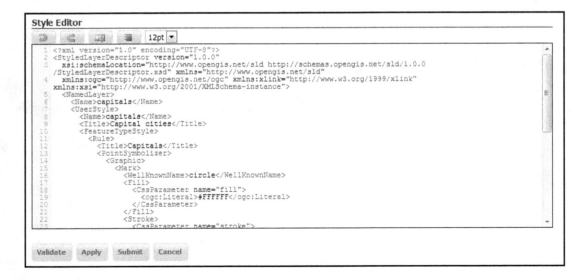

3. The **capitals** style is a fairly simple example. You can see the mandatory elements required for a style. There is a `UserStyle` element with a single rule defining a circle symbol with a red fill and a black stroke.

4. Now try to add something wrong. Insert the following line of code after the `<Rule>` element at line 11:

```
<Title>This is a clever rule</Title>
```

5. Click on the **Validate** button. GeoServer checks your file and reports an error occurring where you inserted your code. It complains about line 13 because you can't have two instances of `<Title>` inside a rule:

```
line 13: cvc-complex-type.2.4.a: Invalid content was found
starting with element 'Title'. One of "
{"http://www.opengis.net/sld":Abstract,
"http://www.opengis.net/sld":LegendGraphic,
"http://www.opengis.net/ogc":Filter,
"http://www.opengis.net/sld":ElseFilter,
"http://www.opengis.net/sld":MinScaleDenominator,
"http://www.opengis.net/sld":MaxScaleDenominator,
"http://www.opengis.net/sld":Symbolizer}" is expected.
```

6. Remove the line you inserted and click on the **Validate** button again. Now GeoServer shows the following message:

```
No validation errors.
```

7. Load other styles and take a look at the syntax. You do not need to fully understand them; we will cover it in the remaining part of the chapter.

8. If you scroll up, you can see other elements in the page. Switching to the **Publishing** tab, you will find a list of layers. From here, you can associate the style you are working with to several layers:

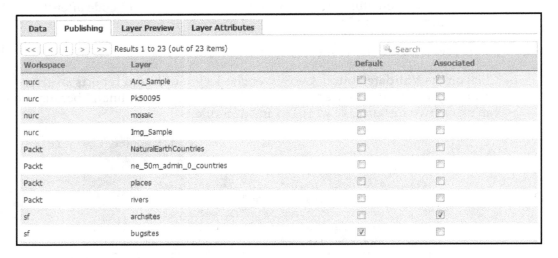

9. The **Layer Preview** tab offers a map view of the style, applied to a layer selected by the user. It is very useful if you are creating a complex style and want to check the result while composing it:

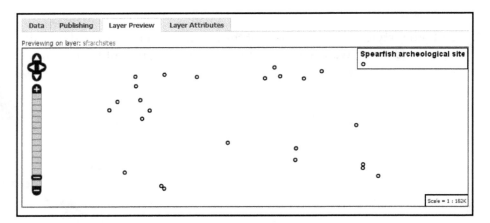

10. The last one is the **Layer Attribute** tab. Here, you can explore the properties of the layer associated with the style and calculate some simple statistics. Click on the **Compute** button and you will see the maximum and minimum value for the attribute:

name	type	sample	min	max	computeStats
the_geom	Point	POINT (593493 4914730)			Compute
cat	Long	1	1	25	Compute
str1	String	Signature Rock	Bob Miller	Whitewood Flats	Compute

Data **Publishing** **Layer Preview** **Layer Attributes**

Previewing on layer: sf:archsites
For reference, here is a listing of the attributes in this data set.

We took a brief look at the GeoServer style editor and the styles bundled. A very important feature of the style editor is the **Validate** button. You can compose your styles with an external tool and have them validated before starting to use them.

Loading data for styling

In order to create pretty maps, we need some more data than the default layers packaged with GeoServer. We will use the freely available Natural Earth dataset. We already used a shapefile with administrative boundaries in Chapter 4, *Adding Your Data*.

Natural Earth provides several datasets in the shapefile format, packaged in three different reference scales. In the styles examples of this chapter, we will use a subset; you need to download the following datasets:

- http://www.naturalearthdata.com/http//www.naturalearthdata.com/download/50m/cultural/ne_50m_populated_places.zip

- http://www.naturalearthdata.com/http//www.naturalearthdata.com/download/50m/physical/ne_50m_rivers_lake_centerlines.zip

- http://www.naturalearthdata.com/http//www.naturalearthdata.com/download/10m/cultural/ne_10m_roads.zip

- http://www.naturalearthdata.com/http//www.naturalearthdata.com/download/10m/cultural/ne_10m_railroads.zip

Save all of them in the same folder you used for the administrative boundaries. Then repeat the procedure to add them to your GeoServer configuration. Refer to Chapter 4, *Adding Your Data*, for details about data store and layer configuration. When you publish the shapefiles, you may use the default styles for points, polylines, and polygons; you may take a first look at the data. All the data is in geographic coordinates--WGS84. The SRID is ESPG:4326.

Saving the shapefiles in a folder and publishing them is the easiest way. In Chapter 4, *Adding Your Data*, you learned how to load data into a PostGIS database. For what concerns styling and SLD, there is no difference in using the Natural Earth data as shapefile or inside PostGIS. The second option makes them faster; hence, you can load them and take this as a small challenge to check that you really learned the lesson from Chapter 4, *Adding Your Data*.

Apart from this data, you may find some resources in the code files accompanying this book that you can download from the Packt website. Code files contain XML files for all the styles we will write in this chapter, but I would suggest you take them just as a reference and a graphic resource used in styling.

Working with point symbols

We will start with a basic example. What is the simplest geometry type? A point feature; hence, we will start with styles for point features. The Populated places shapefile fits our purposes perfectly. Did you publish it using the default style for points? If you did it, you should see it rendered with a small red square, as shown in the following screenshot:

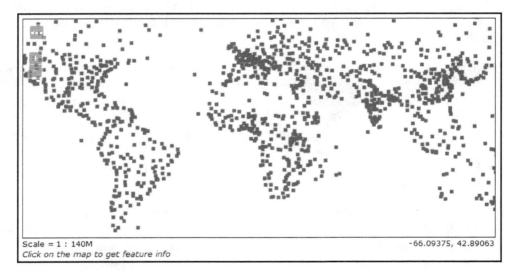

To modify the map, you need to add a new style and associate it to the layer. For setting point symbol properties, you have to use the <PointSymbolizer> element and its children.

Creating a simple point style

To familiarize you with SLD file creation, we will compose a simple style to apply a small red circle to all the point features:

1. Open your favorite text editor. We will expect you have already inserted the XML declaration and the `<StyledLayerDescriptor>` part of the code. So, start by inserting a `<NamedLayer>` element. Then, add a `<Name>` element and write the name you want for your layer inside it, as shown here:

```
<NamedLayer>
 <Name>PopulatedPlaces</Name>
</NamedLayer>
```

2. Now you need to define at least one style for the layer. We use the `<Title>` element to assign a descriptive name to the style:

```
<NamedLayer>
 <Name> PopulatedPlaces </Name>
 <UserStyle>
   <Title>Geoserver Beginners Guide: Populated Places simple
     mark</Title>
 </UserStyle>
</NamedLayer>
```

3. You want to apply the style to features represented by points. Hence, you need to insert a `<FeatureTypeStyle>` element and a `<Rule>` element for a `<PointSymbolizer>` element. The last one contains drawing rules for point data:

```
<NamedLayer>
 <Name> PopulatedPlaces </Name>
 <UserStyle>
   <Title>Geoserver Beginners Guide: Populated Places simple
     mark</Title>
   <FeatureTypeStyle>
     <Rule>
       <PointSymbolizer>
       </PointSymbolizer>
     </Rule>
   </FeatureTypeStyle>
 </UserStyle>
</NamedLayer>
```

4. You have now arrived at the core of our style. The elements you will add define the symbol used to draw the point features. You use a predefined graphic with the WellKnownName element (options are circle, square, triangle, star, cross, and x). A Fill element defines the point color with the CssParameter element. The color is in the #RRGGBB form. Finally, you define how many pixels the circle should be with the Size element:

```
<NamedLayer>
 <Name> PopulatedPlaces </Name>
 <UserStyle>
    <Title>Geoserver Beginners Guide: Populated Places simple
mark</Title>
    <FeatureTypeStyle>
      <Rule>
        <PointSymbolizer>
          <Graphic>
            <Mark>
              <WellKnownName>circle</WellKnownName>
              <Fill>
                <CssParameter
                name="fill">#FF0000</CssParameter>
              </Fill>
            </Mark>
            <Size>5</Size>
          </Graphic>
        </PointSymbolizer>
      </Rule>
    </FeatureTypeStyle>
  </UserStyle>
</NamedLayer>
```

5. Now save your document as PopulatedPlaces.xml and open the **Styles** list in GeoServer.

6. Click on the **Add a new style** link to open the editor form:

7. Click on the **Browse** button, then go to the folder containing your file and select it.

8. Click on the **Upload** link next to the **Browse** button; your file is loaded in the editor form.

9. Click on **Validate** to check if you misspelled something. When it returns no errors, click on the **Apply** button.

10. Switch to the **Publishing** section and click on the **ne_50m_populated_places** flag to make this style the default for that layer:

11. Click on the **Submit** button. Go to the **Layer Preview** section and open up the **OpenLayers** preview for the **PopulatedPlaces** layer. Your map should now look as shown in the following screenshot:

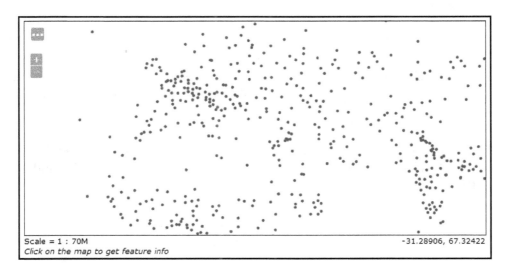

You just created a new style for a simple point symbol and assigned it as default to a layer. This is the first step in creating custom maps, where you decide how and what has to be drawn.

Adding a stroke value

Now we will continue exploring the point symbology by changing the shape and adding a stroke value:

1. Take the `PopulatedPlaces.xml` file, make a copy of it, and name it as `PopulatedPlacesStroke.xml`. Edit the new file in your text editor.

2. Go to line 4 and replace the text inside the `<Name>` element with the following:

   ```
   <Name>PopulatedPlacesStroke</Name>
   ```

3. Find the text inside the `<Title>` element and replace it with the following lines of code:

   ```
   <Title>Geoserver Beginners Guide: Populated Places square mark
   with stroke</Title>
   ```

4. We will change the shape form used to represent points on map. Replace the text inside the `<WellKnownName>` element with the following line of code:

   ```
   <WellKnownName>square</WellKnownName>
   ```

5. To add a stroke to your shape, you have to add a `<Stroke>` element just after the `<Fill>` element. Use the `<CssParameter>` element to set the color and width of the stroke:

   ```
   <Stroke>
    <CssParameter name="stroke">#000000</CssParameter>
    <CssParameter name="stroke-width">1</CssParameter>
   </Stroke>
   ```

6. Now save your document and upload it to GeoServer. Instead of making it the default style for the populated places layer, flag the associate option, as shown in the following image:

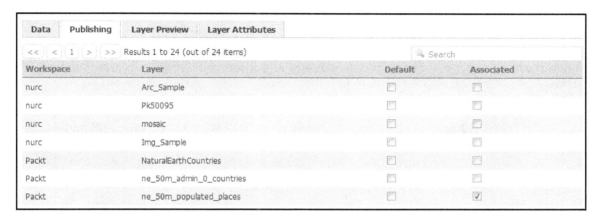

7. Open the **Layer Preview** map. Your map is still presenting the simple marker; indeed, you didn't change the default style. Click on the button on the top left of the map to show the options toolbar. From the **Styles** drop-down list, select **PopulatedPlacesStrokes**. Your map will suddenly be updated with the new point symbol. If you zoom to North America, it should look as shown in the following screenshot:

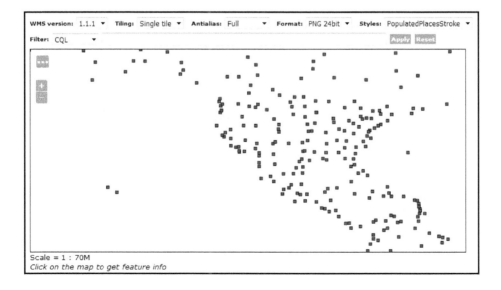

We modified a simple style by adding a stroke. You also learned that a layer may be associated to more than one style, and you can decide at runtime which one to use to render maps.

Dealing with angles and transparency

When representing a point marker, you can add a rotation angle to those shapes where it makes sense. You can also set opacity to make the fill, stroke, or both more or less transparent. Let's create a new style experimenting with these features:

1. Take the `PopulatedPlacesStrokes.xml` file, make a copy of it, and name it as `PopulatedRotateTransparent.xml`. Edit the new file in your text editor. Replace the text inside the `<Name>` element with the following line of code:

   ```
   <Name>PopulatedRotateTransparent</Name>
   ```

2. Replace the text inside the `<Title>` element with the following lines of code:

   ```
   <Title>Geoserver Beginners Guide: Populated Places rotated
   mark
   with transparency</Title>
   ```

3. Now, we will change the size for marker. Replace the text inside the `<Size>` element with the following line of code:

   ```
   <Size>9</Size>
   ```

4. In order to rotate the marker, add a line after the `<Size>` element, setting an angle of 45 degrees:

   ```
   <Rotation>45</Rotation>
   ```

5. To set transparency, add the following line after the `<CssParameter>` element's fill color setting:

   ```
   <CssParameter name="fill-opacity">0.35</CssParameter>
   ```

6. Now save your document and upload it to GeoServer. Instead of making it the default style for the populated places layer, flag the associated option.

7. Open the Layer Preview map and change the style used to **PopulatedRotateTransparent**, as you did in the previous section. Your map now shows the rotated square marker with a transparent fill:

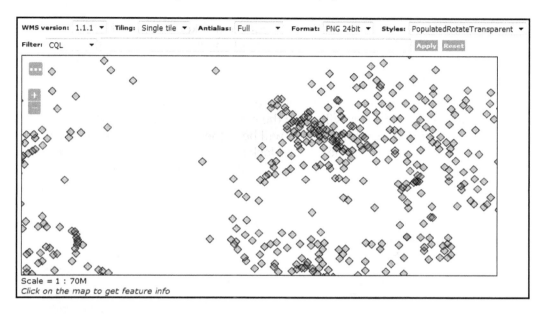

You have learned how to set a rotating angle to markers and set transparency. Step-by-step, you are discovering how flexible SLD is and how many different symbols you can create from quite simple shapes. Are you wondering if you can mix them? You can; let's jump to the next section.

Composing simple shapes

You've learned you can specify a specific marker using the <WellKnownName> element; however, if you need something more complex, you can always merge two or more basic shapes to create a new marker. In the following steps, you will see how to do so:

1. Take the PopulatedPlacesStrokes.xml file, make a copy, and name it as PopulatedPlacesComplex.xml. Edit the new file in your text editor. Replace the text inside the <Name> element with the following line of code:

```
<Name>PopulatedPlacesComplex</Name>
```

2. Replace the text inside the `<Title>` element with the following lines of code:

    ```
    <Title>Geoserver Beginners Guide: mark composed of three basic
    shapes</Title>
    ```

3. Now we will change the size for the square marker. Replace the text inside the `<Size>` element with the following line of code:

    ```
    <Size>10</Size>
    ```

4. To compose a complex marker, you need to add other markers as in a pile. Keep in mind that GeoServer will draw the markers in the inverse order; hence, the first marker you insert in the rule will be at the bottom of others on the map. We want to have a green circle with a black stroke containing the square marker. Insert a new `<PointSymbolizer>` element after the existing one:

    ```
    <PointSymbolizer>
      <Graphic>
       <Mark>
         <WellKnownName>square</WellKnownName>
         <Fill>
           <CssParameter name="fill">#FF0000</CssParameter>
         </Fill>
         <Stroke>
           <CssParameter name="stroke">#000000</CssParameter>
           <CssParameter name="stroke-width">1</CssParameter>
         </Stroke>
       </Mark>
       <Size>10</Size>
      </Graphic>
    </PointSymbolizer>
    ```

5. Now we want to have a small black circle inside the square. After the closure of the previous `<PointSymbolizer>` element, add a new one as follows:

    ```
    <PointSymbolizer>
      <Graphic>
        <Mark>
          <WellKnownName>circle</WellKnownName>
          <Fill>
            <CssParameter name="fill">#000000</CssParameter>
          </Fill>
        </Mark>
       <Size>5</Size>
      </Graphic>
    </PointSymbolizer>
    ```

6. Now save your document and upload it to GeoServer. Instead of making it the default style for the populated places layer, flag the associate option.

7. Open the **Layer Preview** map and select the **PopulatedPlacesComplex** style from the drop-down list. The symbol is quite large, so you may have to zoom out a little to take a look at it without overlapping:

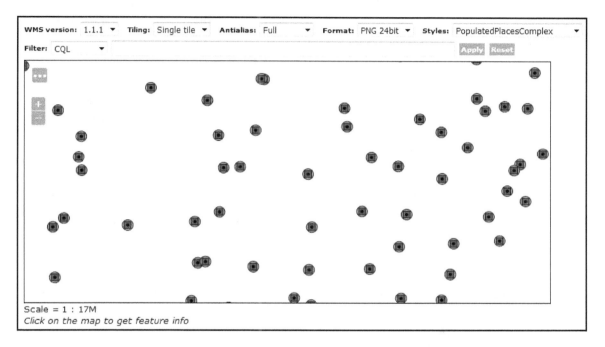

We created a complex symbol merging three basic markers. Playing with size, colors, and positions, you may think of quite a few possibilities with this technique. However, eventually, you will find something too hard to mimic with the markers. Then what do you do? It is time to use external graphics. Go ahead to the next section.

Using external graphics

When merging markers and setting colors and transparency can't help you realize the symbol you need, it's time to use external graphics. External graphics are vector or raster files containing a complex image. The supported formats are the common graphic files you use in web applications such as PNG, JPG, and SVG. The resources are referred to by a URL, so you can store it in your GeoServer data folder, as in this example, or get it from an online resource:

1. Take the `town.svg` file from the source code and copy it to the `<GEOSERVER_HOME>/data/styles` folder.

2. Take the `PopulatedPlacesStrokes.xml` file, make a copy, and name it as `PopulatedPlacesGraphics.xml`. Edit the new file in your text editor. Replace the text inside the `<Name>` element with the following line of code:

   ```
   <Name>PopulatedPlacesGraphic</Name>
   ```

3. Replace the text inside the `<Title>` element with the following lines of code:

   ```
   <Title>Geoserver Beginners Guide: Populated Places with external
   graphics</Title>
   ```

4. Remove the Mark section and insert an `<ExternalGraphic>` element. The value of `href` can be absolute, or as in this case relative to the location of the SLD file:

   ```
   <ExternalGraphic>
    <OnlineResource xlink:type="simple" xlink:href="town.svg" />
    <Format>image/svg+xml</Format>
   </ExternalGraphic>
   ```

5. Change the size to `20`:

   ```
   <Size>20</Size>
   ```

6. Now save your document and upload it to GeoServer. Instead of making it the default style for the populated places layer, flag the associate option.

7. Open the **Layer Preview** map and select the **PopulatedPlacesGraphic** style from the drop-down list. As in the previous section, the symbol is quite large; zoom in a little on a populated area on Earth and your map will look as shown in the following screenshot:

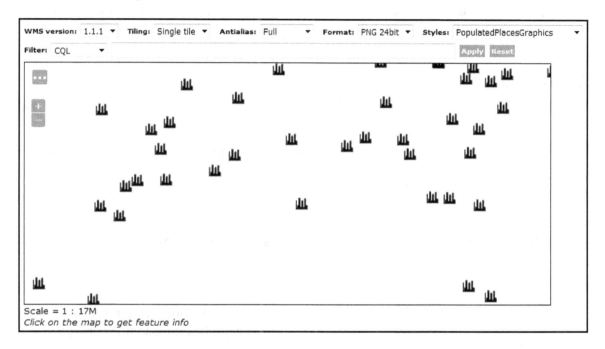

We have used a small vector file to add a complex symbol on a map. Using external graphics will open your map to an infinite variety of symbols. You can draw your own or search for a resource file on the Internet, minding the copyright obviously. After exploring what SLD offers to render point features, you are ready to jump to line features.

Composing your symbol

Did you like the possibility of adding external graphics to your map? You can compose them on your own. A great open source tool to create/modify graphic files is Inkscape. It is available in binary packages for Linux and Windows, and it has an excellent set of tools to work with vector graphics. You can save your creations in SVG, an XML-based specification from W3C for vector graphics. Are you ready to use your creative side? Then go to http://inkscape.org/ and try it.

LineString symbols

Lines are other simple features you can draw on your map. Inside a rule for lines, you have the `<LineSymbolizer>` element where you define color, thickness, and the type of line to draw (for example, a continuous or a dashed line). As for points, we will start with a simple symbol and then move to examples that are more complex.

Creating a simple line style

We will use a rivers and lake centerlines shapefile from Natural Earth to create a map of the rivers of the world with a light sky blue color:

1. Take the `PopulatedPlaces.xml` file, make a copy to `Rivers.xml`, and then edit the new file in your text editor. Find the text inside the `<Name>` element and replace it with the following line of code:

    ```
    <Name>Rivers</Name>
    ```

2. Replace the text inside the `<Title>` element with the following lines of code:

    ```
    <Title> Geoserver Beginners Guide: Rivers simple stroke
    </Title>
    ```

3. Now replace the `<FeatureTypeStyle>` code with the following piece of code. We are using a continuous line, which is the default, setting a width of 2 pixels and a specific color:

    ```
    <LineSymbolizer>
     <Stroke>
       <CssParameter name="stroke">#82CAFA</CssParameter>
       <CssParameter name="stroke-width">2</CssParameter>
     </Stroke>
    </LineSymbolizer>
    ```

4. Now save your document and upload it to GeoServer. Make it the default style for the **ne_50m_rivers_lake_centerlines** layer flag:

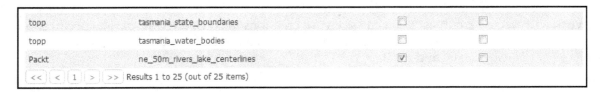

topp	tasmania_state_boundaries	☐	☐
topp	tasmania_water_bodies	☐	☐
Packt	ne_50m_rivers_lake_centerlines	☑	☐
`<<` `<` `1` `>` `>>` Results 1 to 25 (out of 25 items)			

5. Open the **Layer Preview** map. When you zoom to North America, it should look as shown in the following screenshot:

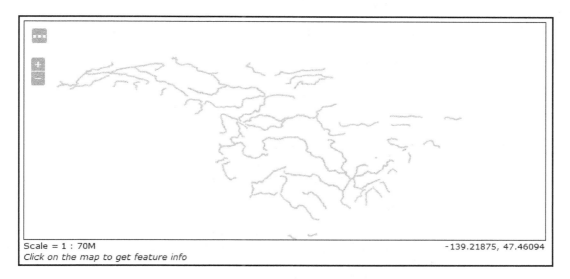

```
Scale = 1 : 70M                                    -139.21875, 47.46094
Click on the map to get feature info
```

We created a new style for a simple line symbol to draw rivers. As for points, there are several options to draw something prettier than a colored line. As you may have guessed, you can apply the merging technique that we used for points for lines too.

Adding a border and a centerline

On maps, major roads, such as highways, are often represented with a more complex symbol than a continuous colored line (in cartographers' slang this is also known as road casing). You will use three line symbols to build a representation of highways, as follows:

1. Take the Rivers.xml file, make a copy to Roads.xml, and then edit the new file in your text editor. Replace the text inside the <Name> element with the following line of code:

```
<Name>Roads</Name>
```

2. Replace the text inside the `<Title>` element with the following lines of code:

```
<Title>Geoserver Beginners Guide: Roads complex symbol</Title>
```

3. Edit the `<CssParameter>` element, setting the color to red, as shown here:

```
<CssParameter name="stroke">#FF0000</CssParameter>
```

4. Again, edit it, setting the width to 5, as in this example:

```
<CssParameter name="stroke-width">5</CssParameter>
```

5. Insert a new `<LineSymbolizer>` section as shown in the following code fragment. Use a width of seven and set the color to black. The black line, using a larger symbol, will result in a border on both sides of the line feature:

```
<LineSymbolizer>
  <Stroke>
   <CssParameter name="stroke">#000000</CssParameter>
   <CssParameter name="stroke-width">7</CssParameter>
  </Stroke>
</LineSymbolizer>
```

6. After the previous code and the existing `<LineSymbolizer>` element, insert a new one. Use a width of one and set the color to black. A black line will appear in the center of the line feature:

```
<LineSymbolizer>
  <Stroke>
   <CssParameter name="stroke">#000000</CssParameter>
   <CssParameter name="stroke-width">1</CssParameter>
  </Stroke>
</LineSymbolizer>
```

7. Now save your document and upload it to GeoServer. Make it the default style for the **ne_10m_roads** layer flag.

8. Open the **Layer Preview** map. The shapefile contains a lot of features and the symbol is too big for a full zoom map. Zoom into a small area, for example, the Los Angeles area, as shown in the following screenshot:

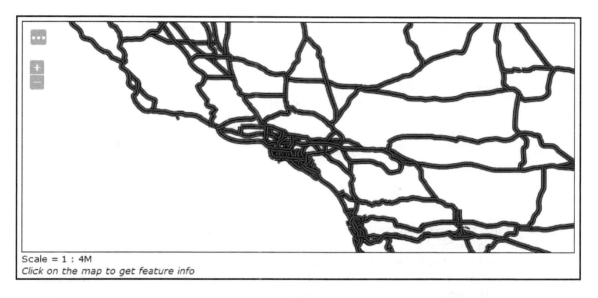

Scale = 1 : 4M
Click on the map to get feature info

You have learned to create complex line symbols. By merging lines of different sizes and colors, you can create symbols to represent almost all types of roads you would find on a Rand McNally© Atlas. However, what happens if you leave for a trip on a railroad?

Using hatching

Until now, we have used standard SLD syntax; you may take the styles and use them on another map server and it will produce the same maps. Nevertheless, this book focuses on a specific map server, and we can use a vendor option--a small trick that is only available on GeoServer--to create a symbol that resembles railroads:

1. Take the `Rivers.xml` file, make a copy to `RailRoads.xml`, and then edit the new file in your text editor. Find the text inside the `<Name>` element and replace it with the following line of code:

   ```
   <Name>RailRoads</Name>
   ```

2. Replace the text inside the `<Title>` element with the following lines of code:

```
<Title>Geoserver Beginners Guide: RailRoads with
hatching</Title>
```

3. Edit the `<CssParameter>` element, changing the color to black:

```
<CssParameter name="stroke">#000000</CssParameter>
```

4. Go to the end of the `<Rule>` element and add another `<Rule>` for a new `<LineSymbolizer>` element as follows:

```
<Rule>
  <LineSymbolizer>
    <Stroke>
    </Stroke>
  </LineSymbolizer>
</Rule>
```

5. In this rule, we will configure the hatching; you need to specify how the hatch line has to be drawn. Insert the following code fragment inside the stroke element. In the fourth line, you specify a `<WellKnownName>` element to inform GeoServer that the line has to be drawn perpendicular to the geometric feature. In the 6th and 7th lines, you set the color to black and width of the hatching line to `1`. Finally, at line 10, you set the length of the hatching line, as in the following code fragment:

```
<GraphicStroke>
 <Graphic>
   <Mark>
     <WellKnownName>shape://vertline</WellKnownName>
     <Stroke>
       <CssParameter name="stroke">#000000</CssParameter>
       <CssParameter name="stroke-width">1</CssParameter>
     </Stroke>
   </Mark>
   <Size>8</Size>
 </Graphic>
</GraphicStroke>
```

This book focuses on GeoServer, but if you are going to use the SLD code of this example in another Map Server you will get an error. This is because the `shape://vertline` value is a vendor parameter; it is not a part of SLD standard, but an extension to the standard provided by the GeoServer development Team.

6. Now save your document and upload it to GeoServer. Make it the default style for the **ne_10m_railroads** layer flag.

7. Open the **Layer Preview** map. Zoom to a small area and look at the result, as shown in the following image:

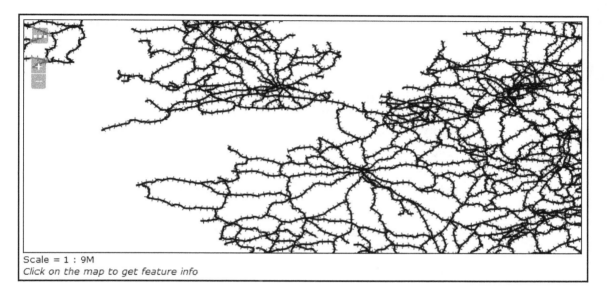

Scale = 1 : 9M
Click on the map to get feature info

You used a vendor option to enable hatching lines. Although this way of a styling feature is not portable, it helps you greatly in composing pretty maps. We will now explore another variation for lines in next section.

Using dashed lines

On many paper maps, a common symbol to represent roads under construction or planned is a couple of parallel dashed lines. Can you imagine how to do it with SLD? It requires a couple of lines merged together with a new SLD element. We will see that element in this section:

1. Take the `Roads.xml` file and make a copy to `DashedRoads.xml`, then edit the new file in your text editor. Find the text inside the `<Name>` element and replace it with the following line of code:

```
<Name>DashedRoads</Name>
```

2. Replace the text inside the `<Title>` element with the following lines of code:

```
<Title>Geoserver Beginners Guide: Roads under construction
with
dashing</Title>
```

3. Edit the `<CssParameter>` element, changing the width of the symbol to 5, as shown here:

```
<CssParameter name="stroke-width">5</CssParameter>
```

4. Add a line just after the previous one, setting dashing for the black lines as follows. The 15 10 values indicate to GeoServer to create a dashed line with filled and empty segments with length proportional to the numeric values:

```
<CssParameter name="stroke-dasharray">15 10</CssParameter>
```

5. Edit the other `<LineSymbolizer>` element, changing the color to white and width to 3:

```
<CssParameter name="stroke">#FFFFFF</CssParameter>
<CssParameter name="stroke-width">3</CssParameter>
```

6. Add a line just after the previous one to set dashing for the white lines:

```
<CssParameter name="stroke-dasharray">15 10</CssParameter>
```

7. Remove the last `<LineSymbolizer>` code. The third line is no longer needed to represent roads with parallel dashed lines.
8. Now save your document and upload it to GeoServer. Instead of making it the default style for the **ne_10m_roads** layer, flag the associate option.
9. Open the **Layer Preview** map and select the **DashedRoads** style from the drop-down list. As this is a complex symbol, you have to zoom into a small area to have a clear view of how the symbol looks, as shown in the following screenshot:

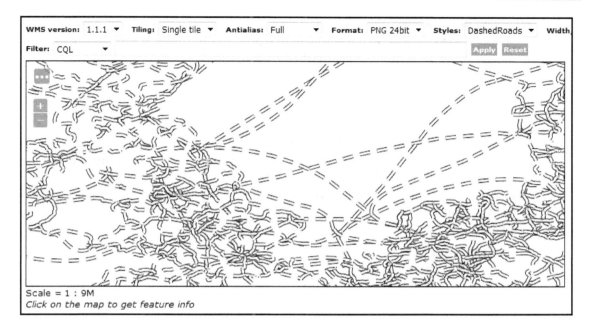

You built a dashing symbol by merging two lines. However, there is more that you can do with merging; you can mix dashing lines and marker symbols.

Mixing dashing lines and markers

Natural Earth does not provide a data set for aqueducts, but you may wonder how you can create an appropriate symbol to represent them. Aqueducts are usually represented in maps with a dashed line alternated with a small circle, all colored in light blue. We are going to create a new style for this:

1. Take the `DashedRoads.xml` file, make a copy to `DashingAndMarkers.xml`, and then edit the new file in your text editor. Find the text inside the `<Name>` element and replace it as follows:

   ```
   <Name>DashingAndMarkers</Name>
   ```

2. Replace the text inside the `<Title>` element as follows:

   ```
   <Title>Geoserver Beginners Guide: Aqueducts with dashing and
   circle</Title>
   ```

3. Locate the first `<LineSymbolizer>` element and change the setting of the element. Set the color to a hexadecimal value for light blue, set a width of 2, and a dasharray of 10 10 to have regularly-spaced dashing, as shown here:

```
<CssParameter name="stroke">#ADD8E6</CssParameter>
<CssParameter name="stroke-width">2</CssParameter>
<CssParameter name="stroke-dasharray">10 10</CssParameter>
```

4. Now delete all the code inside the following `<LineSymbolizer>` element. We need a totally different symbolizer, something similar to what we used for hatching. Insert the following code fragment. You can see that on the 6th line, we add a `<WellKnownName>` element and set it to a circle. Then, we set its color to light blue and width to 1. The circle width is set to 5 to make it larger than the dashed line:

```
<Stroke>
  <GraphicStroke>
    <Graphic>
      <Mark>
        <WellKnownName>circle</WellKnownName>
        <Stroke>
          <CssParameter name="stroke">#ADD8E6</CssParameter>
          <CssParameter name="stroke-width">1</CssParameter>
        </Stroke>
      </Mark>
      <Size>5</Size>
    </Graphic>
  </GraphicStroke>
  <CssParameter name="stroke-dasharray">5 15</CssParameter>
  <CssParameter name="stroke-dashoffset">7.5</CssParameter>
</Stroke>
```

5. Now save your document and upload it to GeoServer. Instead of making it the default style for the `50m-rivers-lake-centerlines` layer, flag the associate option.

6. Open the **Layer Preview** map and select the **DashingAndMarkers** style from the drop-down list. Zoom to North America and check if your map looks as shown in the following screenshot. Do you see that big aqueduct that covers all the Middle West lands?

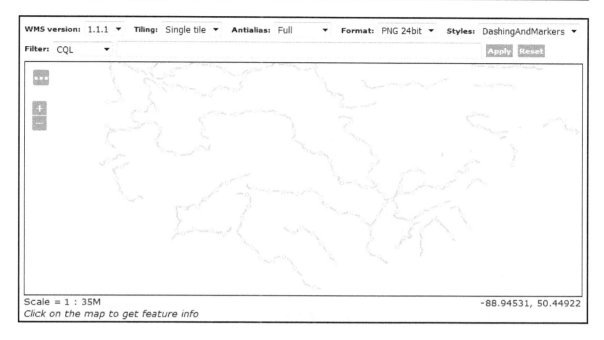

We have merged markers for points and lines. In the previous examples, you learned how to use them for a point or line features. In this last example, you discovered they can be mixed to achieve a new kind of symbology. It's now time to switch to the last type of shapes-- polygons.

Working with polygon symbols

Polygons are defined by a set of rings, a closed lineString, so it is not surprising that you have the possibility of setting the stroke color and width. By defining a closed area, you may also set how this area has to be filled. The key element is <PolygonSymbolizer>; include it inside any rule you are defining for polygons. We will start with a fairly simple example.

Creating a simple polygon style

Since you were a kid, you have been familiarized with the political maps of the world. Countries were rendered with brown boundaries and there were different colors for each country. Isn't this a wonderful example for your first polygon styling?

You may wonder how many different colors you need to build a map where each adjacent country does not share the same color. The answer is not trivial; indeed, it is a surprisingly little number. Four different colors are enough for a map with any number of polygonal features. Take a look at http://en.wikipedia.org/wiki/Four_color_theorem for more information.

We will create a map with all features rendered with the same color and outline, to start with a simple example, but we will return to this style in the thematic mapping section:

1. Take the `Rivers.xml` file, make a copy to `Countries.xml`, and then edit the new file in your text editor. Replace the text inside the `<Name>` element with the following line of code:

   ```
   <Name>Countries</Name>
   ```

2. Locate the `<Title>` element and replace the text inside it with the following lines of code:

   ```
   <Title> Geoserver Beginners Guide: Countries with outline and
   fill</Title>
   ```

3. As we are using polygons, you will need to replace the `<LineSymbolizer>` element with a `<PolygonSymbolizer>` element:

   ```
   <PolygonSymbolizer>
   </PolygonSymbolizer>
   ```

4. Set the outline color to brown and the width to 2, as in the following code:

   ```
   <CssParameter name="stroke">#A52A2A</CssParameter>
   <CssParameter name="stroke-width">2</CssParameter>
   ```

5. Lines are rendered with stroke but polygons may have a fill defined too. Insert the following three lines of code just after the `<PolygonSymbolizer>`element starts. This will set the fill color to a complementary color for brown:

   ```
   <Fill>
   <CssParameter name="fill">#29A6A6</CssParameter>
   </Fill>
   ```

6. Now save your document and upload it to GeoServer. Instead of making it the default style for the `ne_50m_admin_0_countries` layer, flag the associated option.

7. Open the **Layer Preview** map and zoom in Europe. Select the **Countries** style from the drop-down list. Your map should look as shown in the following screenshot:

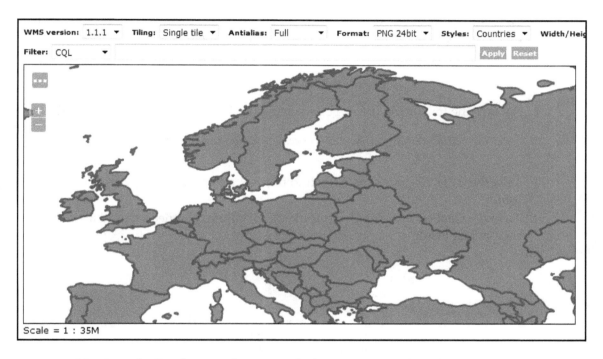

You have built a basic polygon symbol. You may work with outlines much the same way as with lineStrings, applying dashing, transparency, and different colors and widths. We will explore the different ways of filling polygons in the next section.

Using a graphic filling

Colors may help you in pointing out some areas, but you may need something different. If you want to represent wooded areas in topographic maps, you can insert many little markers, each one representing a circle. Patterns of markers are widely used in mapping. As we did with points and lines, the solution is using an external graphic resource. A bitmap or a vector, for example, an SVG file, can be used to fill a polygon:

1. Take the `Countries.xml` file, make a copy to `CountriesGraphics.xml`, and then edit the new file in your text editor. Replace the text inside the `<Name>` element with the following line of code:

   ```
   <Name>CountriesGraphics</Name>
   ```

2. Replace the text inside the `<Title>` element with the following lines of code:

   ```
   <Title>Geoserver Beginners Guide: Countries with graphics
   filling</Title>
   ```

3. Take the `fill.svg` file and copy it to the `<GEOSERVER_HOME>/data/styles` folder.

4. To make GeoServer using the graphic fill for filling, you need to add a `<Fill>` section just inside `<PolygonSymbolizer>`:

   ```
   <Fill>
     <GraphicFill>
       <Graphic>
         <ExternalGraphic>
           <OnlineResource xlink:type="simple"
            xlink:href="fill.svg"/>
           <Format>image/svg+xml</Format>
         </ExternalGraphic>
       </Graphic>
     </GraphicFill>
   </Fill>
   ```

5. Now save your document and upload it to GeoServer. Instead of making it the default style for the `ne_50m_admin_0_countries` layer, flag the associate option.

6. Open the **Layer Preview** map and select the **CountriesGraphics** style from the drop-down list. Zoom to North America and check if your map looks as shown in the following screenshot:

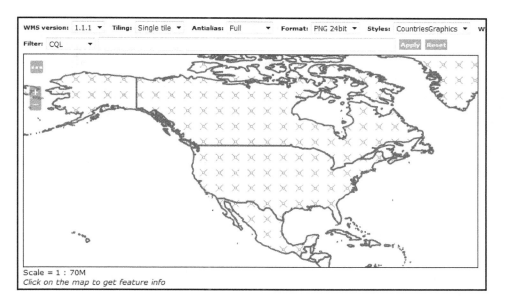

Working with external graphic lets you build any pattern you may need, but GeoServer offers you yet another possibility. Go to the next section and see.

Using hatching with polygons

Hatching a polygon is a different way to produce maps similar to those seen in the previous example. The pros are that you do not need to search for or build a graphical resource; you have a set of hatching patterns ready for you. It is also faster for GeoServer to render a map without using external graphic resources. When it is feasible to achieve the same results with internal resources, stick to hatching!

1. Take the `CountriesGraphics.xml` file, make a copy to `CountriesHatching.xml`, and then edit the new file in your text editor. Replace the text inside the `<Name>` element with the following line of code:

   ```
   <Name>CountriesHatching</Name>
   ```

2. Replace the text inside the `<Title>` element with the following lines of code:

```
<Title>Geoserver Beginners Guide: Countries with
hatching</Title>
```

3. To add code for hatching, you need to replace the `<ExternalGraphic>` element with a `<Mark>` element. Inside it, you set the shape to use with a `<WellKnownName>` element (remember that the `shape://` notation is only supported in GeoServer):

```
<Graphic>
  <Mark>
    <WellKnownName>shape://dot</WellKnownName>
    <Stroke>
       <CssParameter name="stroke">#29A6A6</CssParameter>
       <CssParameter name="stroke-width">3</CssParameter>
    </Stroke>
  </Mark>
  <Size>16</Size>
</Graphic>
```

4. Now save your document and upload it to GeoServer. Instead of making it the default style for the `ne_50m_admin_0_countries` layer, flag the associate option.

5. Open the **Layer Preview** map and select the **CountriesHatching** style from the drop-down list, then zoom to Australia. Can you see how similar hatching is to use an external graphic resource?

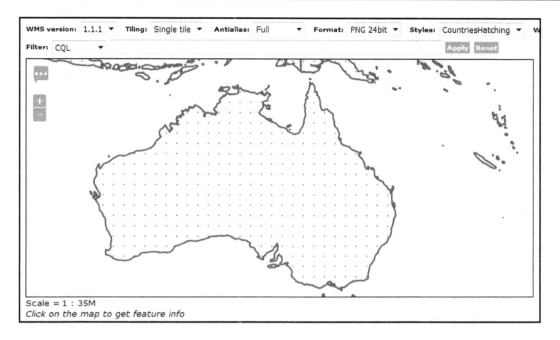

We used point markers to fill an area enclosed in a polygon. Thanks to the GeoServer extension, this can be done not only with a limited set of point markers supported by standard SLD, but also by using the following markers:

- `shape://vertline`: This is a vertical line
- `shape://horline`: This is a horizontal line
- `shape://slash`: This is a diagonal line leaning forwards like the slash (/) keyboard symbol
- `shape://backslash`: This is the same as the previous marker, but oriented in the opposite direction (\)
- `shape://dot`: This is a very small circle with space around it
- `shape://plus`: This is a + symbol, without space around it
- `shape://times`: This is an X symbol, without space around it
- `shape://oarrow`: This is an open arrow symbol
- `shape://carrow`: This is a closed arrow symbol

Adding labels

We had a full exploration of styling for geometry features, but we have produced maps without any text. Are you wondering how you can represent textual attributes on maps? As in paper maps, you need a labeling engine and GeoServer provides you with the right tool. You can add labels to any kind of feature; let's start with points.

Labeling points

You are probably a geography geek and you know what a place's name is at the first look at the map. However, maps are not always so expressive and common people tend to get confused without some reference text. Do you remember the pretty maps you styled with the Populated Places layer? They would look much better with some labels next to their markers:

1. Take the `PopulatedPlacesStroke.xml` file; make a copy to `PopulatedPlacesLabeled.xml`, and then edit the new file in your text editor. Replace the text inside the `<Name>` element with the following line of code:

   ```
   <Name>PopulatedPlacesLabeled</Name>
   ```

2. Replace the text inside the `<Title>` element with the following lines of code:

   ```
   <Title>Geoserver Beginners Guide: Populated Places with styled
   labels</Title>
   ```

3. Change the marker to a `circle` as follows:

   ```
   <WellKnownName>circle</WellKnownName>
   ```

4. Change the size to `8`, as shown here:

   ```
   <Size>8</Size>
   ```

5. After the `<PointSymbolizer>` element, add a new `<TextSymbolizer>` element. Inside it, you have to specify which field of the layer attributes will be used to extract text strings (be aware that the attribute's name is case sensitive). You can use the `<Label>` element to do it. Then, add a `<Font>` element to specify which font family GeoServer will use to draw labels and text properties:

```
<TextSymbolizer>
 <Label>
   <ogc:PropertyName>NAME</ogc:PropertyName>
 </Label>
 <Font>
   <CssParameter name="font-family">Arial</CssParameter>
   <CssParameter name="font-size">12</CssParameter>
   <CssParameter name="font-style">normal</CssParameter>
   <CssParameter name="font-weight">italic</CssParameter>
 </Font>
</TextSymbolizer>
```

6. Now you have to set the position of labels. The position is relative to the point feature; you add a `<LabelPlacement>` element for this. We want to have a label relative to points on the top right, so we use an `<AnchorPoint>` element, setting it to 0 and a `<Displacement>` element, setting it to 2 pixels along the x-axis and 5 pixels along the y-axis:

```
<LabelPlacement>
 <PointPlacement>
   <AnchorPoint>
     <AnchorPointX>0</AnchorPointX>
     <AnchorPointY>0</AnchorPointY>
   </AnchorPoint>
   <Displacement>
     <DisplacementX>2</DisplacementX>
     <DisplacementY>5</DisplacementY>
   </Displacement>
 </PointPlacement>
</LabelPlacement>
```

7. Eventually, you need to set a color for your label. Use a `<Fill>` element and set it to black. Include the following code snippet just after the `<LabelPlacement>` section:

```
<Fill>
 <CssParameter name="fill">#000000</CssParameter>
</Fill>
```

8. Now save your document and upload it to GeoServer. Instead of making it the default style for the `ne_50m_populated_places` layer, flag the associate option.

9. Open the **Layer Preview** map and select the **PopulatedPlacesLabeled** style from the drop-down list, then zoom in to get a better preview of the labels:

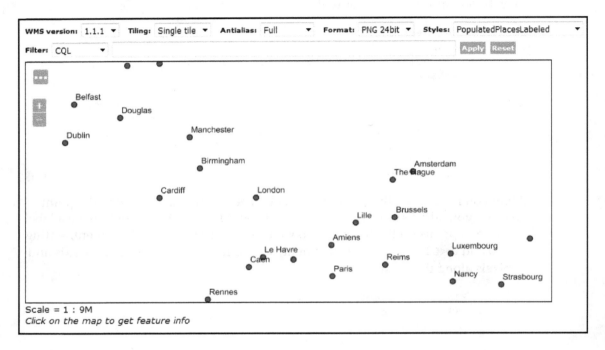

We added pretty labels using the font (be aware that fonts must be available on the server side) and placement properties.

Labeling lines

Place names are useful, but a roadmap without a road name, or at least road codes, is almost useless. You need to get back to the roads style and add code to enable road labeling:

1. Take the `Roads.xml` file, make a copy to `RoadsLabeled.xml`, and then edit the new file in your text editor. Replace the text inside the `<Name>` element with the following line of code:

```
<Name>RoadsLabeled</Name>
```

2. Replace the text inside the `<Title>` element with the following lines of code:

    ```
    <Title>Geoserver Beginners Guide: Roads with labels along the
    line</Title>
    ```

3. Remove the last `<LineSymbolizer>` element. We need a simpler symbol to have a pretty map.
4. Set the width of the black line to 4 as follows:

    ```
    <CssParameter name="stroke">#000000</CssParameter>
    <CssParameter name="stroke-width">4</CssParameter>
    ```

5. Set the width of the red line to 2 as follows:

    ```
    <CssParameter name="stroke">#FF0000</CssParameter>
    <CssParameter name="stroke-width">2</CssParameter>
    ```

6. After the last `<LineSymbolizer>` element, add a new `<TextSymbolizer>` element. Inside it, you have to specify which field of the layer attributes will be used to extract the text string. This is done with the `<Label>` element. Then, add a `<LabelPlacement>` element to specify where the label has to be placed, relative to the line:

    ```
    <TextSymbolizer>
     <Label>
       <ogc:PropertyName>STATE</ogc:PropertyName>
     </Label>
     <LabelPlacement>
       <LinePlacement>
         <PerpendicularOffset>10</PerpendicularOffset>
       </LinePlacement>
     </LabelPlacement>
    </TextSymbolizer>
    ```

7. Add a `<Fill>` element just after the `<LabelPlacement>` section. Set the label color to black:

    ```
    <Fill>
     <CssParameter name="fill">#000000</CssParameter>
    </Fill>
    ```

8. Now save your document and upload it to GeoServer. Instead of making it the default style for the `ne_10m_roads` layer, flag the associate option.

9. Open the **Layer Preview** map and zoom to a very little area. Open the controls and select the RoadsLabeled style from the drop-down list. Yes, you are in the UK, in the great London!

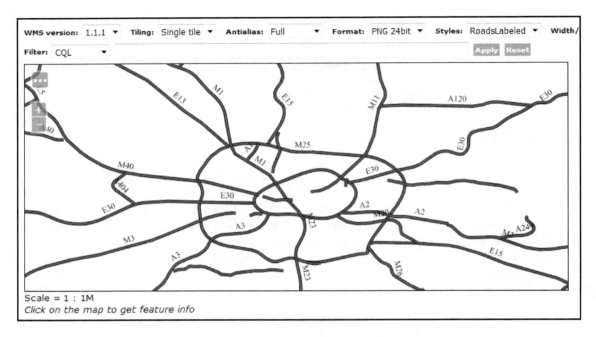

10. Now we will add some GeoServer extensions. After the `<Fill>` element, add an option to have labels following bending roads and set a maximum angle value for bending. The maximum displacement of the label sets how many pixels the GeoServer label engine may shift text labels to avoid overlapping. The last parameter makes GeoServer repeat labels every 300 pixels for long roads.

```
<VendorOption name="followLine">true</VendorOption>
<VendorOption name="maxAngleDelta">90</VendorOption>
<VendorOption name="maxDisplacement">400</VendorOption>
<VendorOption name="repeat">300</VendorOption>
```

11. After you updated the style, go back to the OpenLayers map and refresh the view. Do you see any changes in the following screenshot of the map?

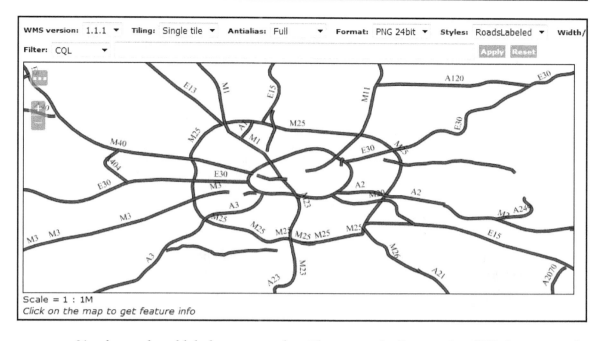

You have placed labels upon roads with your style. By merging SLD features and options only available in GeoServer, you can create pretty labels and place them in a well-readable form.

Labeling polygons

We will now come back to our countries dataset to add labeling to the countries style. While most of the properties are what we already saw in the labeling of points and lines, we will add code to make halos around our labels. Halos could enhance the readability of labels:

1. Take the `Countries.xml` file, make a copy to `CountriesLabeled.xml`, and then edit the new file in your text editor. Replace the text inside the `<Name>` element with the following line of code:

   ```
   <Name>CountriesLabeled</Name>
   ```

2. Replace the text inside the `<Title>` element with the following lines of code:

   ```
   <Title>Geoserver Beginners Guide: Countries with
   labels</Title>
   ```

3. Add a `<TextSymbolizer>` element just after the `<PolygonSymbolizer>` element. Inside it, define the feature field containing the text and the font name and the style to draw the label, as in the following code:

```
<TextSymbolizer>
 <Label>
   <ogc:PropertyName>NAME</ogc:PropertyName>
 </Label>
 <Font>
   <CssParameter name="font-family">Arial</CssParameter>
   <CssParameter name="font-size">11</CssParameter>
   <CssParameter name="font-style">normal</CssParameter>
   <CssParameter name="font-weight">bold</CssParameter>
 </Font>
</TextSymbolizer>
```

4. The placement of polygon labels is very similar to points. After the `<Font>` section, add `<LabelPlacement>` and set the `<AnchorPoint>` element:

```
<LabelPlacement>
 <PointPlacement>
   <AnchorPoint>
     <AnchorPointX>0.5</AnchorPointX>
     <AnchorPointY>0.5</AnchorPointY>
   </AnchorPoint>
 </PointPlacement>
</LabelPlacement>
```

5. Set the text color to black by adding a `<Fill>` element as follows:

```
<Fill>
 <CssParameter name="fill">#000000</CssParameter>
</Fill>
```

6. After the `<Fill>` element, add a couple of vendor options. The first line ensures that long labels are split across multiple lines by setting line wrapping on the labels to 50 pixels, and the second sets 150 pixels as the maximum displacement for places where labels crowd:

```
<VendorOption name="autoWrap">50</VendorOption>
<VendorOption name="maxDisplacement">150</VendorOption>
```

7. Lastly, add the code for halos. We will use a white halo, to maximize contrast, with a 3-pixel width around the text:

```
<Halo>
 <Radius>3</Radius>
 <Fill>
   <CssParameter name="fill">#FFFFFF</CssParameter>
 </Fill>
</Halo>
```

8. Now save your document and upload it to GeoServer. Instead of making it the default style for the `ne_50m_admin_0_countries` layer, flag the associate option.

9. Open the **Layer Preview** map and zoom to Europe. Open the controls and select the **CountriesLabeled** style from the drop-down list:

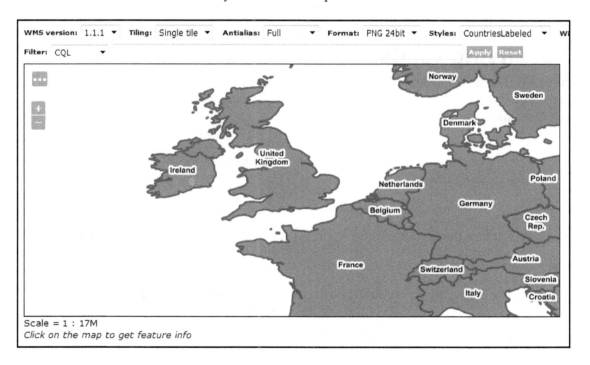

We used standard SLD elements and GeoServer extensions to build pretty labels for the polygon feature. You may have noticed that, apart from labels, all the styles we created use the same symbol for all features. It is now time to explore thematic mapping.

Thematic mapping

Very simple maps may be well-defined with just one symbol per layer, but this is not the case for the vast majority of maps you can find, nor for what you will create with your GeoServer. To fully express the meaning of features, you need to apply a symbology that can make it easy to recognize different real features on a map. Think of the road layer containing North America's roads--a map where interstates have a different symbol to intrastate roads, or where the federal road is much more readable. Countries symbolized according to their GDP can be mapped as the richest area of the world.

There are many different kinds of thematic maps. One of the most common is the choropleth map; we talked about it in `Chapter 1`, *GIS Fundamentals*.

Of course, SLD can be used to build choropleth maps; you just have to define a classification rule and a symbol for each class.

Classifying roads

The roads dataset provided by Natural Earth has some attributes that can be used to classify roads. You may use the `level` field for thematic mapping, assigning a different symbol to each class, as in the following example:

1. Take the `Roads.xml` file, make a copy to `RoadsThematic.xml`, and then edit the new file in your text editor. Replace the text inside the `<Name>` element with the following line of code:

    ```
    <Name>RoadsThematic</Name>
    ```

2. Replace the text inside the `<Title>` element with the following lines of code:

    ```
    <Title>Geoserver Beginners Guide: Roads thematic map</Title>
    ```

3. The `level` field contains six different values--Interstate, Federal, State, Other, Closed, and U/C. We will reuse the symbol for the first value, Interstate. You need to add a filter inside the rule so that the symbol will be applied only to features with the Interstate value in the `level` field. Add a Name element inside the Rule element and set it to Interstate:

    ```
    <Name>Interstate</Name>
    ```

4. Now add a `<Filter>` element and use `<PropertyIsEqualTo>` to set the filter operator. `<PropertyName>` sets what field to search for and `<Literal>` sets the value to be searched:

```
<ogc:Filter>
 <ogc:PropertyIsEqualTo>
   <ogc:PropertyName>level</ogc:PropertyName>
   <ogc:Literal>State</ogc:Literal>
 </ogc:PropertyIsEqualTo>
</ogc:Filter>
```

5. Now create a new `<FeatureTypeStyle>` element and set its Filter for Federal roads:

```
<FeatureTypeStyle>
 <Rule>
   <Name>Federal</Name>
   <ogc:Filter>
     <ogc:PropertyIsEqualTo>
       <ogc:PropertyName>level</ogc:PropertyName>
       <ogc:Literal>Federal</ogc:Literal>
     </ogc:PropertyIsEqualTo>
   </ogc:Filter>
 </Rule>
</FeatureTypeStyle>
```

6. For Federal roads, use an orange line with black borders:

```
<LineSymbolizer>
 <Stroke>
   <CssParameter name="stroke">#808080</CssParameter>
   <CssParameter name="stroke-width">4</CssParameter>
 </Stroke>
</LineSymbolizer>
<LineSymbolizer>
 <Stroke>
   <CssParameter name="stroke">#FF7F00</CssParameter>
   <CssParameter name="stroke-width">2</CssParameter>
 </Stroke>
</LineSymbolizer>
```

7. Now add a `Rule` for State roads; use a symbol--yellow with black borders:

```
<FeatureTypeStyle>
 <Rule>
   <Name>State</Name>
   <ogc:Filter>
     <ogc:PropertyIsEqualTo>
       <ogc:PropertyName>level</ogc:PropertyName>
       <ogc:Literal>State</ogc:Literal>
     </ogc:PropertyIsEqualTo>
   </ogc:Filter>
   <LineSymbolizer>
     <Stroke>
       <CssParameter name="stroke">#000000</CssParameter>
       <CssParameter name="stroke-width">4</CssParameter>
     </Stroke>
   </LineSymbolizer>
   <LineSymbolizer>
     <Stroke>
       <CssParameter name="stroke">#FFFF00</CssParameter>
       <CssParameter name="stroke-width">2</CssParameter>
     </Stroke>
   </LineSymbolizer>
 </Rule>
</FeatureTypeStyle>
```

8. To remember the old times when paper maps were all you could count on when driving around the country, we will add a rule for Other roads using a blue symbol with gray borders:

```
<FeatureTypeStyle>
 <Rule>
   <Name>Other</Name>
   <ogc:Filter>
     <ogc:PropertyIsEqualTo>
       <ogc:PropertyName>level</ogc:PropertyName>
       <ogc:Literal>Other</ogc:Literal>
     </ogc:PropertyIsEqualTo>
   </ogc:Filter>
   <LineSymbolizer>
     <Stroke>
       <CssParameter name="stroke">#808080</CssParameter>
       <CssParameter name="stroke-width">4</CssParameter>
     </Stroke>
   </LineSymbolizer>
   <LineSymbolizer>
     <Stroke>
```

```
    <CssParameter name="stroke">#0000FF</CssParameter>
    <CssParameter name="stroke-width">2</CssParameter>
   </Stroke>
  </LineSymbolizer>
 </Rule>
</FeatureTypeStyle>
```

9. We are not interested in closed roads, so you don't add a rule for them. Hence they will not appear on the map. Add a rule for U/C, that is, under construction roads, and use a grey dashed line:

```
<FeatureTypeStyle>
 <Rule>
   <Name>Under Construction</Name>
   <ogc:Filter>
     <ogc:PropertyIsEqualTo>
       <ogc:PropertyName>level</ogc:PropertyName>
       <ogc:Literal>U/C</ogc:Literal>
     </ogc:PropertyIsEqualTo>
   </ogc:Filter>
   <LineSymbolizer>
     <Stroke>
       <CssParameter name="stroke-dasharray">15
        10</CssParameter>
       <CssParameter name="stroke">#808080</CssParameter>
       <CssParameter name="stroke-width">4</CssParameter>
     </Stroke>
   </LineSymbolizer>
 </Rule>
</FeatureTypeStyle>
```

10. Now save your document and upload it to GeoServer. Instead of making it the default style for the ne_10m_roads layer, flag the associate option.

11. Open the **Layer Preview** map and zoom to the East Coast of the USA. Open the controls and select the **RoadsLabeled** style from the drop-down list:

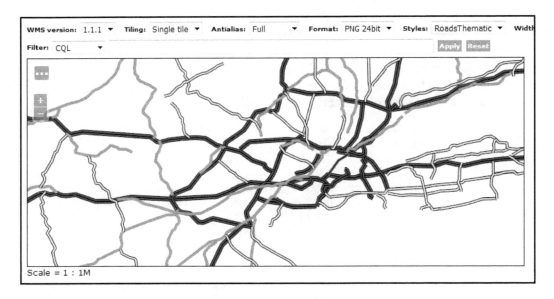

We made a choropleth roadmap. It was not more difficult than doing a single symbol map; it just took a bit longer. Using the `<Filter>` element, you can classify your features and group them in homogeneous sets to which you can apply a single symbol.

Setting visibility

When you look at Google maps or another web-mapping application, you can see that the map changes its style according to the zoom level. When you are looking at an entire continent, symbols are simple and there are a few features drawn on the map. As you get closer, you can see more labels--major roads change their symbols and minor roads appear.

This approach permits us to insert a large quantity of information on a web map while avoiding producing an almost unreadable crowd of labels and symbols. As an example, you can think of a cadastral map containing all USA parcels with a label showing owners. When you are looking at the entire country, it is impossible to show all this information without owning a several thousand inch wide display! A good approach would be to just show the country's boundaries and major roads and places on smaller scales and avoid showing parcels until you are not so close to see just a county.

The way to build such a map with SLD is by using zoom thresholds. We will try them in the following section.

Enhancing thematic roads maps

In the previous section, we styled a thematic roads map. It is a pretty map, but it lacks something to be ready for publication. As a user, you would expect roads to be drawn on different scales according to their classification. SLD has elements to define a scale range where a rule must be applied; they are called `<MinScaleDenominator>` and `<MaxScaleDenominator>`. Let's use them!

1. Take the `RoadsThematic.xml` file, make a copy to `RoadsThematicScale.xml`, and then edit the new file in your text editor. Replace the text inside the `<Name>` element with the following line of code:

   ```
   <Name>RoadsThematicScale</Name>
   ```

2. Replace the text inside the `<Title>` element with the following lines of code:

   ```
   <Title>Geoserver Beginners Guide: Roads thematic map with scale
   ranges</Title>
   ```

3. We want Interstate roads to appear at any scale, so we leave the first Rule unchanged. Federal roads will appear only at a 1:10,000,000 scale and closer. Add the following line of code just after the `<Filter>` section:

   ```
   <MaxScaleDenominator>10000000</MaxScaleDenominator>
   ```

4. Add a scale condition filter to make State roads only visible from a 1:1,500,000 scale:

   ```
   <MaxScaleDenominator>1500000</MaxScaleDenominator>
   ```

5. Other and Under Construction roads would only be visible from a 1:500,000 scale. For both filters, you need to add a scale condition filter as follows:

   ```
   <MaxScaleDenominator>500000</MaxScaleDenominator>
   ```

6. Now save your document and upload it to GeoServer. Instead of making it the default style for the `ne_10m_roads` layer, flag the associate option.

7. Open the **Layer Preview** map and zoom to scale 1:17,000,000. Open the controls and select the **RoadsThematicScale** style from the drop-down list. As the map redraws, you can see that many roads disappear:

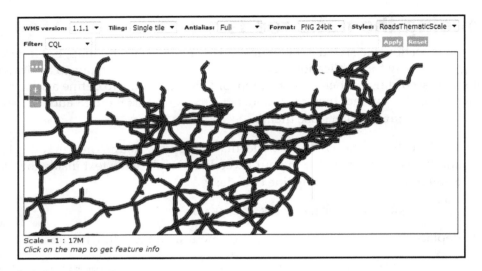

8. Zoom in to get closer and you will see that other road classes appear. As you go under the 1:500,000 scale, all roads are drawn as shown in the previous example.

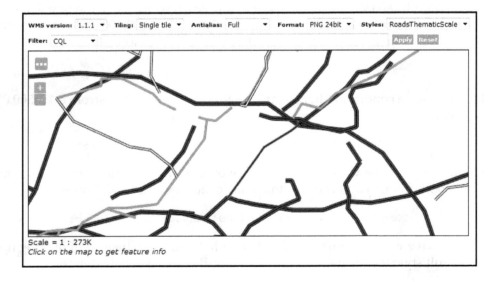

You have made road maps much more readable by setting scale range for your feature classes. Setting scale range is a powerful tool and it is usually required in maps, unless you are composing a map with a tiny number of features. Using scale range is quite easy; you just add it inside your rule.

Besides `MaxScaleDenominator`, there is another element to set scale range-- `MinScaleDenominator`. Using them together, you can define the upper and lower scale where a rule has to be applied. You may define two rules for the same layer with different scale ranges; this way, as the user zooms in or out, the symbols applied to features will change.

Putting it all together

A common map contains more than a layer, each one styled with one or more symbols according to its complexity and the map purpose. How can you create a multilayer document with SLD? You can't. As the acronym states, an SLD document can contain a rule relative to just one layer.

By publishing your layers with one or more styles associated on GeoServer, you can compose a map with an external client supporting a WMS protocol, for example, an OpenLayers JavaScript client or a desktop GIS such as QGIS.

Another possibility offered by GeoServer is the layer group. A **layer group** is a set of layers with a drawing order. Using layer groups, you can compose and publish a full map as if it was a single layer. Your client will have to do a single WMS request to get all the layers.

Grouping layers

To compose a full map, we will use a couple of styles created in this chapter and one bundled with GeoServer. We will not create new styles; it is just a matter of selecting layers and setting map properties:

1. On the GeoServer web interface, go to **Data** | **Layer Groups**.

2. Click on the **Add new layer group** link:

3. Insert the name you would like to give to the new layer group, for example, `myLayerGroup`.

4. Select the **Add layer...** link and choose the **states** layer from the list.

poly_landmarks	nyc	tiger
tiger_roads	nyc	tiger
states	states_shapefile	topp
tasmania_cities	taz_shapes	topp
tasmania_roads	taz_shapes	topp
<< < 1 2 > >> Results 1 to 25 (out of 27 items)		

5. Repeat the previous step to add the **10m_roads** and **50m_rivers_lake_centerlines** layers.

6. In the **Coordinate Reference System** textbox, insert the **EPSG:4326** string. Then click on the **Generate Bounds** button.

You could also build a map with a different SRS than that of layers.

In this case, data will be projected at runtime.

7. You composed the map; however, as you selected the layers, they were added with their default style. Click on the style name for the roads layer and select the **RoadsThematicScale** style, then click on **Save**.

8. Go to the **Layer Preview** section and search for your new layer group. Notice the different icon showing you that the item is composed of multiple layers:

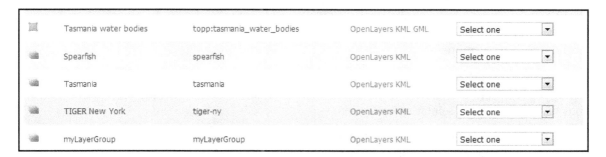

	Tasmania water bodies	topp:tasmania_water_bodies	OpenLayers KML GML	Select one
	Spearfish	spearfish	OpenLayers KML	Select one
	Tasmania	tasmania	OpenLayers KML	Select one
	TIGER New York	tiger-ny	OpenLayers KML	Select one
	myLayerGroup	myLayerGroup	OpenLayers KML	Select one

9. Explore your map and zoom in closer to make all roads appear in the map.

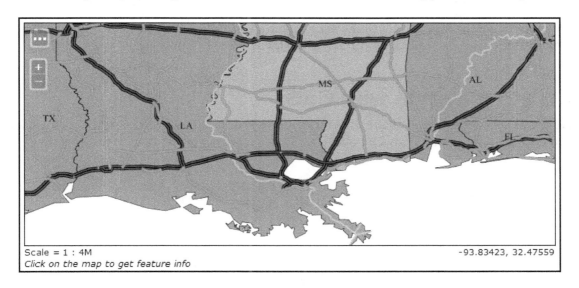

Scale = 1 : 4M -93.83423, 32.47559
Click on the map to get feature info

We have composed a nice starting point for a map of the USA. It has thematic mapping, scale range, and different layers properly overlapped.

Styling with CSS

In this chapter, you learned a lot about SLD and how to use its elements to produce graphical effects on your maps. While SLD is a powerful tool and enables you to create a complex and pretty rendering of data, it is also famous for being quite hard to write and understand for humans.

Cascading Style Sheets (CSS) (`http://en.wikipedia.org/wiki/CSS`) is a convenient and easier replacement alternative to long SLD documents. When using CSS, you must be aware that this is GeoServer specific.

While SLD is a standard approach that can be reused with other WMS implementations or a desktop application such as QGIS, CSS is a GeoServer-specific module. For instance, you can't use the CSS syntax with MapServer, but you can, of course, reuse the styles on another GeoServer WMS server, assuming that layers with similar details are published on them.

If you followed the instructions at the start of this chapter, you already installed the CSS module; so, now we are ready to duplicate the thematic roads map with the CSS syntax.

Creating a style with CSS

We previously created a thematic map for roads with a scale-dependent renderer. How can you create a similar map with CSS code? Again, it's a matter of creating filters. This time, you will use the concise CSS syntax.

 The entire CSS style for the recipe is located in the `WorldRoad.css` file.

1. As you did previously, open the style editor to create a new one. Call it WorldRoads and select CSS as the format:

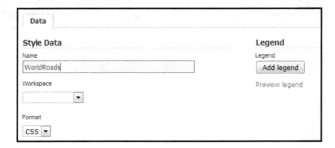

2. Insert the following lines of code in the textbox and click on the **Apply** button:

```
/* @title Major Highway */
[type = 'Major Highway'] [@scale > 10000000]
{
  stroke: red;
  stroke-width: 1;
}
```

3. Now switch to the **Layer Preview** tab and zoom to the North of Europe:

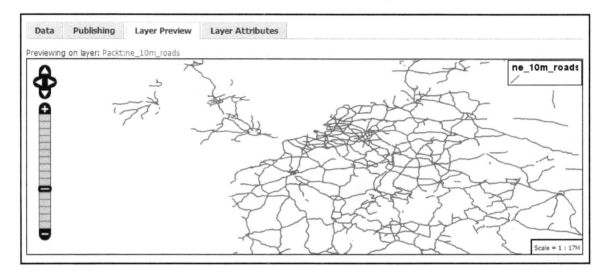

4. Now add the following piece of code to draw more roads as you zoom in:

```
/* @title Road */
[type = 'Road'] [@scale < 5000000]
{
  stroke: #000000, #FFFF00;
  stroke-width: 4, 2;
  z-index: 0, 1;
}
/* @title Major Highway */
[type = 'Major Highway'] [@scale < 10000000]
{
  stroke: black, red, black;
  stroke-width: 7, 3, 1;
  z-index: 0, 1, 2;
}
/* @title Secondary Highway */
```

```
[type = 'Secondary Highway'] [@scale < 5000000]
{
  stroke: #808080, #FF7F00;
  stroke-width: 4, 2;
  z-index: 0, 1;
}
/* @title Track */
[type = 'Track'] [@scale < 5000000]
{
  stroke: #808080;
  stroke-width: 2;
  stroke-dasharray: 15 10;
}
```

5. Zoom your map to a 1:4,000,000 scale, and now, you will see more roads with different symbols:

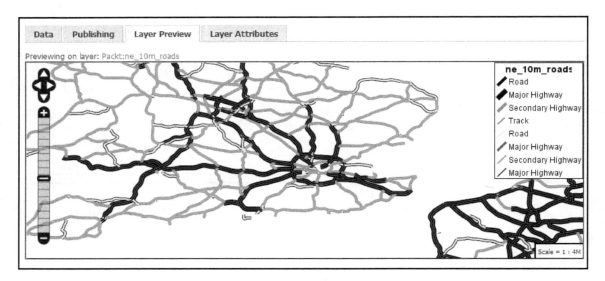

6. Now, let's add the final part of the code. We will draw a label and ferry route:

```
[@scale < 5000000]
{
  label: [label];
  font-fill: black;
}
/* @title Ferry Route */
[type = 'Ferry Route'] [@scale < 5000000]
{
  stroke: #6699CD;
```

```
      stroke-width: 1;
      stroke-dasharray: 6 2;
    }
    /* @title Ferry, seasonal */
    [type = 'Ferry, seasonal'] [@scale < 5000000]
    {
      stroke: blue;
      stroke-width: 1;
      stroke-dasharray: 6 2;
    }
```

7. Refresh the map; now, your view should look like this:

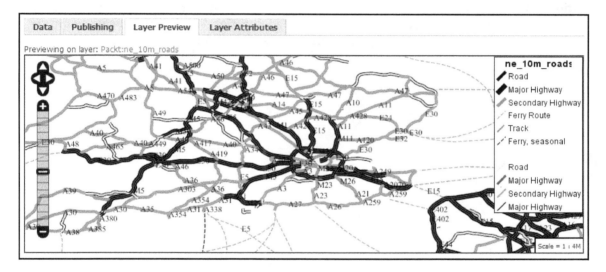

We created a beautiful map of World roads using the CSS syntax. The result is quite similar to the previous one we created with standard SLD. Did you notice the CSS syntax is simpler and more concise than the standard SLD?

Summary

We had a complete introduction to styling in this chapter. Although there are some features we didn't explore, you learned techniques that will help you build 90% of your maps, and your comprehension of styling should make you comfortable with looking for more in rare cases where you need it.

Styles and layers are the building blocks of maps. You are now ready to jump to the client side and create a code that can use what you are configuring on your GeoServer.

In the next chapter, we will use the maps you could compose on GeoServer. There are a few options to build a client application that will be able to deal with the WMS protocol. We will explore client-side JavaScript with some specialized libraries. We will also create examples in detail using Google Map API, OpenLayers, and LeafLet library.

7
Creating Simple Maps

In Chapter 6, *Styling Your Layers*, you learned how to style your layers. You also composed maps by combining more layers. It is now time to learn how you can use maps on the client side.

In this chapter, we will explore how to build client applications with a few JavaScript frameworks. JavaScript is a powerful and widespread language and, unsurprisingly, it is one of the best choices when developing a web application. We will build some sample maps using the Google Maps API (https://developers.google.com/maps/), OpenLayers (http://openlayers.org/), and Leaflet (http://leafletjs.com/)--the new kid on the block. Throughout the chapter, we will use a lot of simple yet useful code examples. We will use many of the layers you configured in the previous chapters.

In this chapter, we will cover the following topics:

- Google map with GeoServer layer
- Google map with GeoServer as base layer
- Google map with GeoServer as base layer and Google as overlay
- OpenLayers map with GeoServer layer
- OpenLayers map with GeoRSS
- Leaflet map

Start up your favorite IDE or text editor. These sample maps will show you how to use GeoServer layers on your website.

Exploring the Google Maps API

If you have been reading this book from the beginning, you probably remember that we have already encountered Google Maps previously. As a map geek, you probably might have used Google Maps on your websites.

The map application uses the Google Maps API, a JavaScript framework that you can incorporate in your application to build maps. Most users utilize the Google Maps API to build maps with the datasets from Google, the same that you can see when using the Google application.

However, the API also supports the WMS standard, thereby enabling you to get data from any Map Server compliant with the standard. We will go over several examples using version 3 of the Google Maps API, and how to incorporate the GeoServer layers.

Let's start with a very simple map.

 The Google Maps API is not an Open Source software. Before you use it, you should carefully read the terms of agreement and usage limits at `https://developers.google.com/maps/documentation/javascript/usage`. You also need to get an API Key to use them. Follow the procedure at `https://developers.google.com/maps/documentation/javascript/get-api-key` to get a key and replace `INSERT_YOUR_API_KEY` with this value in the examples.

Adding a GeoServer layer as overlay

We will build a basic map with data from Google Maps API and Natural Earth Data published by GeoServer. The full code of the following example is contained in the `google/geoserver_wms/index.html` file from the code bundle. You can use the file as a reference; we will create it from scratch in the following steps:

1. Open your text editor and create a new file, call it `map.html` and save it in the `webapps/ROOT/geoserver_wms` folder. The root folder is exposed, via HTTP protocol, from Tomcat. So the fastest way to publish your code is putting it there. Insert the following piece of code; it contains the basic for a static HTML page and a `div` element that is a reference to a map object we will create further:

```
<!DOCTYPE html />
<html xmlns="http://www.w3.org/1999/xhtml" lang="en">
<head>
```

```
<meta name="viewport" content="initial-scale=1.0">
<meta charset="utf-8">
<title>Google Map with Geoserver WMS Overlay</title>
</head>
<body>
   <div id="map"></div>
</body>
</html>
```

2. We want to add some styling properties for the HTML page. Paste this code just after the row containing the `<title>` element:

```
<style>
#map {
   height: 550px;
   width: 800px;
}
html, body {
   height: 100%;
   margin: 10px;
}
</style>
```

3. Now add the following code just after the row containing the `<title>` element. The following code adds the link to the Google Maps API. Remember to insert your key:

```
<script type="text/javascript" src="http://maps.google.com/
   maps/api/js sensor=false"></script>
<script src="map.js" type="text/javascript"></script>
<script src="https://maps.googleapis.com/maps/api/js?
   key=INSERT_YOUR_API_KEY&callback=initMap" async defer></script>
```

4. In the previous code snippet, you may have seen a reference to an external file, `map.js`. It is the file containing the code for creating the map and loading the data. Create a new file, then paste the following code snippet inside it:

```
(function () {
  window.onload = function () {
    var mapOptions = {
      zoom: 5,
      center: new google.maps.LatLng(45.5, 10.5),
      mapTypeId: google.maps.MapTypeId.TERRAIN
    };
```

```
        map = new google.maps.Map(document.getElementById('map'),
           mapOptions);
     };
   }) ();
```

5. Now, open the browser and point it to
   `http://localhost:8080/geoserver_wms/index.html`. The map should show you
   a portion of Europe. We specified the cartography in this code: `mapTypeId:`
   `google.maps.MapTypeId.TERRAIN`. This is shown in the following screenshot:

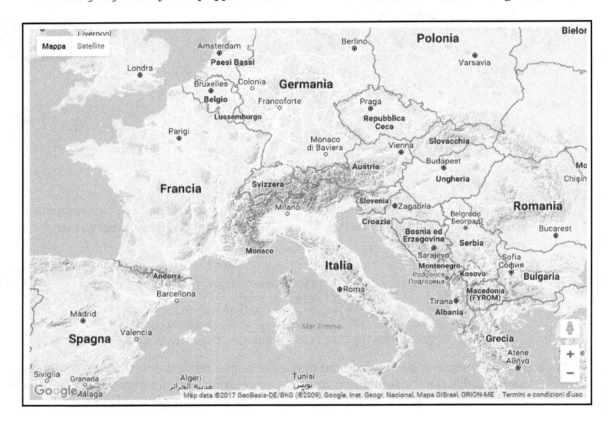

6. It is a nice map, but it still uses data only from Google. Now we want to include data from GeoServer, so add the following piece of code to map.js, just after the map creation row:

```
var placesLayer = new google.maps.ImageMapType(
{
  getTileUrl:
  function (coord, zoom) {
    var s = Math.pow(2, zoom);
    var twidth = 256;
    var theight = 256;
    var gBl = map.getProjection().fromPointToLatLng( new
        google.maps.Point(coord.x * twidth / s,
        (coord.y + 1) * theight / s));
    var gTr = map.getProjection().fromPointToLatLng( new
        google.maps.Point((coord.x + 1) * twidth / s,
        coord.y * theight / s));
    var bbox = gBl.lng() + "," + gBl.lat() + "," + gTr.lng()
        + "," + gTr.lat();
    var url = "http://localhost:8080/geoserver/Packt/wms?";
    url += "&service=WMS";
    url += "&version=1.1.0";
    url += "&request=GetMap";
    url += "&layers=ne_50m_populated_places";
    url += "&styles=PopulatedPlacesComplex";
    url += "&format=image/png";
    url += "&TRANSPARENT=TRUE";
    url += "&srs=EPSG:4326";
    url += "&bbox=" + bbox;
    url += "&width=256";
    url += "&height=256";
    return url;
  },
  tileSize: new google.maps.Size(256, 256),
    opacity: 0.85,
    isPng: true
});
map.overlayMapTypes.push(placesLayer);
```

7. Save the file and refresh the page opened in your browser. Does the map look different? You can recognize the points from the populated places data, styled with the complex symbol you created in the previous chapter:

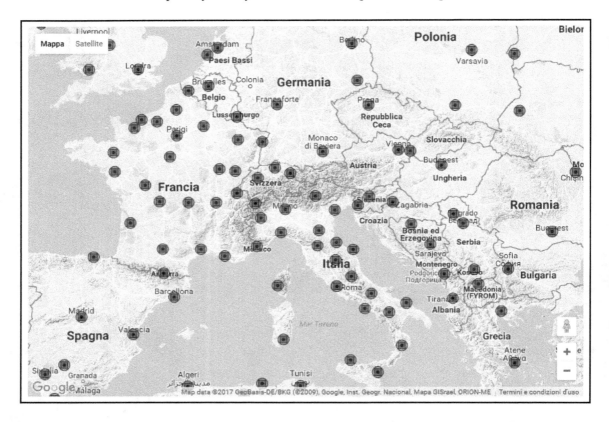

We built a basic Google Map and calculated the `bbox` parameters to query GeoServer's WMS server. Just like the other examples in this chapter, you will see the WMS parameters that we pass to GeoServer. Another way to do this would be to use the GeoServer reflector, which can take the `x`, `y`, and `zoom` parameters instead of `bbox`.

Adding a GeoServer layer as a base layer

In the previous example, we used the Google Maps API cartography as a base map and overlaid a WMS layer to it. This is a common use of the Google Maps API, but you can also use the API only loading data from GeoServer. We will now modify the previous code to add another layer as a base map:

1. Open the `map.js` file with your editor, locate the row just after the declaration of the `window.onload` function, and paste the following piece of code. Here, we will define the options for a layer to be used as a base map:

```
var maptypeOptions = {
  getTileUrl: function(coord, zoom)
  {
   var s = Math.pow(2, zoom);
   var twidth = 256;
   var theight = 256;
   var gBl = map.getProjection().fromPointToLatLng( new
       google.maps.Point(coord.x * twidth / s,
       (coord.y + 1) * theight / s));
   var gTr = map.getProjection().fromPointToLatLng( new
       google.maps.Point((coord.x + 1) * twidth / s,
       coord.y * theight / s));
   var bbox = gBl.lng() + "," + gBl.lat() + "," +
       gTr.lng() + "," + gTr.lat();
   var url = "http://localhost:8080/geoserver/Packt/wms?";
   url += "&service=WMS";
   url += "&version=1.1.0";
   url += "&request=GetMap";
   url += "&layers=NaturalEarthCountries";
   url += "&styles=";
   url += "&format=image/png";
   url += "&TRANSPARENT=TRUE";
   url += "&srs=EPSG:4326";
   url += "&bgcolor=0xFFFFFF",
   url += "&bbox=" + bbox;
   url += "&width=256";
   url += "&height=256";
   return url;
  },
  tileSize: new google.maps.Size(256, 256),
  isPng: true,
  maxZoom: 15,
  minZoom: 1,
  alt: ''
};
```

2. Add the following line to declare a new custom map:

```
var custommap = new google.maps.ImageMapType(maptypeOptions);
```

3. Now, edit the declaration of the `mapOptions` variable and replace the existing code with the following:

```
var mapOptions = {
  zoom: 5,
  center: new google.maps.LatLng(45.5,10.5),
  mapTypeControl:false,
  mapTypeId:'mapid',
  backgroundColor: "#badbff"
}
```

4. The last step is to set the custom map as your base map. Insert the following line of code just after the creation of the `map` variable:

```
map.mapTypes.set('mapid', custommap);
```

5. Save the file and close it. Now open your browser and point to the `index.html` file. The following map will now show you the data from the populated places layer overlaid on the administrative boundaries from Natural Earth:

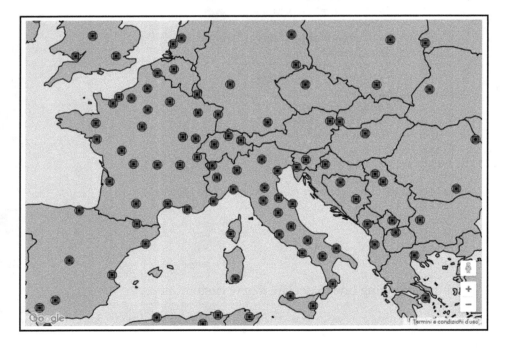

You saw an example of how you can use a GeoServer layer as a base layer using the Google Maps API. Normally, you would have specified **ImageMapType** of **ROADMAP**, **SATELLITE**, **HYBRID**, or **TERRAIN**, but in our example, we created our own **ImageMapType** called `custommap`.

Using OpenLayers

The Google Maps API is not the only option to develop a JavaScript mapping application. OpenLayers is one of the oldest and frequently used frameworks. It is an open source project constantly maintained and developed by a growing crowd of enthusiastic developers. As you have noticed, it is used with the GeoServer previews.

The Layer preview uses OpenLayers 2, but the 4.x release has been out for a while. As long as you are building a new mapping application, you should use this release. Although the following examples are basic, they will show you how to incorporate GeoServer data using the WMS protocol.

Integrating GeoServer and OpenLayers

To discover OpenLayers' capabilities, we will start with a simple map interacting with GeoServer WMS as follows:

1. Open your text editor and create a new file; we will call it `basemapWMS.html`. As usual, we will start with the basic elements for an HTML file, plus the reference to the OpenLayers library. Paste the following piece of code inside the file:

```
<!DOCTYPE html>
<html>
<head>
  <title>OpenStreetMap and GeoServer WMS</title>
  <link rel="stylesheet" href="https://openlayers.org/en/
    v4.2.0/css/ol.css" type="text/css">
  <script src="https://openlayers.org/en/v4.2.0/
    build/ol.js"></script>
</head>
<body>
</body>
</html>
```

2. Now, we will add the map control, for example, the canvas where your data will be drawn. Paste the following line of code inside the `<body>` block:

```
<div id="map" class="map"></div>
```

3. We do not want a full-page map, so we add a CSS section with some properties for the map canvas. Paste the following code snippet just after the `<script>` block loading the OpenLayers JS library:

```
<style type="text/css">
html { height: 100% }
body {
   height: 100%;
   margin: 20px;
}
.map {
   border: 1px solid black;
   width: 800px;
   height: 550px;
}
</style>
```

4. We are now ready to insert the core that will create the map and load the data. Insert the following piece of code, just after the `<div>` declaration. There are two variables--the `layers` variable is a collection of objects that point to spatial data. In this case, we are retrieving a tiled map from OpenStreetMap. The map object is where you set the general properties of the map layout, such as projection, zoom level, and area of interest:

```
<script>
var layers = [
  new ol.layer.Tile({
    source: new ol.source.OSM()
  })
];
var map = new ol.Map({
layers: layers,
target: 'map',
view: new ol.View({
  projection: 'EPSG:4326',
  center: [-75, 45],
  zoom: 7
  })
});
</script>
```

5. Now save the file and open the following URL in your browser:
   `http://localhost:8080/openlayers/basemapWMS.html`. The map should look
   like this:

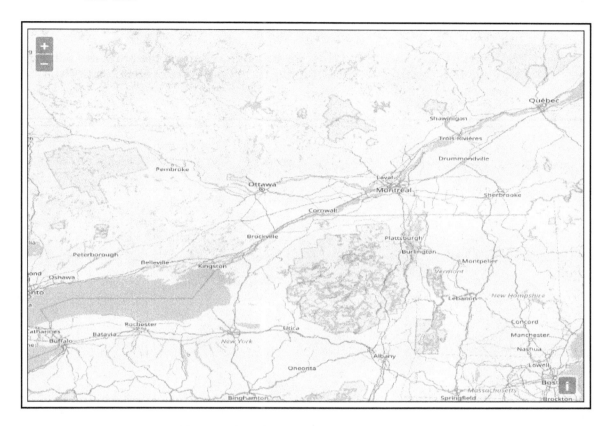

6. How can we add some data from GeoServer? You are probably guessing it needs
   another object in the **Layers** collection. In fact, we need a new one, and a different
   one, with properties to retrieve data from your GeoServer. Replace the code block
   for the `layers` variable with the following code block:

```
var layers = [
  new ol.layer.Tile({
    source: new ol.source.OSM()
  }),
  new ol.layer.Image({
      source: new ol.source.ImageWMS({
          url: 'http://localhost:8080/geoserver/wms',
          params: {'LAYERS': 'myLayerGroup'},
```

```
        ratio: 1,
        serverType: 'geoserver'
    }),
    opacity: 0.7
  })
];
```

7. You can now save the file and close the text editor. Refresh the browser's window and your map should now show the data from GeoServer overlaid on the `OpenStreetMap` tiles:

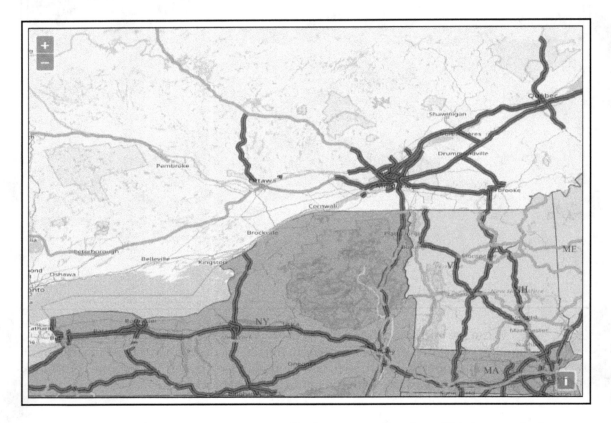

We created a basic OpenLayers map using GeoServer to serve data. This is a good place to start when we want to use OpenLayers with GeoServer, as the GeoServer previews don't work if you copy and paste them into your own applications.

Using tiled WMS

The previous example showed you how to use OpenLayers to create a map and send a WMS request to GeoServer. Any action by the user, for example, a pan or zoom-in action, the simple app creates a new WMS request for a single image and sends it to GeoServer. We now want to use the tiles. Perform the following steps:

1. Open the HTML file of the previous example and save it as `tiledWMS.html`. We want to focus on a WMS request to GeoServer; therefore, we will remove the layer from `OpenStreetMap`. Remove the following lines of code and save the file:

```
new ol.layer.Tile({
    source: new ol.source.OSM()
}),
```

2. Now open your browser and enable the developer console, the following screenshot shows it for Firefox, and then open the URL pointing to the `tiledWMS.html` file. In the network log, you can see the request sent from your app. Can you locate the single GetMap request?

3. To split that request into several tiles, we need a different layer type. Remove all the code blocks creating `ol.layer.Image` variable and replace it with the following. Apart from the different objects, you can see that there is only one parameter more than the previous one:

```
new ol.layer.Tile({
    source: new ol.source.TileWMS({
        url: 'http://localhost:8080/geoserver/wms',
        params: {'LAYERS': 'myLayerGroup', 'TILED': true},
        ratio: 1,
        serverType: 'geoserver'
    })
})
```

4. Now save the file and open it in your browser; your map should be similar to the previous one, without the base map from OpenStreetMap. Consider the following screenshot:

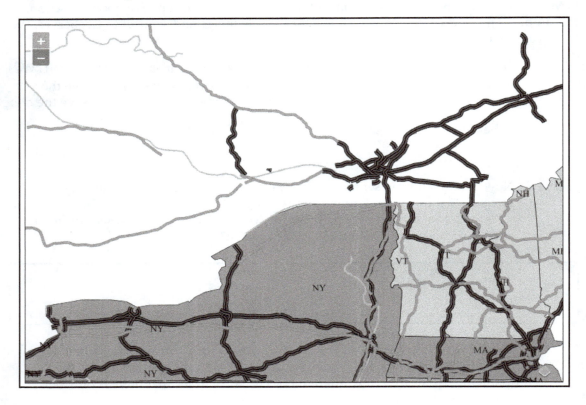

5. Open the developer toolbar and look at the network log. Can you see the difference? Several GetMap requests are now listed, each representing a small portion of the map:

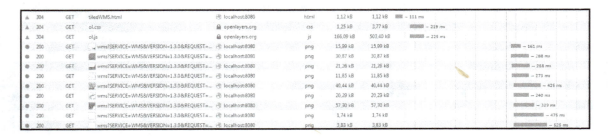

We discovered how to send tiled WMS requests. As we already discussed in previous chapters, this is a more efficient way to compose a map.

Mixing WMS and WFS

As we have seen in the previous examples, using OpenLayers, you can create maps by mixing data from different servers. Although WMS is an excellent way to get a representation of data, sometimes, you may want to retrieve data in a raw form and process them on the client side. OpenLayers lets you create WFS requests to retrieve vector data. In this example, we will mix WMS and WFS requests.

1. Open your text editor and insert the following piece of code in a new file. We will use the same properties of the previous examples. Call it WMSandWFS.html and save it in the Tomcat folder to publish it:

```
<!DOCTYPE html>
<html>
<head>
<title>WFS - GetFeature</title>
<link rel="stylesheet" href="https://openlayers.org/
    en/v4.2.0/css/ol.css" type="text/css">
<script src="https://openlayers.org/en/v4.2.0/
    build/ol.js"></script>
<style type="text/css">
html { height: 100% }
body {
    height: 100%;
    margin: 20px;
}
.map {
    border: 1px solid black;
    width: 800px;
    height: 550px;
}
</style>
</head>
<body>
<div id="map" class="map"></div>
</body>
</html>
```

2. Now, add the code section inside `<body>` element. This section adds the `baseMap` from OpenStreetMap:

```
<script>
var baseMap = new ol.layer.Tile({
  source: new ol.source.OSM()
});
var map = new ol.Map({
  layers: [ baseMap],
  target: document.getElementById('map'),
  view: new ol.View({
     projection: 'EPSG:4326'
  })
});
</script>
```

3. Just after the code, create the `baseMap` variable, add the creation of a WMS layer and add it to the `layers` collection inside the code for the `map` variable:

```
var placesLayer = new ol.layer.Image({
  source: new ol.source.ImageWMS({
    url: 'http://localhost:8080/geoserver/wms',
    params: {'LAYERS': 'Packt:ne_50m_populated_places'},
    ratio: 1,
    serverType: 'geoserver'
  }),
  opacity: 0.7
})

var map = new ol.Map({
layers: [ baseMap, placesLayer],
```

4. Your map is now showing the `OpenStreetMap` data with the WMS image overlaid:

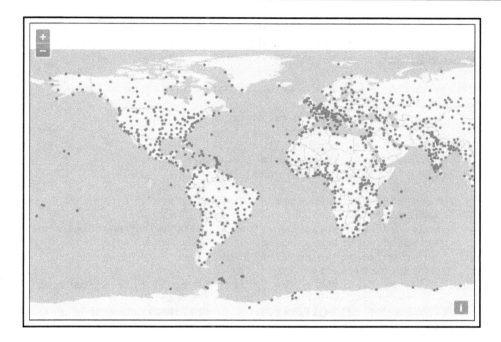

5. We will now add the code for the WFS request. Just after the previous layer declaration, insert the following piece of code. As you see, it introduces a new layer type, `ol.layer.Vector`. As you retrieve raw data, without any decoration, you need to supply a style to the client:

```
var vectorSource = new ol.source.Vector();
var riverLayer = new ol.layer.Vector({
  source: vectorSource,
  style: new ol.style.Style({
    stroke: new ol.style.Stroke({
        color: 'rgba(0, 0, 255, 1.0)',
        width: 3
    })
  })
});
```

6. After the code creating the `map` variable, you need to insert this block. It creates a WFS `GetFeature` request and assigns the response to the vector layer you created before:

```
var featureRequest = new ol.format.WFS().writeGetFeature({
  srsName: 'EPSG:4326',
  featureNS: 'https://www.packtpub.com/',
  featurePrefix: 'Packt',
  featureTypes: ['rivers'],
  outputFormat: 'application/json',
});

fetch('http://localhost:8080/geoserver/wfs', {
  method: 'POST',
  body: new XMLSerializer().serializeToString(featureRequest)
}).then(function(response) {
  return response.json();
    }).then(function(json) {
      var features = new ol.format.GeoJSON().readFeatures(json);
      vectorSource.addFeatures(features);
      map.getView().fit(vectorSource.getExtent());
});
```

7. Now, open the file in your browser and your map should look like this:

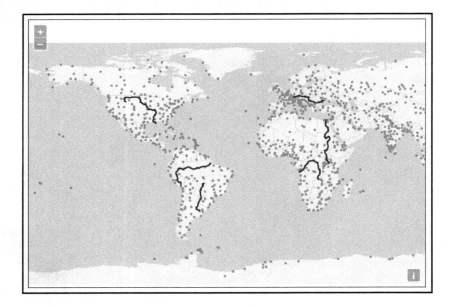

8. The rivers layer contains just a few features, but how can you avoid retrieving thousands of features when you are querying a huge layer? We need a filter. Insert the following code snippet inside the vector layer declaration:

```
filter: ol.format.filter.or(
    ol.format.filter.equalTo('name', 'Amazon'),
    ol.format.filter.equalTo('name', 'Mississipi')
)
```

9. Now refresh the map. The following screenshot shows the output:

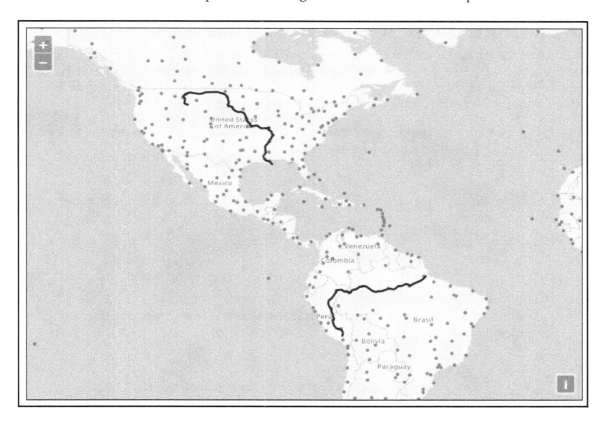

Working with vector data is more complex than using WMS. You have to retrieve data and process on the client side. You cannot just set a style among those configured in GeoServer; you need to set the drawing properties in your code. However, with the full geometry on the client side, you can use them in a more flexible way, also transforming the geometry.

Exploring Leaflet

The Leaflet project focuses on simplicity, performance, and usability. It does not offer all the tools and functionalities available in OpenLayers, but it is easier to implement and understand. And, it is lightweight--the main package is only 38 KB.

Mobile devices are given equal attention with bug fixes and features. These examples will work well on iOS, Android, and other HTML5 mobile browsers.

Creating a basic map with Leaflet

In this first example, we will build a basic map with Natural Earth Data. We will incorporate Leaflet in a simple HTML page. The full code of the following example is contained in the `leaflet/map.html` file from the code bundle. You can use the file as a reference; we will create it from scratch in the following steps:

1. Open your text editor and create a new file; call it `map.html`. Insert the following code block--the basic for a static HTML page:

```
<!DOCTYPE html>
<html>
<head>
  <title>WMS basic map - Leaflet</title>
</head>
<body>
</body>
</html>
```

2. Now, add the following piece of code just after the row containing the `<title>` element, which adds the link to the Leaflet library:

```
<meta charset="utf-8" />
<meta name="viewport" content="width=device-width,
  initial-scale=1.0">
<link rel="shortcut icon" type="image/x-icon"
  href="docs/images/favicon.ico" />
<link rel="stylesheet" href=
  "https://unpkg.com/leaflet@1.1.0/dist/
  leaflet.css"integrity="sha512-wcw6ts8Anuw10Mzh9Ytw4pylW8+
  NAD4ch3lqm9lzAsTxg0GFeJgoAtxuCLREZSC5lUXdVyo
  /7yfsqFjQ4S+aKw==" crossorigin=""/>
<script src="https://unpkg.com/leaflet@1.1.0/dist/
```

```
leaflet.js" integrity="sha512-mNqn2Wg7tSToJhvHcqfzLMU6J4mk
OImSPTxVZAdo+lcPlk+GhZmYgACEe0x35K7YzW1zJ7XyJV/TT
1MrdXvMcA==" crossorigin=""></script>
```

3. We will now add a map to this simple page. The map canvas is the element that the users will be using to interact with spatial data. Add the following code snippet after the last row of the previous snippet:

```
<style>
#map {
  width: 600px;
  height: 400px;
  background-color:#badbff
}
</style>
```

4. In the previous snippet, we set the properties for the canvas; now, we add the map canvas. Insert the following lines of code inside the <body> element:

```
<div id='map'></div>
<script type="text/javascript">
var map = L.map('map', {
  center: [45.4, 12.5],
  zoom: 4
});
```

5. Save the file and move it to the webapps/ROOT folder of your Tomcat installation. Then, open your browser and point it to http://localhost:8080/map.html; you should see an empty map, as shown in the following image:

6. We have now arrived at the final step: adding data from GeoServer. We will use the WMS protocol. Let's start adding a layer with administrative boundaries. Take the following code snippet and paste it inside the previous `<script>` element, just after the creation of the map:

```
var wmsLayer = L.tileLayer.wms('http://localhost:8080/
    geoserver/Packt/wms?', {
    layers: 'Packt:ne_50m_admin_0_countries',
    format: 'image/png',
    transparent: true
}).addTo(map);
```

7. Refresh the browser's window, pointing at `http://localhost:8080/map.html`; you should see an empty map, as shown in the following image:

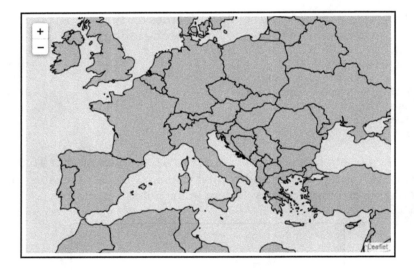

8. Isn't that great? You just created your Leaflet map with a few code rows. As you pan and zoom with your mouse, the JavaScript API sends requests to GeoServer, asking for the data. Try adding another two layers to have a more complex map. Pay attention to the fact that each layer is subsequently layered on top of the other, so you need to add the countries as the first layer, so it avoids covering the other features:

```
var wmsLayer = L.tileLayer.wms('http://localhost:8080/
    geoserver/Packt/wms?', {
    layers: 'Packt:ne_50m_rivers_lake_centerlines',
    format: 'image/png',
    transparent: true
```

```
}).addTo(map);
var wmsLayer = L.tileLayer.wms('http://localhost:8080/
  geoserver/Packt/wms?', {
  layers: 'Packt:ne_50m_populated_places',
  format: 'image/png',
  transparent: true
}).addTo(map);
```

9. The final look of your map should be equivalent to the following image:

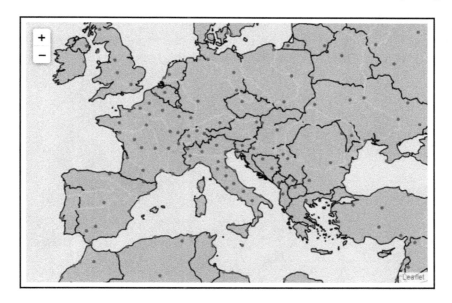

This very basic example showed you the simplicity of Leaflet. Incorporating a map in your web application is very easy, as long as you configured your data on GeoServer.

Summary

By now, you should be able to select among several choices to build your web-based GeoServer maps. Specifically, in this chapter, we covered how to use the Google Maps API to show a GeoServer layer as a base layer and an overlay. We also covered OpenLayers and Leaflet, two open source projects that offer you a ready-to-use framework. OpenLayers, at the moment, is considered more powerful, but a little bit harder to learn. Leaflet is really straightforward to use and its capabilities are growing more and more.

In the next chapter, we will cover the cached layers in detail. We will describe why caching is important and how can you configure it in GeoServer. Moreover, we will also explore the integrated GeoWebCache that ships with GeoServer in greater detail.

8
Performance and Caching

In previous chapters, you learned how to style layers to compose maps. Then you built a JavaScript code snippet, exploring several possibilities to include maps in your web application.

Whatever technology you prefer, or are constrained to use, you will have to submit a `GetMap` request to GeoServer. For each request, GeoServer has to perform a complex set of operations--loading data, applying styles, rendering the result to a bitmap, and pushing it back to the client who performed the request. As your web application gains popularity, more and more concurrent requests will hit your server, and you may run out of resources to satisfy them all.

Having to build the map from scratch every time does not make sense, especially if your web application does not offer the user the possibility to modify styles for layers. In many cases, the styles are defined just once, or very rarely, updated. Therefore, your GeoServer instance will render many identical maps.

This is, of course, a great place to do something to boost performance. As with other web document sharing, the keyword here is caching.

Indeed, when you are requesting a map to GeoServer, chances are that the same map was already produced before. We need a procedure to store and retrieve maps when needed and to match them for equality. This is a more general problem, not specifically linked to GeoServer. Several systems to implement map caching exist. Earlier, GeoServer releases did not include any caching mechanism and you had to set software in front of GeoServer, intercepting map requests and forwarding only those that can't get a hit from the cache to GeoServer.

In this chapter, we will cover the following topics in detail:

- What is GeoWebCache and how can you use it?
- Setting general parameters to integrate GWC
- Configuring new gridsets
- Configuring **Tile Layers**

This time, we will work with GeoServer's administrative interface; you can keep your favorite IDE or text editor closed.

Exploring GeoWebCache

A prominent member of the tile map caching software family is *GeoWebCache* (`http://geowebcache.org/`), a Java open source project. Just as with any caching system, it acts as a proxy between the clients and the map server. If you use the standalone version, your map server can be any that complies with the WMS standard. Indeed, GeoWebCache uses the WMS syntax to retrieve tiles from the map server. It exposes the tiles in several ways; with the GeoServer integrated version, you can use the following:

- **WMS (Web Mapping Service)**
- **WMS-C (WMS Tiling Client Recommendation)**
- **WMTS (Web Map Tiling Service)**
- **TMS (Tile Map Service)**

You can use an external instance of GeoWebCache, disabling the one that is included, but there are many advantages in using the internal one. You can use a single interface to administer both GeoServer and GeoWebCache, and you do not have to use a custom URL or a special endpoint; all the layers you publish on GeoServer are automatically configured as cached. You just have to set the caching properties on layers and layer groups.

Configuring GeoWebCache

Although you did not know it, you have already used caching. GeoWebCache is shipped with GeoServer, and caching is enabled by default when you add a new layer to the GeoServer configuration. However, you may want to customize the **caching configuration**. Most of the parameters may be tuned from the GeoServer's web interface. The repository for tiles is not one of them. To change it, you need to edit the configuration files.

Caching will produce a lot of files, and storage requires quite a lot of space on your disk. By default, all the files are stored on the same filesystem where you installed GeoServer. A common issue is that you can run out of free space or available inodes on Linux filesystems. The result is the same--you won't be able to store anything more on the filesystem, and you may also crash your system. We will use a custom location for the cache files:

1. Locate your `webapps/geoserver/WEB-INF` folder inside the Apache Tomcat installation folder:

   ```
   ~$ cd /opt/apache-tomcat-8.0.56/webapps/ geoserver/WEB-INF/
   ```

2. Open the `web.xml` file and locate the line containing the following code:

   ```
   <display-name>GeoServer</display-name>
   ```

3. After this, there are several parameters defined. We will insert a new parameter to set the `GeoWebCache` folder location. You can enter the following piece of code just after the previous line. The `param-value` syntax is valorized with a folder location that is valid on the Linux filesystem. On a Windows filesystem, use the proper syntax:

   ```
   <!-- Setting GeoWebCache folder -->
     <context-param>
       <param-name>GEOWEBCACHE_CACHE_DIR</param-name>
       <param-value>/opt/gwc</param-value>
     </context-param>
   ```

4. Save the file and close it.
5. Now, go to the Tomcat Manager Application to reload GeoServer. The parameters that you change from the web administration interface don't need a reload to be effective. GeoServer reads the `web.xml` file on startup, so any changes to the file are effective only after an application reload.
6. Open your browser and enter the following URL:

   ```
   http://localhost:8080/manager/html/list
   ```

7. Locate **GeoServer** in the application list and click on the **Reload** button:

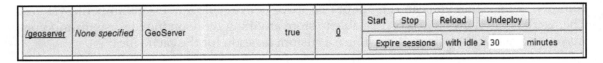

8. After a while, depending on the complexity of your configuration, a success message will appear, as shown in the following screenshot:

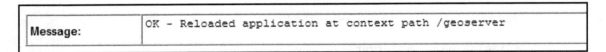

9. Now, go to the **Tile Layers** section on the web administration interface of GeoServer and browse through the list to find the **Packt:ne_50_m_populated_places** layer:

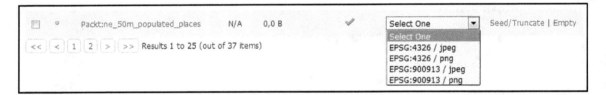

10. From the drop-down list, select a combination of SRS and image format (for example, **EPSG:4326/png**); a new map preview will show up in the browser window.

This preview is not the same as the one you can access from the **Layer Preview** page. While both use JavaScript code with the **OpenLayers** library, the latter is optimized to use the integrated GeoWebCache.

11. Navigate the map by panning and zooming it. Each operation will request tiles from GeoWebCache. For the first time you use it, they have to be requested to GeoServer and stored for future reuse.

12. Now, close the map and click on the **Tile Layers** link in the administration interface. Going to the row that shows information for your layer, you can see that there is now a number showing the disk storage used by tiles:

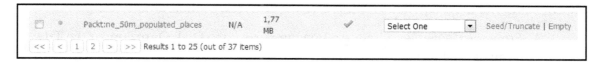

13. Open a system console and go to the folder you configured for GeoWebCache in step 4. You should see that it contains a folder for the tiles of the layer:

```
drwxr-xr-x 5 root root 4096 Jul 24 13:35 ./
drwxr-xr-x 4 root root 4096 Jul 24 13:35 ../
drwxr-xr-x 2 root root 4096 Jul 24 13:48 diskquota_page_store_h2/
drwxr-xr-x 1 root root 406 Jul 24 13:50 /tmp
drwxr-xr-x 8 root root 4096 Jul 24 14:08 Packt_ne_50m_
populated_places/
```

14. Open the folder and check whether the folder content actually uses the size that GeoServer showed you:

```
/opt/gwc/Packt_ne_50m_populated_places$ du -sh
1.8M  .
```

You configured the storage location for your tiles. By default, GeoWebCache stores them in the `temp` folder located inside the Tomcat installation location. For the production site, it is a good idea to use a folder on a different device. Also, try to avoid storing tiles on the same disk where the data is stored. Having tiles and data on the same disk will cause a resource contention; that is, a conflict over access to a shared resource.

Configuring Disk Quota

Whether you prefer seeding your layers, as we will do moreover in this chapter, or just setting the cache on and waiting for your client's requests to populate it, the tiles can grow to a huge number of files and sizes. The folder configured to contain them may fill, and you may run the filesystem on a shortage of resources. By default, the integrated GeoWebCache comes with unlimited disk usage for cached tiles. It is a good practice to configure it to a known value and to set a policy for tiles recycling. This can be done as follows:

1. From the GeoServer administration interface, go to **Disk Quota** under the **Tile caching** section, as shown here:

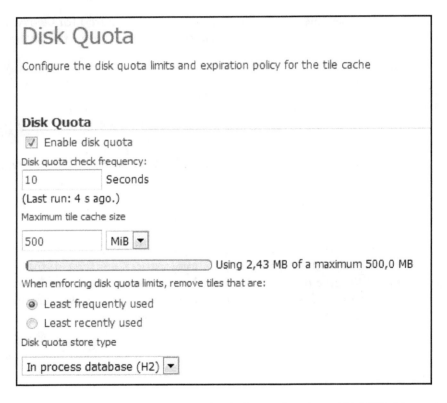

2. As you can see, there is an upper limit for cache size--**500 MiB**. You might wonder what happens when your cache size hits the limit. Set the limit at 5 megabytes and click on the **Submit** button.

3. Now go to the **Tile Layers** form and open the cache preview for **myLayerGroup**, which you created in `Chapter 6`, *Styling Your Layers*. Browse the map, panning and zooming a little, until you see that the layer's cache size exceeds 5 megabytes (you have to manually refresh the interface for the new size value to show up):

4. Go back to the **Disk Quota** form and you will see that all your tiles are there; the total size is over the upper bound and the maximum size value acts just as a warning. This is because GeoServer does not delete tiles immediately, but checks for the total size periodically, every 10 seconds by default:

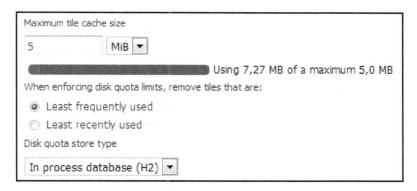

5. Wait for 10 seconds, then refresh the page. GeoServer should have deleted the tiles exceeding the quota. GeoServer deletes blocks of tiles, so it may happen that some tiles more than the strictly required number to get in the quota are permanently removed:

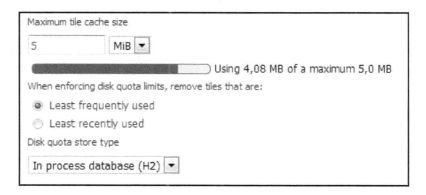

6. Now, you will set the parameters to more realistic values. Restore the size values of 500.0 GBytes or more. The upper limit for your cache size depends on how many layers you have to cache and, of course, on how much space is available. If you are using a non-dedicated filesystem for your tiles, consider that there may be other processes creating temporary objects on the filesystem and select a conservative value that leaves at least 20 percent of the filesystem always free. On the other hand, if you have a dedicated filesystem for your cache, you may insert a value near to 99 percent of the total size. Avoid setting it to a value equal to the size of the filesystem, as filling it completely may produce weird errors and corruption. We assume here that you are fine with a 5 GBytes cache size.

7. Then you may want to set the time interval for GeoWebCache performing checks on the cache size. Although 10 seconds is a good trade-off, you might want to insert a higher value as a very low value will degrade performance.

8. Lastly, you have to choose the criteria for tile removal when the upper limit is hit. The default option selects **Least frequently used**, which is usually a good choice as long as your site contains a static set of layers. If you frequently add new layers, there is a chance that older layers are used less, so select the **Least recently used** option.

9. Now that all the parameters are valorized, you can click on the **Submit** button:

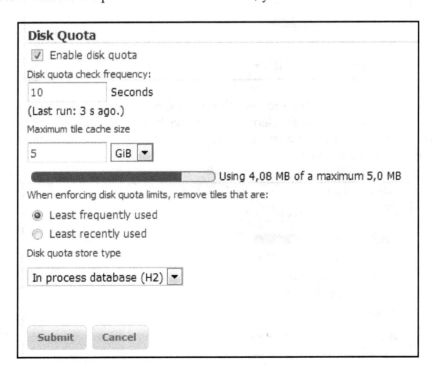

You completed the storage configuration for GeoWebCache. Did you see the last parameter in the **Disk Quota** configuration page? It lets you choose where the information will be stored. In fact, GeoServer saves tiles on the filesystem, but there is other information about them and their properties that are persisted in a database. By default, you can locate an H2 database in the same folder where you find the tiles.

You can change this option by choosing a **PostgreSQL** or **Oracle** database to save the information. Select **External Database** and insert the connection parameters. The following screenshot shows you the connection to a PostgreSQL database:

When you press the **Submit** button, GeoServer creates two tables in the database-- tilepage and tileset:

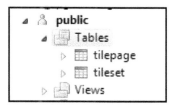

The following `tileset` table contains the information about the gridset configured for each layer:

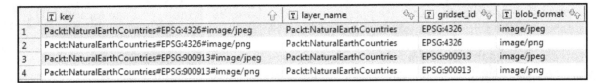

	T key	T layer_name	T gridset_id	T blob_format
1	Packt:NaturalEarthCountries#EPSG:4326#image/jpeg	Packt:NaturalEarthCountries	EPSG:4326	image/jpeg
2	Packt:NaturalEarthCountries#EPSG:4326#image/png	Packt:NaturalEarthCountries	EPSG:4326	image/png
3	Packt:NaturalEarthCountries#EPSG:900913#image/jpeg	Packt:NaturalEarthCountries	EPSG:900913	image/jpeg
4	Packt:NaturalEarthCountries#EPSG:900913#image/png	Packt:NaturalEarthCountries	EPSG:900913	image/png

The following `tilepage` table contains information about each tile. This information is used by GeoServer to retrieve tiles and clean the cache:

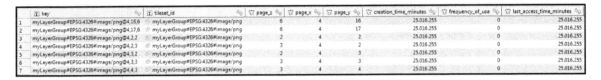

	T key	T tileset_id	page_z	page_x	page_y	creation_time_minutes	frequency_of_use	last_access_time_minutes
1	myLayerGroup#EPSG:4326#image/png@4,16,6	myLayerGroup#EPSG:4326#image/png	6	4	16	25.016.255	0	25.016.255
2	myLayerGroup#EPSG:4326#image/png@4,17,6	myLayerGroup#EPSG:4326#image/png	6	4	17	25.016.255	0	25.016.255
3	myLayerGroup#EPSG:4326#image/png@4,2,2	myLayerGroup#EPSG:4326#image/png	2	4	2	25.016.255	0	25.016.255
4	myLayerGroup#EPSG:4326#image/png@4,2,3	myLayerGroup#EPSG:4326#image/png	3	4	2	25.016.255	0	25.016.255
5	myLayerGroup#EPSG:4326#image/png@4,3,2	myLayerGroup#EPSG:4326#image/png	2	4	3	25.016.255	0	25.016.255
6	myLayerGroup#EPSG:4326#image/png@4,3,3	myLayerGroup#EPSG:4326#image/png	3	4	3	25.016.255	0	25.016.255
7	myLayerGroup#EPSG:4326#image/png@4,4,3	myLayerGroup#EPSG:4326#image/png	3	4	4	25.016.255	0	25.016.255

Setting Caching Defaults

As mentioned previously, the included GeoWebCache comes with a default configuration. Although the default configuration is ready to use, you can manage almost all parameters from the web interface.

The **Caching Defaults** form includes general parameters. The first section is about services used to expose tiles:

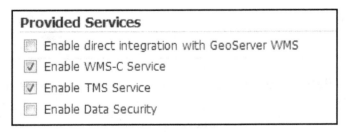

Direct integration

The first option is disabled by default. Direct integration is about the endpoint used in the WMS GetMap requests. If you go with the default option, you will have to use a custom endpoint to tell GeoServer that you want to retrieve a map from the cache if there are tiles available to fulfill your request:

```
http://localhost:8080/geoserver/gwc/service/wms?
```

Enabling direct integration lets you use the same syntax you would use against a non-cached layer:

```
http://localhost:8080/geoserver/<workspace>/wms?tiled=true
```

The endpoint is not the only condition required to use cache. Any WMS request has to meet several other conditions in order to use tiles from the cache. We can explore both methods using a command-line utility to send GetMap requests to GeoServer.

 The curl tool is a computer software project providing a library and command-line tool to transfer data using various protocols (https://curl.haxx.se/).

With the direct integration not enabled, send the following request to GeoServer:

```
curl -v
"http://localhost:8080/geoserver/Packt/wms?SERVICE=WMS&VERSION=1.1.1&REQUES
T=GetMap&FORMAT=image/png&TRANSPARENT=true&tiled=true&STYLES=Countries&LAYE
RS=Packt:ne_50m_admin_0_countries&tilesOrigin=-180,-89.99892578124998&WIDTH
=256&HEIGHT=256&SRS=EPSG:4326&BBOX=22.5,33.75,33.75,45" > tile.png
```

You will receive the following answer:

```
< HTTP/1.1 200
...
< Content-Type: image/png
< Transfer-Encoding: chunked
...
{ [16207 bytes data]
100 19417    0 19417    0     0   135k      0 --:--:-- --:--:-- --:--:--
135k
```

Now enable the direct integration as follows; you will see that GeoServer looks for tiles in the cache and uses them if available:

```
< HTTP/1.1 200
< geowebcache-tile-bounds: 22.5,33.75,33.75,45.0
< geowebcache-tile-index: [18, 11, 4]
...
< geowebcache-cache-result: HIT
< geowebcache-crs: EPSG:4326
...
< geowebcache-layer: Packt:ne_50m_admin_0_countries
< geowebcache-gridset: EPSG:4326
...
< Content-Type: image/png
< Transfer-Encoding: chunked
...
{ [15865 bytes data]
100 17019     0 17019     0     0   117k      0 --:--:-- --:--:-- --:--:--
117k
```

WMS-C

The second option listed is for the WMS-C service. **WMS-C** is the acronym for **Web Mapping Services Cached**. It is the default way to query for tiles and is available at the endpoint:

```
http://localhost:8080/geoserver/gwc/service/wms
```

If you disable the option when performing a request to the endpoint, you will receive a `Service is disabled` message and a `400` (bad request) HTTP response code from GeoServer.

TMS and WMTS

These two options enable endpoints specific to the **TMS (Tiled Map Services)** and **WMTS (Web Map Tiled Services)** specifications. The latter is an OGC standards to retrieve tiled maps; the main difference is the incorporation of a query by location request (`GetFeatureInfo`) in WMTS. The endpoints are as follows:

```
http://localhost:8080/geoserver/gwc/service/tms/1.0.0
http://localhost:8080/geoserver/gwc/service/wmts?
```

TMS is not an OGC standard but it is widely used. You can find more information about it at: `https://wiki.osgeo.org/wiki/Tile_Map_Service_Specification`.

More information about WMTS can be retrieved at: `http://www.opengeospatial.org/standards/wmts`.

Default layers options

By default, any layer on GeoServer is configured for caching. Configuring a layer for caching does not use space on your cache storage until someone starts requesting maps of it. You may consider removing this option if, on your site, you may add a large number of frequently updated layers. Note that by disabling this flag you will need to manually enable caching for each layer you publish.

As you did in `Chapter 6`, *Styling Your Layers*, you can configure more than one style for your layers; by default, all the styles are cached. If you add a lot of styles but only one is important, you may want to avoid wasting space in your cache storage and store only tiles rendered with the default style. Consider the following screenshot:

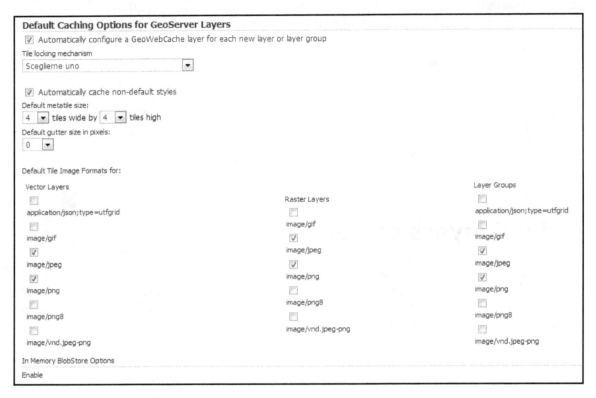

The default metatile size sets dimensions of the map produced by GeoServer when it gets a request for a tile not already stored in the cache. By default, the map produced is composed of 16 tiles. When a request arrives, GeoWebCache checks if there are tiles to create the corresponding map. If the required tiles are not stored, GeoWebCache sends a `GetMap` request for a map, with dimensions equal to four times the tile's height size and four times the tile's width size. Once produced, the map is sliced and each tile is stored in the GeoWebCache repository. Using a metatile is useful to reduce a layer's seeding time and for label placement. When you ask GeoWebCache to seed a layer (we will discuss this in detail later), all the tiles are produced and many `GetMap` requests are sent to GeoServer. It is much more efficient to produce larger maps and then slice them than producing many tiny maps.

With regards to label placement, you have to consider that GeoServer's labeling engine places the label according to the map's dimension. So, with bigger maps, you have a small chance of label duplication and overlapping. So you may wonder why the default metatile size is not bigger than a mere 4 x 4. The problem is that when producing a map, the memory consumption of GeoServer grows proportionally to the map's dimensions; however, having a big metatile size may produce errors in caching. According to the memory resource on your installation, you may increase the size, but be careful with a metatile size higher than 8 x 8.

The gutter size defines an extra edge on the map used for label and feature placements. The edges won't be rendered in the map, but setting it larger than zero may help in reducing the label's conflicts.

In the **Default Tile Image Formats for** section, you can set those formats you want to enable. It is a good idea to go with the default here as **png8** (an 8-bit color depth version of PNG) and **gif** are not much used in web mapping.

Default Cached Gridsets

This section shows the gridsets that will be automatically configured for cached layers. A gridset is a schema for tiles; it contains CRS, tile dimensions, and zoom levels.

By default, there are two gridsets configured for all layers. They are the ones most commonly used in web mapping:

- **EPSG:4326** (geographic) with **22** maximum **Zoom levels** and **256 x 256** pixel tiles.
- **EPSG:900913** (spherical Mercator) with **31** maximum **Zoom levels** and **256 x 256** pixel tiles. This is shown in the following screenshot:

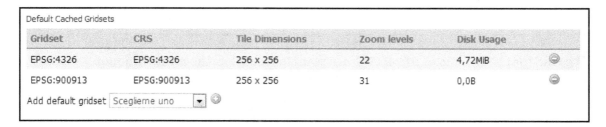

Gridset	CRS	Tile Dimensions	Zoom levels	Disk Usage	
EPSG:4326	EPSG:4326	256 x 256	22	4,72MiB	
EPSG:900913	EPSG:900913	256 x 256	31	0,0B	
Add default gridset	Sceglierne uno				

Configuring gridsets

Gridsets are caching schemas. When you decide to store tiles for a layer, you have to define the common properties for the tiles set. The logical entities where you store those properties are the gridsets.

The properties you can configure in a gridset are the CRS, the tile sizes in pixels, the number and scale of zoom levels, and the bounds of the gridset. Once you define a gridset and bind it to a layer, your client requests must conform to the caching schema; that is, the gridset or GeoWebCache will be unable to fulfill your request.

For your convenience, GeoServer comes with a common gridset already configured. Nevertheless, you can create a custom gridset for your layers.

Creating a custom gridset

We want to add national parks boundaries for the United States.

Download the data from `https://catalog.data.gov/dataset/national-park-boundariesf0a4c`, select the ZIP file, download the archive, then extract it, and publish it on GeoServer as you learned in previous chapters:

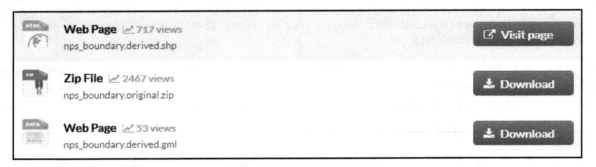

The CRS for this layer is **EPSG:4269**. If we want to create a cache for it without projection, we need to create a specific gridset. Perform the following steps:

1. In the GeoServer web interface, select the gridset URL on the left panel.

2. GeoServer will show you a list of existing gridsets. Click on the **Create a new gridset** link, as shown in the following screenshot:

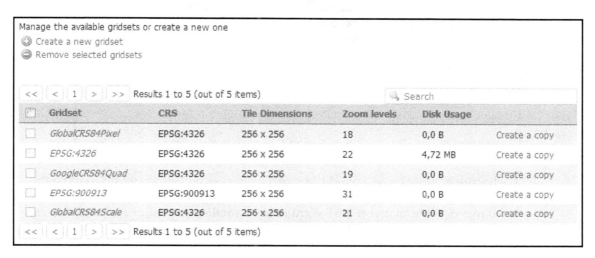

Manage the available gridsets or create a new one
⊕ Create a new gridset
⊖ Remove selected gridsets

<< | < | 1 | > | >> | Results 1 to 5 (out of 5 items)   🔍 Search

	Gridset	CRS	Tile Dimensions	Zoom levels	Disk Usage	
☐	GlobalCRS84Pixel	EPSG:4326	256 x 256	18	0,0 B	Create a copy
☐	EPSG:4326	EPSG:4326	256 x 256	22	4,72 MB	Create a copy
☐	GoogleCRS84Quad	EPSG:4326	256 x 256	19	0,0 B	Create a copy
☐	EPSG:900913	EPSG:900913	256 x 256	31	0,0 B	Create a copy
☐	GlobalCRS84Scale	EPSG:4326	256 x 256	21	0,0 B	Create a copy

<< | < | 1 | > | >> | Results 1 to 5 (out of 5 items)

3. In the creation form, you have to insert the values for creating parameters. Choose a name for the new gridset; using the CRS is a good idea, so insert the **EPSG:4269** value.

4. In the **Coordinate Reference System** section, enter the EPSG:4269 value. The **Units** and **Meters per unit** parameters are updated from GeoServer as it retrieves the projection parameters. Note that we inserted the same string in the title and CRS textbox, but they have completely different meanings; the title is just a label that you can set to a string convenient for you, while the CRS has to be a value recognized by the GeoServer projection engine:

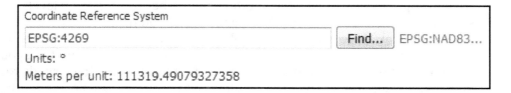

Coordinate Reference System

EPSG:4269   [Find...] EPSG:NAD83...
Units: °
Meters per unit: 111319.49079327358

5. Click on the **Compute from maximum extent of CRS** link; the **Gridset bounds** will be automatically calculated by GeoServer. If you want your gridset limited to a smaller extent, you may manually insert values in the textboxes. As we will use this gridset for the USA inland counties, we will enter custom bound values, as shown in the following screenshot:

Gridset bounds			
Min X	Min Y	Max X	Max Y
-180	10	-60	80
Compute from maximum extent of CRS			

6. Each gridset must have a fixed tile size. GeoServer will prompt you to have the default values of 256 x 256 pixels; this is usually a good choice, so we will leave it unchanged. Note that you may want to set a smaller or greater size and you can also have rectangular tiles, but you might run into trouble with clients requesting your tiles:

Tile width in pixels *
256

Tile height in pixels *
256

7. You now have to set the zoom levels for your gridsets. Keep in mind that when using cached maps, you are constrained to precalculated zoom levels. Here, you have the opportunity to set what and how many they are. Creating levels is quite simple; first, you need to decide how many levels you need. Click on the **Add zoom level** link. A new line is added, showing you the level's parameters. The first column shows you the level's index (the list is zero based), and then you will find the **Pixel Size**. GeoServer calculates the first level for having a single row of tiles covering all of your layer extent. Optionally, you may set a name for the level. In the **Tiles** column, you can see how many tiles would compose the levels; the syntax is column x rows. The red symbol at the end of the row lets you remove a level:

8. Keep adding levels until you add level **10**. As you can see, each level is calculated doubling the columns and the rows; hence, it contains 4x the tiles of the previous level. The total number of tiles grows fast; at level **10**, you already have almost 2 million tiles, plus those of the other levels:

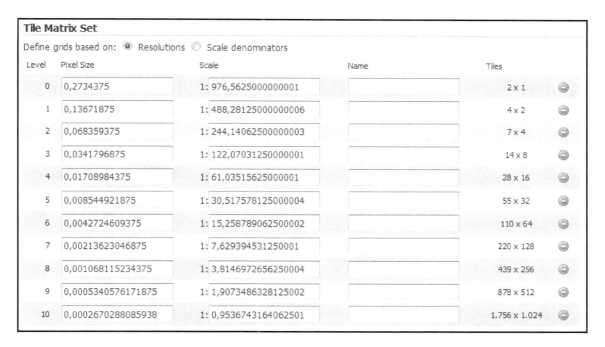

Tile Matrix Set

Define grids based on: ◉ Resolutions ○ Scale denominators

Level	Pixel Size	Scale	Name	Tiles	
0	0,2734375	1: 976,5625000000001		2 x 1	⊝
1	0,13671875	1: 488,28125000000006		4 x 2	⊝
2	0,068359375	1: 244,14062500000003		7 x 4	⊝
3	0,0341796875	1: 122,07031250000001		14 x 8	⊝
4	0,01708984375	1: 61,03515625000001		28 x 16	⊝
5	0,008544921875	1: 30,517578125000004		55 x 32	⊝
6	0,0042724609375	1: 15,258789062500002		110 x 64	⊝
7	0,00213623046875	1: 7,629394531250001		220 x 128	⊝
8	0,001068115234375	1: 3,8146972656250004		439 x 256	⊝
9	0,0005340576171875	1: 1,9073486328125002		878 x 512	⊝
10	0,0002670288085938	1: 0,9536743164062501		1.756 x 1.024	⊝

9. Now click on the **Save** button. The gridset is added to the list. You may also want to add a custom gridset to the default gridset list, but this is not the case with the **EPSG:4269** gridset that we created for the county layer.

10. Go to the **Layers** panel and select **Packt:nps_boundary**. In the **Configuration** form, go to the **Tile Caching** tab. At the end of the page, there is the **Gridset** section; here, you can configure the available gridsets for your layer. Note that all the default settings we configured in the previous paragraph may be overridden in the layer configuration. From the drop-down list, select the EPSG:4269 gridset you just created, then click on the plus symbol on the right. The new gridset is added to the list of those available for your layer. Note that you can optionally have only a subset of the levels published and/or cached:

Gridset	Published zoom levels	Cached zoom levels	Grid subset bounds	
EPSG:900913	Min ▼ / Max ▼	Min ▼ / Max ▼	Dynamic	⊖
EPSG:4326	Min ▼ / Max ▼	Min ▼ / Max ▼	Dynamic	⊖
EPSG:4269	Min ▼ / Max ▼	Min ▼ / Max ▼	Dynamic	⊖

We created a new gridset with custom properties to cache a specific layer and a specific area of the world. You can have as many gridsets as you need for your layers. Remember that clients requesting maps shall conform to the gridset's properties (for example, tile sizes); otherwise, you will get an error from GeoWebCache.

Configuring Tile Layers

From the web interface, you can access the **Tile Layers** section. All the layers published on GeoServer and configured for caching are listed in this section, and you can review the status and the main parameters for each layer:

	Type	Layer Name	Disk Quota	Disk Used	BlobStore	Enabled	Preview	Actions
☐	▦	nurc:Pk50095	N/A	0,0 B		✓	Select One ▼	Seed/Truncate | Empty
☐	▨	sf:restricted	N/A	0,0 B		✓	Select One ▼	Seed/Truncate | Empty
☐	▤	Packt:rivers	N/A	0,0 B		✓	Select One ▼	Seed/Truncate | Empty
☐	∘	sf:archsites	N/A	0,0 B		✓	Select One ▼	Seed/Truncate | Empty
☐	▨	Packt:nps_boundary	N/A	0,0 B		✓	Select One ▼	Seed/Truncate | Empty

The first two columns display the **Type** and **Layer Name** values, and the third is for per layer **Disk Quota**. In GeoServer, this feature cannot be configured as in the GeoWebCache standalone version, so you can only see an **N/A** value here. The next column contains the size occupied on disk by the layer's tiles.

The next column shows you if the layer, configured for caching, is enabled to store tiles in the cache. Disabling caching on a layer without removing it from cached layers is useful when you want to temporarily disable layers from caching without losing the configuration.

If caching is enabled on a specific layer, you see a drop-down list with the gridsets associated to that layer, and by clicking on it, you can open a new webpage with a preview application. It is very similar to the page raised by the layer preview list, but it ensures that the request conforms to the caching schema that is, the gridset and maps that are requested are retrieved from the cache.

Eventually, you will find the link to **Seed** or **Truncate** one or more levels of the cache.

Pressing the **Empty** link will erase all tiles for that specific layer, including all gridsets and styles.

Configuring layers and layer groups for caching

By default, each layer you publish on GeoServer is added to GeoWebCache's configuration. If your layer contains data that is updated very often, caching may be a bad idea. You would waste space to store tiles that will soon become outdated. Let's see how to configure caching on a specific layer:

1. From the web interface, open the **Tile layers** section.
2. Scroll through the list to find the **Packt:ne_10m_railroads** layer and click on the layer name.
3. The layer configuration page opens with a focus on the **Publishing** panel; switch to the **Tile Caching** tab.

4. The very first section contains flags to insert layers among the cached layers and to enable caching. If you uncheck the first radio button, all the other settings become unavailable, and the caching configuration is lost. By default, unless you modified the **Caching Defaults** section, all layers added to the GeoServer configuration are also configured as cached layers.

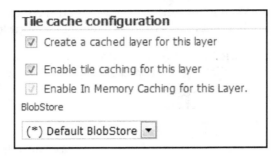

5. Metatiling factors, gutter size, and image formats let you override the values set for these parameters in the **Caching Defaults** section. For example, you may want to increase metatiling sizes and gutter sizes on layers where labeling is critical. Acting on a per layer basis avoids stress on overall performance. You can also set the available image formats for this layer, as well as customized expiration times:

Metatiling factors

4 ▼ tiles wide by 4 ▼ tiles high

Gutter size in pixels

0 ▼

Tile Image Formats

☐ application/json;type=utfgrid

☐ image/gif

☑ image/jpeg

☑ image/png

☐ image/png8

☐ image/vnd.jpeg-png

Expire server cache after n seconds (set to 0 to use source setting)

0

Expire client cache after n seconds (set to 0 to use server setting)

0

6. You can set which gridset will be used to cache your layer. By default, both the gridsets defined in the **Caching Defaults** section are enabled. You can add others or remove the defaults. You can also set zoom levels for each gridset that you want to be published and/or cached:

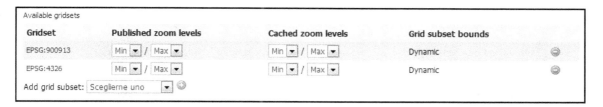

You reviewed all the options available for fine tuning on cache configuration. While **Caching Defaults** are fine to have a working set of properties, each time you add a new layer, you should configure it to maximize performance and optimize disk space.

Using tiles with OpenLayers

Now that you know how to manage caching configuration, we will explore how clients can use it. In this section, you will use an **OpenLayers** client to consume cached layers. You took a look at the **OpenLayers** library in the previous chapter, and, as usual, you do not need to be an expert; we will guide you to fully understand the basic code of the following example:

1. We will create a new HTML file. It should be published with Apache Tomcat, so you can create it in the `webapps/ROOT` folder inside your Tomcat installation.

2. Insert the following code snippet. As we are creating an HTML file, the code contains some mandatory elements. We also want to include a title for our page:

```
<!DOCTYPE html>
<html>
  <head>
    <title>plain WMS</title>
  </head>
  <body>
  </body>
</html>
```

3. Now we have to include a reference to the **OpenLayers** library. We will use a reference to the online release. Note that this only works if you are connected to the internet in your development environment; otherwise, you may want to download the library and deploy it on Tomcat:

```
<link rel="stylesheet"
 href="https://openlayers.org/en/v4.2.0/css/ol.css"
   type="text/css">
<script src="https://openlayers.org/en/v4.2.0/build/ol.js">
</script>
```

4. Now, add the following CSS code to add a style to the HTML element that will host the map canvas:

```
<style type="text/css">
  html { height: 100% }
  body {
    height: 100%;
    margin: 20px;
    }
  .map {
    border: 1px solid black;
    width: 800px;
    height: 550px;
    }
</style>
```

5. Inside the <body> element, we will insert the core of the small web app. We will create the map object and add the following piece of code to load a WMS layer:

```
<div id="map" class="map"></div>
<script>
  var projection = ol.proj.get('EPSG:4326');

  var map = new ol.Map({
    layers: [
      new ol.layer.Image({
        opacity: 0.7,
        source: new ol.source.ImageWMS({
          url: 'http://localhost:8080/geoserver/wms',
          params: {'LAYERS': 'Packt:NaturalEarthCountries'},
          ratio: 1,
          serverType: 'geoserver'
        })
      })
    ],
    target: 'map',
```

```
view: new ol.View({
  projection: projection,
  center: [10, 40],
  zoom: 4
})
});
</script>
```

6. Save the file as `plainWMS.html`. Now open your browser and enter `http://localhost:8080/plainWMS.html` as the URL:

7. There is only a GetMap request to GeoServer and GeoWebCache is not used:

● 200	GET	plainWMS.html	localhost:8080	document	html	1,16 kB	1,16 kB	⊢ 15 ms	
● 200	GET	ol.css	openlayers.org	stylesheet	css	1,25 kB	3,77 kB		⊣ 750 ms
● 200	GET	ol.js	openlayers.org	script	js	166,09 kB	503,40 kB		⊣ 754 ms
● 200	GET	wms?SERVICE=WMS&VERSION=1.3.0&REQUEST=...	localhost:8080	img	png	96,28 kB	96,28 kB		

8. How can we modify this simple app to leverage on the GeoWebCache capabilities? Go back to the folder where you saved the `wmsPlain.html` file, make a copy of it, and rename the copy as `WMTS.html`.

9. Open the new file with your editor and replace the title with the following:

```
<title>WMTS example</title>
```

10. We need a different type of layer, hence we will to replace all the code block creating the `layers` variable with the following. As you can see, we use a WMTS layer, using one of the standards supported by GeoWebCache. It requires a different URL and some properties:

```
layers: [
  new ol.layer.Tile({
    opacity: 0.7,
    source: new ol.source.WMTS({
      url: 'http://localhost:8080/geoserver/gwc/service/wmts',
      layer: 'Packt:NaturalEarthCountries',
      matrixSet: 'EPSG:4326',
      format: 'image/png',
      projection: projection,
      tileGrid: new ol.tilegrid.WMTS({
        origin: ol.extent.getTopLeft(projectionExtent),
        resolutions: resolutions,
        matrixIds: matrixIds
      })
    })
  })
],
```

11. In the WMTS layers, we inserted a reference to `resolutions` and `matrixIds`. The former contains a set of values for each zoom level in the gridset we will use. We selected the `EPS:4326` projection, so we need to get the same values contained in that default gridset. Insert the following code snippet just before the map creation:

```
var resolutions = [
  0.703125, 0.3515625, 0.17578125, 0.087890625,
  0.0439453125, 0.02197265625, 0.010986328125,
  0.0054931640625, 0.00274658203125, 0.001373291015625,
  6.866455078125E-4, 3.4332275390625E-4, 1.71661376953125E-4,
  8.58306884765625E-5, 4.291534423828125E-5,
  2.1457672119140625E-5,
  1.0728836059570312E-5, 5.364418029785156E-6,
  2.682209014892578E-6,
  1.341104507446289E-6, 6.705522537231445E-7,
  3.3527612686157227E-7
];
```

You do not really need to add all the zoom levels to your maps; you can select a subset of them. This way, you can constrain your user to explore data only at a specific zoom range.

12. We also need to define the identifier for each zoom level. Insert the following code snippet just after the `projection` declaration:

```
var projectionExtent = projection.getExtent();
var matrixIds = new Array(22);
for (var z = 0; z < 22; ++z) {
  matrixIds[z] = "EPSG:4326:" + z;
}
```

13. Save the file. Now open your browser and enter `http://localhost:8080/WMTS.html`. As before, navigate your maps by panning and zooming around the world; this time, the requests sent to GeoServer are different:

●	200	GET	WMTS.html	👤 localhost:8080	📄 document	html	2,11 kB	2,11 kB	I — 16 ms
●	200	GET	ol.css	🔒 openlayers.org	stylesheet	css	1,25 kB	3,77 kB	▬▬▬▬▬ — 929 ms
●	200	GET	ol.js	🔒 openlayers.org	script	js	166,09 kB	503,40 kB	▬▬▬▬▬ — 981 ms
●	200	GET	wmts?layer=Packt:NaturalEarthCountries&tilemat...	👤 localhost:8080	🖼 img	png	16,08 kB	16,08 kB	
●	200	GET	wmts?layer=Packt:NaturalEarthCountries&tilemat...	👤 localhost:8080	🖼 img	png	20,90 kB	20,90 kB	
●	200	GET	wmts?layer=Packt:NaturalEarthCountries&tilemat...	👤 localhost:8080	🖼 img	png	12,02 kB	12,02 kB	
●	200	GET	wmts?layer=Packt:NaturalEarthCountries&tilemat...	👤 localhost:8080	🖼 img	png	18,53 kB	18,53 kB	
●	200	GET	wmts?layer=Packt:NaturalEarthCountries&tilemat...	👤 localhost:8080	🖼 img	png	12,05 kB	12,05 kB	
●	200	GET	wmts?layer=Packt:NaturalEarthCountries&tilemat...	👤 localhost:8080	🖼 img	png	15,25 kB	15,25 kB	
●	200	GET	wmts?layer=Packt:NaturalEarthCountries&tilemat...	👤 localhost:8080	🖼 img	png	14,19 kB	14,19 kB	
●	200	GET	wmts?layer=Packt:NaturalEarthCountries&tilemat...	👤 localhost:8080	🖼 img	png	11,94 kB	11,94 kB	
●	200	GET	wmts?layer=Packt:NaturalEarthCountries&tilemat...	👤 localhost:8080	🖼 img	png	13,97 kB	13,97 kB	
●	200	GET	wmts?layer=Packt:NaturalEarthCountries&tilemat...	👤 localhost:8080	🖼 img	png	2,43 kB	2,43 kB	

14. Let's analyze one of the requests; the following are the parameters:

```
layer=Packt:NaturalEarthCountries
tilematrixset=EPSG:4326
Service=WMTS
Request=GetTile
Version=1.0.0
Format=image/png
TileMatrix=EPSG:4326:3
TileCol=8
TileRow=2
```

15. And this is the response header where you can see that GeoWebCache searched for a tile and found it in the cache:

```
HTTP/1.1 200
geowebcache-cache-result: HIT
geowebcache-tile-index: [8, 5, 3], [8, 5, 3]
geowebcache-tile-bounds: 0.0,22.5,22.5,45.0
geowebcache-gridset: EPSG:4326
geowebcache-crs: EPSG:4326
Last-Modified: Fri, 28 Jul 2017 14:06:17 GMT
Content-Disposition: inline; filename=geoserver-dispatch.image
Content-Type: image/png
Content-Length: 16462
Date: Sat, 29 Jul 2017 10:11:15 GMT
```

You built a very simple web mapping application and integrated it with GeoWebCache. Apart from the trivial interface, you explored how to properly build map requests that can access a cache. You can use this knowledge to apply caching in a real application.

Seeding a layer

As of now, we have used the GeoWebCache to store tiles produced by user requests. Of course, the following requests with equal parameters will hit the cache and GeoServer will not render a new map for them.

However, you can also precalculate the tiles for a layer to avoid some users experiencing a delay when requesting zoom levels and areas not yet cached.

The process of precalculating tiles is called seeding. This section will guide you in understanding how it works:

1. Go to the **Tile Layers** page and look for the **Packt:ne_50m_rivers_lake_centerlines** layer. Click on the **Seed/Truncate** link for it:

2. A new page will open. The GeoWebCache seeding is not integrated in the GeoServer web interface. What you see is the GeoWebCache interface:

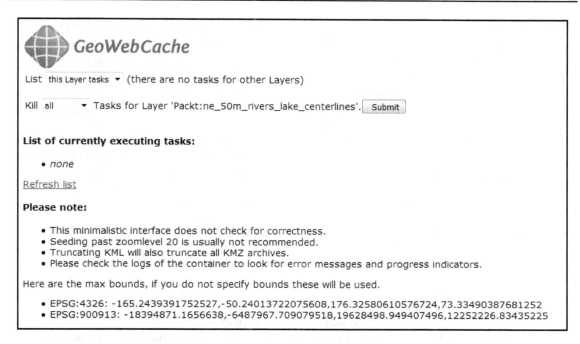

3. Scroll to the **Create a new task** section. You have to set the parameters for the seeding. The first one is the number of parallel processes; that is, threads that will request maps to GeoServer. As we have a single GeoServer instance, there is no gain in running too many processes. Select **04** from the drop-down list.(in fact, the best number to select depends on the number of cores available on your server. A rule of thumb is to select a number of threads equal to the 50 percent of the available cores):

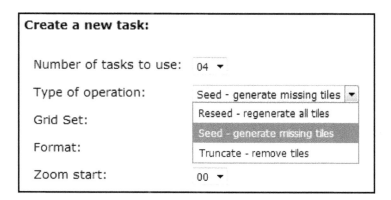

4. Then, select the operation type. You can select **Seed**, which will generate only the missing tiles, or **Reseed**, which will regenerate all tiles. This is the case if you changed the style for the layer and do not want your user to see a mixed map. Note that the **Truncate** operation is a little different from the **Empty** operation integrated into the GeoServer interface. Here you will have the option to select a set of zoom levels to truncate, while the Empty operation will always remove all tiles. Select **Seed - generate missing tiles**. You have to select a gridset and an image format for the seeding. If you want to precalculate cache for more than one gridset and/or image format, you can start another operation just after starting this. Select **Grid Set** as **EPSG:4326** and **Format** as **image/png**, as shown here:

Grid Set:	EPSG:4326 ▼
Format:	image/png ▼

5. You can start a seeding operation only on a subset of the specified gridset. You can select a levels range and an area. If you do not want to restrict seeding to a specific area, leave the **Bounding box** textboxes empty, and the operation will use the gridset bounds. Select **00** as **Zoom start** and **10** as **Zoom stop**. We want to generate tiles with the **Rivers** style. Now, start the seeding operation by clicking on the **Submit** button:

Zoom start:	00 ▼
Zoom stop:	10 ▼
Modifiable Parameters:	STYLES: Rivers ▼
Bounding box:	
	These are optional, approximate values are fine.
	Submit

6. Once the tasks start, the web interface shows you the list of currently running tasks. If you are seeding more layers concurrently, you can filter the tasks per layer and also kill one or all of the tasks that are running. Clicking on the **Refresh list** link will update the list with the number of **Tiles completed**, **Time elapsed**, and **Time remaining** columns. The number of tiles grows quickly at more detailed zoom levels. Seeding not only requires a lot of disk space, it also requires a lot of time, depending on your system's capacity:

List of currently executing tasks:

Id	Layer	Status	Type	Estimated # of tiles	Tiles completed	Time elapsed	Time remaining	Tasks	
1	Packt:ne_50m_rivers_lake_centerlines	RUNNING	SEED	1,845,730	3,472	1 minute 19 s	2 hours 53 m	(Task 1 of 4)	Kill Task
2	Packt:ne_50m_rivers_lake_centerlines	RUNNING	SEED	1,845,730	3,760	1 minute 19 s	2 hours 40 m	(Task 2 of 4)	Kill Task
3	Packt:ne_50m_rivers_lake_centerlines	RUNNING	SEED	1,845,730	3,728	1 minute 19 s	2 hours 41 m	(Task 3 of 4)	Kill Task
4	Packt:ne_50m_rivers_lake_centerlines	RUNNING	SEED	1,845,730	3,808	1 minute 19 s	2 hours 38 m	(Task 4 of 4)	Kill Task

7. When your tasks end, you should see an empty list. Go back to the **Tile layers** page and now there will be a lot of disk space allocated for your layer's tiles:

Seeding your layers can have a huge impact on performances. Every map request from your clients, in the levels range you precalculated, will hit the cache now. You can expect performances to increase from 10 to 90 times.

Using an external GeoWebCache

The integrated GeoWebCache is a convenient way to use a powerful caching tool while avoiding the complexity of an external installation and configuration. So, what is the point of using an external instance of GeoWebCache?

In a production environment, you will often have to deal with multiple GeoServer instances, running in parallel like a cluster. Indeed, we will see how to configure such a scenario in Chapter 11, *Tuning GeoServer in a Production Environment*. When more than one GeoServer publishes the same data, you cannot efficiently use the integrated GeoWebCache. There is no way to connect all the GeoServers to a single GeoWebCache. Anyway, it would make no sense as you will introduce a single point of failure in your architecture.

So, you have two ways to go--using the integrated GeoWebCache on each GeoServer node, duplicating the tiles and wasting a lot of space, or installing an external GeoWebCache and linking it to each GeoServer node.

Installing and configuring an external GeoWebCache is out of the scope of this book. You have to turn off the integrated GeoWebCache. You can do this from the **Caching Defaults** page, disabling all services and turning off the automatic creation of a cache configuration for each new layer.

If you used the integrated GeoWebCache before, you may also want to disable each layer and remove tiles.

The standalone GeoWebCache is a Java web application that you can deploy on a Tomcat instance, the same way we did for GeoServer. Once installed, you have to manually configure each layer by editing the `geowebcache.xml` file.

Refer to the online project documentation for detailed instructions and references (`http://geowebcache.org/docs/current/index.html`).

Summary

We explored the integrated GeoWebCache, and how it may affect GeoServer performances. Deploying a properly configured production site requires caching unless your planned users are very few.

Configuring a map cache requires you to act not only on the server side but also on the client side. Clients should know how you cached the data and compiled proper map requests for the benefit of precalculated tiles. We used JavaScript and **OpenLayers** to take a look at the client side.

GeoServer integrates a pretty interface to configure cache; however, as your site grows and you find yourself increasingly adding and removing layers, you may wonder if a way of automating the configuration exists.

In the next chapter, we will explore the GeoServer REST interface. REST exposes most of the GeoServer interfaces through HTTP calls. Using a scripting language, you can build simple procedures that help you in performing repetitive tasks.

We will see how to use the REST interface to add data stores and workspaces, publish layers, and apply changes to your configuration.

9
Automating Tasks - GeoServer REST Interface

In the previous chapters, you learned how to connect GeoServer to your data.

Creating data stores or feature types, configuring layers, and uploading styles can be tedious and overwhelming tasks when your site grows from the data we used in the examples.

If your site intends to deliver a professional map service, it will probably be replicated in more instances. We will see in detail how this can be done, but, for now, you will probably have guessed that it means more effort to configure and synchronize all nodes.

When you are dealing with a repetitive task, you usually look at how you can automate it.

GeoServer's developers did not leave you alone in the dark. GeoServer includes a REST interface that lets you perform most administrative tasks. In this chapter, we will see how you can add, update, and delete your data configuration.

In this chapter, we will cover the following topics in detail:

- Defining REST
- Using REST with cURL and Python
- Configuring Workspaces, Data Stores, and Feature Types
- Configuring Styles and Layers

Introducing REST

So, what is REST? The acronym stands for Representational State Transfer, and defines client-server interaction in terms of state transitions. Each request from the client is a transition to a new state. The response sent by the server represents the application state after the transition.

Does it sound too complicated? From a theory point of view, you may find it unconventional, especially if you are used to a client/server with a stateful interaction. REST is stateless, and, once you get a general idea, you will discover that it is very simple.

Although REST is commonly thought of as a web interface, it actually is much more. The term REST was defined by Roy T. Fielding-one of the most important people behind HTTP protocol design-in his PhD thesis. REST describes the interaction between clients and servers and does it by abstracting from any protocol. It describes a set of operations that a server has to implement and that a client can use. Of course, in implementations, a protocol, for example, HTTP, has to be selected. You can also develop a REST interface without HTTP. Refer to the following links to find out more about REST http://www.ics.uci.edu/~fielding/pubs/dissertation/top.html and http://en.wikipedia.org/wiki/Representational_State_Transfer.

GeoServer's REST interface uses HTTP and defines a set of operations and resources. Operations are derived from HTTP so you can perform GET, POST, PUT, and DELETE operations. Resources are the building blocks of GeoServer's configuration, which includes workspaces, data stores, layers, and so on.

Using REST

REST defines a set of operations defined from the HTTP protocol; so, how can you interact with it? Using a browser can be a common way to send HTTP requests to a server; you do it almost every day when you browse the internet, and you do it with the GeoServer web interface! However, using a browser is not a simple way to automate tasks; it requires human interaction. We need something that enables us to build small programs.

A lot of different tools exist that enable you to interact with REST. You can use programming languages such as Java or PHP, or script languages such as PowerShell in Windows or any Linux shell. In this chapter, we will see examples in a programming language, Python, and with a command-line utility, cURL. Python is a programming language that leverages on simplicity and code readability, and, hence, it is very easy to create small programs with it. cURL is a library and a command-line tool that can be easily incorporated in simple shell scripts. Both of these tools allow users to create REST requests in a very simple manner--that is, by writing a few lines of code. This prevents you from getting distracted by complex syntax.

 In this chapter, it is assumed that you have a working installation of Python and cURL. If you are using a Linux box, it is quite likely that you already have both installed and configured, or you can rely on your distribution package system to install a recent release. For Windows, you can get Python from the project site (http://python.org). cURL is available as a source, for the brave, or as a binary package at http://curl.haxx.se/download.html.

Installing the Requests library

We stated before that Python mainly aims at simplicity and code readability, but, unfortunately, this is not always the case. Interacting with REST using the standard Python libraries can be painfully laborious. Luckily, an open source project can solve this. The project produced a library called Requests, and I have to say it really is an appropriate name. So, let's install it:

1. The easiest way to install requests is using pip. If you are running a Python release higher than 2.7.9, pip is already included. We will cover the installation steps in case you have an older release. On Linux, the best approach is using your distribution's package manager:

```
$ sudo apt-get install python-pip
Reading package lists... Done
Building dependency tree
Reading state information... Done
The following additional packages will be installed:
python-pip-whl
...
Do you want to continue? [Y/n] y
Setting up python-pip (8.1.1-2ubuntu0.4) ...
```

2. On Windows, you can follow the instructions on
   `https://pip.pypa.io/en/stable/installing`.

3. Now we can use `pip` to install requests on the system. The following command
   runs the same on Linux or Windows:

```
$ pip install requests
Collecting requests
 Downloading requests-2.18.2-py2.py3-none-any.whl (88kB)
    100% |                                                      |
92kB 1.5MB/s
    . . .
 Installing collected packages: certifi, chardet, urllib3, idna,
 requests
 Successfully installed certifi chardet-2.3.0 idna-2.0 requests
 urllib3
```

4. Installation is now complete. Check it by opening Python and importing the new
   library in the following manner:

```
$ python
Python 2.7.12 (default, Nov 19 2016, 06:48:10)
[GCC 5.4.0 20160609] on linux2
Type "help", "copyright", "credits" or "license" for more
information.
>>> import requests
>>>
```

You installed the Requests library as a site package inside your Python
installation. You can now use it inside any Python program, leveraging on its
powerful objects for the purpose of interacting with the HTTP protocol.

Requests is an open source project started by Kenneth Reitz. You can
download and use it in a very liberal way. It is released under the Apache
2.0 license. You can also fork it on GitHub and add features. The following
link will lead you to the Requests main page `http://docs.python-requests.org/en/latest/`.

Managing data

The core of each map service is data. We need to create workspaces to group together datasets, connecting databases and folders containing data, adding feature types, and configuring their options. GeoServer's REST interface exposes resources for each one of them.

Working with workspaces and namespaces

A workspace is a logical entity you can use to group data. A workspace is always linked to a namespace URI that defines a web reference for it. The REST interface defines two resources that you can use to access these elements. They are as follows:

- /workspaces
- /namespaces

The GET, POST, PUT, and DELETE operations are defined for both of these resources, which allows you to view, create, update, and delete workspaces and namespaces.

Managing workspaces

We will use REST operations with workspaces. In this section, as in the others contained in this chapter, we will use both cURL and Python to perform the same operation.

The examples are shown in a Linux shell, but cURL and Python syntaxes are identical in a Windows shell.

1. We want to retrieve which workspaces are defined in your GeoServer instance. This requires a GET operation. The following piece of code shows you the syntax. cURL has a lot of options; you can take a look at all of them, by running it with the `curl --help` command from Linux and Windows. On Linux, you can also take a look at the manual with the `man curl` command. Let's look at the different options we use:
   - The first option we use is `-u`. It stands for user authentication; you have to insert the user ID and password you defined when installing GeoServer.
   - The `-v` option tells cURL to run verbosely, so it will output detailed information on the request processing.

- The -X option defines which HTTP operation you want to use to send your requests. If you do not insert it, cURL assumes GET as its default. You can avoid writing the option, although inserting it may make the code clearer.
- The -H option lets you add headers to your requests. You may repeat this option as many times as you need to specify multiple headers. In this case, we are using it to make the server know that we would accept an XML format as a response. After that, we have the URL we want to be requested. The URL is composed of a base part that will be the same for all the operations, that is, `http://yourhostname:yourport/geoserver/rest`, and a variable part specifying the operation. Finally, we add the -o option to write the response to a file:

```
$ curl -u admin:pwd -v -XGET -H 'Accept: text/xml'
http://localhost:8080/geoserver/rest/workspaces -o
workspaces.xml
```

- A lot of information is displayed. This may be very useful when in trouble, when you need to debug what is wrong. A line starting with > means *header data sent by cURL*, while < means *header data received by cURL*. In this case, we just look at the status code received from GeoServer; it reports 200, that is, the HTTP code for OK:

```
* Connected to localhost (::1) port 8080 (#0)
* Server auth using Basic with user 'admin'
> GET /geoserver/rest/workspaces HTTP/1.1
> Host: localhost:8080
> Authorization: Basic YWRtaW46Z2Vvc2VydmVy
> User-Agent: curl/7.54.0
> Accept: text/xml
>
  0     0    0     0    0 --:--:-- --:--:--       0< HTTP/1.1 200
< Date: Mon, 31 Jul 2017 13:25:15 GMT
< Server: Noelios-Restlet-Engine/1.0..8
< Content-Type: application/xml
< Transfer-Encoding: chunked
<
{ [1030 bytes data]
100  1742    0  1742    0  5885       0 --:--:-- --:--:--
5885
* Connection #0 to host localhost left intact
```

2. Before analyzing the response file content, let's execute the same request using Python. Open your favorite text editor and create a new file. Call it `getWorkspaces.py` and insert the following line to import the requests module:

```
import requests
```

3. Now, define a new string variable for the following URL:

```
myUrl = 'http://localhost:8080/geoserver/rest/workspaces'
```

4. We want a response in XML, so we can add a header value using a Python dictionary:

```
headers = {'Accept': 'text/xml'}
```

5. We are ready to send the request; the requests object has a method for each HTTP operation, and, in a really *Pythonic* way, the name is the operation. You have to call the method by passing the parameters for the URL, headers, and authentication:

```
resp = requests.get(myUrl,auth=('admin','pwd'),headers=headers)
```

6. The response was saved in the new variable called `resp`. The Python interpreter didn't throw any exception, so things should be ok; however, how can we check what GeoServer has replied? The `resp` variable is indeed a response object defined in the requests library, and it has methods to extract information about the response. We will inspect the status code of the response. If this is equal to `200`, the HTTP ok code, then we can save the response in a new file, as in the following code fragment:

```
if resp.status_code == 200:
    file = open('workspaces_py.xml','w')
    file.write(resp.text)
    file.close()
```

7. Now, you should have two XML files looking identical. Open one of them and look at its content. It lists the workspaces defined on your GeoServer, and it gives you a URL to reference each one of them. This is shown as follows:

```
<workspaces>
...
 <workspace>
   <name>Packt</name>
   <atom:link xmlns:atom="http://www.w3.org/2005/Atom"
rel="alternate"
```

```
href="http://localhost:8080/geoserver/rest/workspaces/Packt.xml
"  type="application/xml"/>
  </workspace>
 </workspaces>
```

8. We can use the information from the XML file to retrieve information about the first workspace. In cURL, type the following command:

```
$ curl -u admin:pwd -XGET -H "Accept: text/xml"
http://localhost:8080/geoserver/rest/workspaces/Packt.xml -o
Packt.xml
```

9. Edit the getWorkspaces.py file by replacing the following lines of code. We need to get a different URL and save it to another file:

```
myUrl =
'http://localhost:8080/geoserver/rest/workspaces/Packt'
...
file = open('Packt_py.xml','w')
```

10. The information retrieved contains the URL to explore data stores linked to the workspace element:

```
<workspace>
 <name>Packt</name>
 <dataStores>
    <atom:link xmlns:atom="http://www.w3.org/2005/Atom"
rel="alternate"
href="http://localhost:8080/geoserver/rest/workspaces/Packt/dat
a
stores.xml" type="application/xml"/>
 </dataStores>
 ...
 </wmsStores>
</workspace>
```

11. Now retrieve information about namespaces in cURL:

```
$ curl -u admin:pwd -XGET -H 'Accept: text/xml'
http://localhost:8080/geoserver/rest/namespaces -o
namespaces.xml
```

12. In Python, edit the lines of code containing the URL and the filename:

```
myUrl = 'http://localhost:8080/geoserver/rest/namespaces'
...
file = open('namespaces_py.xml','w')
```

13. In the response, you can see the namespace list, which is pretty similar to the workspace list. As we wrote before, they are bounded together, as you can see in the following code:

```
<namespaces>
 <namespace>
...
 <namespace>
   <name>Packt</name>
   <atom:link xmlns:atom="http://www.w3.org/2005/Atom"
rel="alternate"
href="http://localhost:8080/geoserver/rest/namespaces/Packt.xml
"  type="application/xml"/>
 </namespace>
</namespaces>
```

14. Now, take a look at the information about a single namespace. First, in cURL:

```
$ curl -u admin:pwd -XGET -H 'Accept: text/xml'
http://localhost:8080/geoserver/rest/namespaces/Packt -o
PacktNamespace.xml
```

15. Then in Python:

```
myUrl =
'http://localhost:8080/geoserver/rest/namespaces/Packt'
...
file = open('PacktNamespace_py.xml','w')
```

16. The response contains the prefix name for the namespace, that is, the linked workspace, the namespace URI, and a URL to retrieve feature types linked to the namespace:

```
<namespace>
 <prefix>Packt</prefix>
 <uri>https://www.packtpub.com/</uri>
 <featureTypes>
    <atom:link xmlns:atom="http://www.w3.org/2005/Atom"
 rel="alternate"
ref="http://localhost:8080/geoserver/rest/workspaces/Packt/feat
 uretypes.xml" type="application/xml"/>
 </featureTypes>
</namespace>
```

17. Until now, you have retrieved the information; now, you will create a new namespace. To do this, you need to update some information--the XML code containing the information about the namespace to be created. In cURL, we need to specify a different operation with the −X option, and use the −d option to send the XML code:

```
$ curl −u admin:pwd −XPOST −H 'Content-type: text/xml'
 −d '<namespace><prefix>newWorkspace</prefix>
 <uri>http://geoserver.org</uri></namespace>'
 http://localhost:8080/geoserver/rest/namespaces
```

18. To do the same in Python, you need to save the XML code beforehand in a file. Then, create a new Python file like this:

```
import requests

myUrl = 'http://localhost:8080/geoserver/rest/namespaces'
headers = {'Content-type': 'text/xml'}
file = open('requestBody.xml','r')
payload = file.read()
resp = requests.post(myUrl, auth=('admin','pwd'), data=payload,
 headers=headers)
ptint(resp.status_code)
```

19. Open the GeoServer web interface and look at the workspace list; you can now see the one you created, and, if you click on it, you will see the namespace URI you defined:

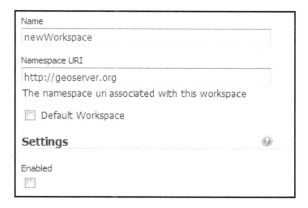

20. Now, we want to set a more appropriate URI for the new workspace. To do so, we will use the PUT operation. In cURL, the syntax is as follows:

```
$ curl -u admin:pwd -XPUT -H 'Content-type: text/xml' -H 'Accept:
  text/xml' -d '<namespace><prefix>newWorkspace</prefix>
  <uri>http://localhost:8080/geoserver</uri></namespace>'
  http://localhost:8080/geoserver/rest/namespaces/newWorkspace
```

21. In Python, it is written as follows:

```
import requests
myUrl =
 'http://localhost:8080/geoserver/rest/namespaces/newWorkspace'
file = open('requestBody.xml','r')
payload = file.read()
headers = {'Content-type': 'text/xml'}
resp = requests.put(myUrl, auth=('admin','pwd'), data=payload,
 headers=headers)
print(resp.status_code)
```

22. The last operation is DELETE. To remove the new workspace from the GeoServer configuration using cURL, run the following command:

```
$ curl -u admin:pwd -XDELETE -H 'Accept: text/xml'
  http://localhost:8080/geoserver/rest/workspaces/newWorkspace
```

23. In Python, run the following script:

```
import requests
myUrl =
 'http://localhost:8080/geoserver/rest/workspaces/newWorkspace'
headers = {'Accept': 'text/xml'}
resp = requests.delete(myUrl, auth=('admin','pwd'),
 headers=headers)
print(resp.status_code)
```

You have learned how to interact with the REST interface. You did it for namespaces and workspaces; however, the basic concepts you learned apply to all REST operations. It is important that you understand that REST is stateless. Each request you sent in the examples were absolutely unaware of what you did previously. You can link REST operations in a chain, but is up to you to extract information from the responses and build requests accordingly.

> If you were a little confused by the Python code, there are many free resources to explore this language. You will learn it very fast and add a powerful tool to your GIS skill. The following links will help you learn Python at http://www.greenteapress.com/thinkpython, http://docs.python.org/tutorial, and https://www.packtpub.com/application-development/learning-python.

Using data stores

Data stores connect GeoServer to your data. You cannot use data that is not supported by GeoServer with a built-in connector or plugin. Of course, the REST interface supports all operations on data stores. The resource exposed is in the form shown as follows:

```
/workspaces/<ws>/datastores
```

Here, ws stands for the workspace to which the data store is linked.

Managing data stores

Did you enjoy using cURL and Python? We hope so, as we are going to use cURL and Python again, since you are now so skilled! So, let's get information about data stores:

1. The GET operation lets you know which data stores are available in the configuration. Retrieve the information in Python using the following code:

```
import requests
myUrl =
 'http://localhost:8080/geoserver/rest/
 workspaces/Packt/datastores'
headers = {'Accept': 'text/xml'}
resp = requests.get(myUrl,auth=('admin','pwd'),headers=headers)
if resp.status_code == 200:
  file = open('datastores_py.xml','w')
  file.write(resp.text)
  file.close()
```

2. In cURL, use the following command:

```
$ curl -u admin:pwd -XGET -H 'Accept: text/xml'
  http://localhost:8080/geoserver/rest/workspaces/
  Packt/datastores -o dataStores.xml
```

3. The response contains all the data stores linked to the workspace. The only attribute is the name and the link to retrieve the detailed information about each one:

```
<dataStores>
  <dataStore>
    <name>gisdata</name>
    <atom:link xmlns:atom="http://www.w3.org/2005/Atom"
     rel="alternate"
     href="http://localhost:8080/geoserver/rest/workspaces/
     Packt/datastores/gisdata.xml" type="application/xml"/>
  </dataStore>
  <dataStore>
    <name>Natural Earth</name>
    <atom:link xmlns:atom="http://www.w3.org/2005/Atom"
     rel="alternate" href="http://localhost:8080/geoserver/rest/
      workspaces/Packt/datastores/Natural+Earth.xml"
      type="application/xml"/>
  </dataStore>
  <dataStore>
    <name>Places</name>
    <atom:link xmlns:atom="http://www.w3.org/2005/Atom"
```

```
     rel="alternate"  href="http://localhost:8080/geoserver/rest/
     workspaces/Packt/datastores/Places.xml"
     type="application/xml"/>
  </dataStore>
</dataStores>
```

 If you are wondering what the request is to get a list of all data stores configured on GeoServer, I am sorry to tell you it does not exist. You have to query each workspace. You may request the workspace list and iterate on items to retrieve all data stores.

4. You created the Places data store in a previous chapter. In case you don't remember what it is about, let's request the information in Python:

```
import requests
myUrl = 'http://localhost:8080/geoserver/rest/workspaces/
 Packt/datastores/Places'
headers = {'Accept': 'text/xml'}
resp = requests.get(myUrl,auth=('admin','pwd'),headers=headers)
if resp.status_code == 200:
    file = open('PlacesDatastores_py.xml','w')
    file.write(resp.text)
    file.close()
```

5. The following command line does the same, using cURL:

```
$ curl -u admin:pwd -XGET -H "Accept: text/xml"
  http://localhost:8080/geoserver/rest/workspaces/
  Packt/datastores/Places -o PlacesDatastore.xml
```

6. Open the XML file. It contains much more information than the previous responses. Data stores are more complicated objects than workspaces. Keep in mind that data stores are heterogeneous; the connection parameter tag may contain very different elements, depending on the data store type, for example, a PostGIS data store will have user ID, password, and a TCP port:

```
<dataStore>
  <name>Places</name>
  <description>Location of famous places around the
   world</description>
  <type>Properties</type>
  <enabled>true</enabled>
  <workspace>
    <name>Packt</name>
    <atom:link xmlns:atom="http://www.w3.org/2005/Atom"
      rel="alternate" href="http://localhost:8080/geoserver/rest/
      workspaces/Packt.xml" type="application/xml"/>
```

```
      </workspace>
      <connectionParameters>
        <entry key="namespace">https://www.packtpub.com/</entry>
        <entry key="directory">c:\opt\Data</entry>
      </connectionParameters>
      <__default>false</__default>
      <featureTypes>
        <atom:link xmlns:atom="http://www.w3.org/2005/Atom"
          rel="alternate" href="http://localhost:8080/geoserver/rest/
          workspaces/Packt/datastores/Places/featuretypes.xml"
          type="application/xml"/>
      </featureTypes>
    </dataStore>
```

7. It is now time to create a new data store. We will start with a single shapefile by duplicating the `Natural Earth ne_10m_roads` file. You have to provide a lot of information; therefore, create a new XML file, insert the following code, and save it as `NaturalEarthRoads.xml`. You should recognize many parameters; you valorized them when adding the data store from the WEB interface. The key part is the `type` element, where you specify which kind of data you are adding. The connection parameters collection, where you insert information on how GeoServer could retrieve the data from the filesystem or a DB, is also important:

```
<dataStore>
  <name>Natural Earth Roads</name>
  <description>Natural Earth roads created
   from REST</description>
  <type>Shapefile</type>
  <enabled>true</enabled>
  <connectionParameters>
    <entry key="memory mapped buffer">false</entry>
    <entry key="create spatial index">true</entry>
    <entry key="charset">ISO-8859-1</entry>
    <entry key="filetype">shapefile</entry>
    <entry key="cache and reuse memory maps">true</entry>
    <entry key="url">file://C:\opt\Data\ne_10m_roads.shp</entry>
    <entry key="namespace">https://www.packtpub.com/</entry>
  </connectionParameters>
  <__default>false</__default>
</dataStore>
```

8. Now call the REST interface in cURL and add the data store:

```
$ curl -u admin:pwd -XPOST -T NaturalEarthRoads.xml -H
  'Content-type:text/xml' -H 'Accept: text/xml'
  http://localhost:8080/geoserver/rest/workspaces/
  Packt/datastores
```

9. Open the web interface and list the configured data store. Was your add request successful?

	Data Type	Workspace	Store Name	Type	Enabled?
		Packt	Natural Earth	Directory of spatial files (shapefiles)	✓
		Packt	Natural Earth Roads	Shapefile	✓

10. Do the same in Python. Note that in a Python dictionary, for example, the headers variable, you can add more than a *key-value* pair. In this case, you specify two header values:

```
import requests
file = open('NaturalEarthRoads.xml','r')
payload = file.read()
file.close()
myUrl = 'http://localhost:8080/geoserver/rest/workspaces/
 Packt/datastores'
 headers = {'content-type':'text/xml','Accept': 'text/xml'}
resp = requests.post(myUrl,auth=('admin','pwd'), data=payload,
 headers=headers)
print(resp.status_code)
```

11. Adding a shapefile data store was quite easy. Let's try to add a new PostGIS source to our configuration. Again, it is better to create an XML file holding all the parameters, name it `postgis.xml`, and insert the code. The mandatory connection parameters are host, port, database, schema, user, and password. In this case, we inserted all the default values you would find by adding the data store from the web interface:

```
<dataStore>
  <name>PostgisRest</name>
  <description>PostGIS connection created with REST</description>
  <type>PostGIS</type>
  <enabled>true</enabled>
  <connectionParameters>
    <entry key="host">localhost</entry>
    <entry key="port">5432</entry>
```

```
            <entry key="database">gisdata</entry>
            <entry key="schema">public</entry>
            <entry key="user">postgres</entry>
            <entry key="passwd">postgres</entry>
            <entry key="dbtype">postgis</entry>
            <entry key="validate connections">true</entry>
            <entry key="Connection timeout">20</entry>
            <entry key="min connections">1</entry>
            <entry key="max connections">10</entry>
            <entry key="Loose bbox">true</entry>
            <entry key="fetch size">1000</entry>
            <entry key="Max open prepared statements">50</entry>
            <entry key="Estimated extends">true</entry>
        </connectionParameters>
        <__default>false</__default>
    </dataStore>
```

12. Now you can send a request with `curl`, including the XML file as content transferred. Use the following syntax:

```
$ curl -u admin:pwd -XPOST -T postgis.xml -H
  'Content-type:text/xml' -H 'Accept: text/xml'
  http://localhost:8080/geoserver/rest/workspaces/
  Packt/datastores
```

13. You can use the following Python file to send the same requests. As usual, if you already created it with cURL, you will get an HTTP 500 error code:

```
import requests
file = open('Postgis.xml','r')
payload = file.read()
file.close()
myUrl = 'http://localhost:8080/geoserver/rest/workspaces/
  Packt/datastores'
headers = {'content-type':'text/xml','Accept': 'text/xml'}
resp = requests.post(myUrl,auth=('admin','pwd'), data=payload,
  headers=headers)
print(resp.status_code)
```

14. You can update a data store configuration. If your PostGIS password was changed from the DBA, you can send a request to update it on GeoServer. Create an XML file with the modified value, as follows:

```
<dataStore>
  <name>PostgisRest</name>
...
    <entry key="user">postgres</entry>
```

```
        <entry key="passwd">new_password</entry>
    ...
</dataStore>
```

15. Then send it in a `PUT` request. In cURL, it is as follows:

```
$ curl -u admin:pwd -XPUT -T updPostGIS.xml -H
  'Content-type: text/xml' -H 'Accept: text/xml'
  http://localhost:8080/geoserver/rest/workspaces/
  Packt/datastores/PostgisRest
```

16. And in Python, the syntax is as follows:

```
import requests
file = open('udpPostgis.xml','r')
payload = file.read()
file.close()
myUrl = 'http://localhost:8080/geoserver/rest/workspaces/
Packt/datastores7PostgisRest'
headers = {'content-type':'text/xml','Accept': 'text/xml'}
resp = requests.put(myUrl,auth=('admin','pwd'), data=payload,
headers=headers)
print(resp.status_code)
```

17. The last supported operation is `DELETE`, for dropping a data store. Clean your configuration by removing the duplicated data store for the roads shapefile we created:

```
$ curl -u admin:pwd -XDELETE -H 'Accept: text/xml'
  http://localhost:8080/geoserver/rest/workspaces/
  Packt/datastores/NaturalEarthRoads
```

18. You can repeat the same for the PostGIS datastore. In Python, we can delete both in a single script:

```
import requests
urls = [
  'http://localhost:8080/geoserver/rest/workspaces/
  Packt/datastores/PostgisRest',
  'http://localhost:8080/geoserver/rest/workspaces/
  tiger/datastores/NaturalEarthRoads']
for url in urls:
  headers = {'Accept': 'text/xml'}
  resp = requests.delete(url, auth=('admin','pwd'),
   headers=headers)
  print(resp.status_code)
```

You have learned how to play with data stores, but there is another way of creating them. In some cases, you may create them implicitly while creating a feature type. We will look at it in the next paragraph.

Using feature types

Feature types are strictly related to data stores; the latter are the data containers and the former are geometrical homogeneous datasets. In some cases, there is a one-to-one relation among feature types and data stores, as in the data store for the single shapefile of Natural Earth roads that we created. More often, a data store contains many feature types. As with other resources, you can use REST operations to list information, add and delete items, and modify the configuration.

The resources are exposed as follows:

```
/workspaces/<ws>/datastores/featuretypes/<ft>
```

Here, `ws` means a workspace existing in your system and `ft` is the feature type on which you want to perform the operation.

Retrieving information about feature types uses the `GET` operation as used by the previous resources. The output is quite long, depending on how many attributes it holds. It looks as follows:

```
<featureTypes>
  <featureType>
    <name>ne_10m_railroads</name>
    <atom:link xmlns:atom="http://www.w3.org/2005/Atom"
     rel="alternate"
     href="http://localhost:8080/geoserver/rest/workspaces/
     Packt/datastores/Natural+Earth/featuretypes/
     ne_10m_railroads.xml" type="application/xml"/>
  </featureType>
  ...
</featureTypes>
```

Adding a new shapefile

We already added a single shapefile data store; in that case, the shapefile was already in the folder on the same server. What we want to accomplish now is uploading a new shapefile and configuring it on GeoServer. And, of course, we will use only HTTP operations to accomplish the task:

1. We will use a new layer from the Natural Earth repository. We will use a small shapefile, that is, the small-scale world admin boundaries:

   ```
   $ wget http://www.naturalearthdata.com/
   http//www.naturalearthdata.com/download/110m/cultural/
   ne_110m_admin_0_countries.zip
   ```

2. Don't extract the archive; we will forward it to GeoServer in the ZIP format, and we will use a PUT operation. Note that, to the header specifying the content type, we are transferring a zip file to GeoServer; this way, we can publish a data set on a remote node without accessing the remote filesystem. We are also creating a new data store, Natural+Earth+Countries; thus the URL points to a nonexistent data store:

   ```
   $ curl -u admin:password -XPUT -H 'Content-type:
   application/zip' -T /home/stefano/110m-admin-0-countries.zip
   http://localhost:8080/geoserver/rest/workspaces/
   Packt/datastores/Natural+Earth+Countries/file.shp
   ```

    Please note that the URL contains a file.shp endpoint, although we are transferring a ZIP file. It is a convention of GeoServer. This syntax tells it that we are uploading a shapefile and we want to create a data store for it.

3. Of course, you can do the same with Python. Note that reading the ZIP file is pretty much the same as reading an XML file. The rb parameter specifies that we will read a binary file:

   ```python
   import requests
   myUrl = 'http://localhost:8080/geoserver/rest/workspaces/
   Packt/datastores/Natural+Earth+Countries/file.shp'
   file = open('110m-admin-0-countries.zip','rb')
   payload = file.read()
   headers = {'Content-type': 'application/zip'}
   resp = requests.put(myUrl, auth=('admin','pwd'), data=payload,
    headers=headers)
   print(resp.status_code)
   ```

4. Now look at the web interface and list the data stores; there is a new one, as shown in the following screenshot:

	Data Type	Workspace	Store Name	Type	Enabled?
☐	▣	Packt	Natural Earth	Directory of spatial files (shapefiles)	✓
☐	▣	Packt	Natural Earth Countries	Shapefile	✓
☐	▣	Packt	Places	Properties	✓

5. And, of course, GeoServer created a new layer for the feature type, populating all parameters and enabling them:

☐	▦	Tasmania water bodies	topp:tasmania_water_bodies	taz_shapes	✓	EPSG:4326
☐	▦	ne_110m_admin_0_countries	Packt:ne_110m_admin_0_countries	Natural Earth Countries	✓	EPSG:4326

6. According to the geometry type, GeoServer assigns a default style so that you can also look at the data preview:

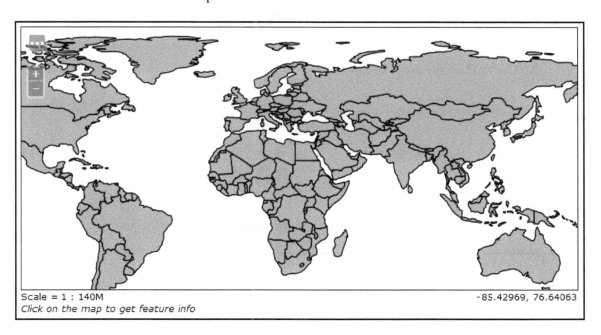

Scale = 1 : 140M   -85.42969, 76.64063
Click on the map to get feature info

You have created a data store, a feature type, and a layer with just one operation. GeoServer can manage retrieving all the needed information from your dataset and can manage using many default values. Of course, you may want to use different styles, but the REST interface truly makes remote administration very easy.

Adding a PostGIS table

The PostGIS data store is one of those connected to many feature types. As time goes by, you will probably have new spatial data to add after creating the data store. Let's see how to do so:

1. In `Chapter 4`, *Adding Your Data*, you loaded data from Natural Earth in PostGIS. Now you have to do the same with the admin boundary's shapefile from Natural Earth by calling the `ne_110m_admin` table. Then you will be using the PostGIS connection to add the table as a new feature type in the NaturalEarth workspace. Note that we need to provide very little information about the feature type to GeoServer; the table name is the only mandatory field:

```
$ curl -u admin:pwd -XPOST -H 'Content-type: text/xml'
  -d '<featureType><name>ne_110m_admin</name></featureType>'
  http://localhost:8080/geoserver/rest/workspaces/
  Packt/datastores/gisdata/featuretypes
```

2. The Python syntax is as follows:

```
import requests
myUrl = 'http://localhost:8080/geoserver/rest/workspaces/
 Packt/datastores/gisdata/featuretypes'
payload = '<featureType><name>ne_110m_admin</name></featureType>'
headers = {'Content-type': 'text/xml'}
resp = requests.post(myUrl, auth=('admin','pwd'), data=payload,
 headers=headers)
print(resp.status_code)
```

3. Looking at the layers list, we can see the newly added workspace:

☐	▥	ne_110m_admin_0_countries	Packt:ne_110m_admin_0_countries	Natural Earth Countries	✓	EPSG:4326
☐	▥	ne_110m_admin	Packt:ne_110m_admin	gisdata	✓	EPSG:4326

4. The new feature type works perfectly, and, of course, we can add more parameters to the XML code to have a better layer configuration. These examples add a more detailed description and some keywords:

```
<featureType>
  <name>World boundaries</name>
  <nativeName>ne_110m_admin</nativeName>
  <title>World boundaries</title>
  <abstract>World administrative boundaries at small
   scale</abstract>
  <keywords>
  string>Political</string>
    <string>World</string>
  </keywords>
<featureType>
```

5. However, there's more. Not only can you add an existing table, you can also create a new one. When creating a new table, you have to specify all the attributes required:

```
<featureType>
  <name>worldrivers</name>
  <nativeName>worldrivers</nativeName>
  <title>World Rivers</title>
  <srs>EPSG:4326</srs>
  <attributes>
    <attribute>
      <name>geom</name>
      <binding>
        com.vividsolutions.jts.geom.MultiLineString
      </binding>
    </attribute>
    <attribute>
      <name>name</name>
      <binding>java.lang.String</binding>
      <length>30</length>
    </attribute>
    <attribute>
      <name>country_code</name>
      <binding>java.lang.String</binding>
      <length>8</length>
    </attribute>
  </attributes>
</featureType>
```

6. Now you have to send a POST request to create the feature. Of course, you have to send it to a PostGIS data store:

```
$ curl -u admin:pwd -XPOST -T newTable.xml -H
  'Content-type: text/xml'
  http://localhost:8080/geoserver/rest/workspaces/
  Packt/datastores/gisdata/featuretypes
```

7. The same request in Python looks like the following piece of code:

```
import requests
myUrl = 'http://localhost:8080/geoserver/rest/workspace/
Packt/datastores/gisdata/featuretypes'
file = open('newTable.xml','r')
payload = file.read()
headers = {'Content-type': 'text/xml'}
resp = requests.post(myUrl, auth=('admin','pwd'),
data=payload, headers=headers)
print(resp.status_code)
```

8. Now look at the layers list; there is a new item:

| | | ne_110m_admin | Packt:ne_110m_admin | gisdata | ✓ | EPSG:4326 |
| | | World Rivers | Packt:worldrivers | gisdata | ✓ | EPSG:4326 |

9. If you go to the layer's detail page, you can see that the SRS was correctly set to 4326. However, as an empty feature type, the bounding boxes are inconsistent. When you populate the feature type with some features you need to manually edit this setting. You can do it via RESt interface again. The attributes mentioned in the following screenshot are the ones you specified:

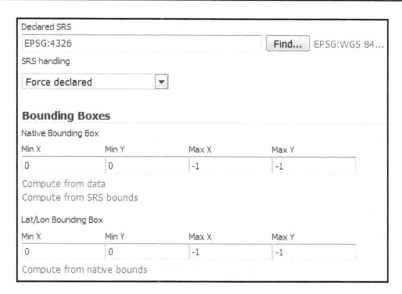

You have learned how to manage feature types--the link to your data. A feature type is strictly connected to a layer, the map representation. You already implicitly created a layer when you added or created a new feature type. To modify the way your data is published, you have to manage the publishing elements.

Publishing data

Once you have configured your data on GeoServer, it is time to publish it. The REST interface gives you the resources to manage layers, styles, and layer groups.

Working with Styles

You learned a lot about styles and SLD in `Chapter 6`, *Styling Your Layers*. Configuring proper visualization requires you to create and publish proper styles.

REST offers you two resources to manage styles. They are as follows:

```
/styles
/workspaces/<ws>/styles
```

The former points to styles that are not associated with a workspace, while the latter contains the styles associated to a specific workspace.

Adding a new style

Adding a new style is a routine task if you are publishing data with REST. We will retrieve an existing style from GeoServer, update it, and then upload it to GeoServer as a new one:

1. We will use `PopulatedPlacesLabeled` as a template for our new style. Send a request to GeoServer to retrieve it and save it to the `PopulatedPlacesBlueLabeled.xml` file. Note that we are sending a header to tell GeoServer that we want the SLD format. If you specify `text/xml`, you will get only a description of what the SLD is:

```
$ curl -u admin:pwd -XGET -H 'Accept:
application/vnd.ogc.sld+xml'
http://localhost:8080/geoserver/rest/
styles/PopulatedPlacesLabeled
-o PopulatedPlacesBlueLabeled.xml
```

2. In Python, the code is as follows:

```
import requests
myUrl = 'http://localhost:8080/geoserver/rest/
styles/PopulatedPlacesLabeled'
headers = {'Accept: application/vnd.ogc.sld+xml'}
resp = requests.get(myUrl, auth=('admin','pwd'), headers=headers)
if resp.status_code == 200:
    file = open('PopulatedPlacesBlueLabeled.xml','w')
    file.write(resp.text)
    file.close()
```

3. Now, open the `PopulatedPlacesBlueLabeled.xml` file and replace the RGB code for black with that for blue. Also, replace the old name with the new name:

```
. . .
<sld:Name>PopulatedPlacesBlueLabeled</sld:Name>
. . .
<sld:CssParameter name="fill">#0000FF</sld:CssParameter>
. . .
```

4. Save the file and close it. Now we will create a new style with this file. Send a POST request to update the `PopulatedPlacesBlueLabeled` style:

```
$ curl -u admin:pwd -XPOST
  -H 'Content-type: application/vnd.ogc.sld+xml'
  -T PopulatedPlacesBlueLabeled.xml
  http://localhost:8080/geoserver/rest/styles
```

5. Or in Python:

```
import requests
myUrl = 'http://localhost:8080/geoserver/rest/styles'
file = open(PopulatedPlacesBlueLabeled.xml','r')
payload = file.read()
headers = {'Content-type': 'application/vnd.ogc.sld+xml'}
resp = requests.post(myUrl, auth=('admin','pwd'), data=payload,
 headers=headers)
print(resp.status_code)
```

6. Go to the WEB interface and list the styles; you should see the new one, as shown here:

PopulatedPlaces

PopulatedPlacesBlueLabeled

PopulatedPlacesComplex

We review just the GET and POST operations for styles, but you can also use DELETE when you want to remove a style from your configuration or PUT when you want to change an existing style. You can mimic the syntax learned in the previous sections.

Working with Layers

Once you are done with configuring styles, you probably want to apply them to layers. Creating or modifying styles is the last step for data publication. Unsurprisingly, it is possible to perform layer operations with the REST interface.

Managing Layers

In the previous section, you created a new style; however, it is useless if you cannot assign it to a layer. We will now update the populated place layer by adding the new style:

1. Retrieve information on the `ne_50m_populated_places` layer:

```
$ curl -u admin:pwd -XGET -H 'Accept: text/xml'
  http://localhost:8080/geoserver/rest/
  layers/ne_50m_populated_places -o ne_50m_populated_places.xml
```

2. In Python, use the following script:

```
import requests
myUrl = 'http://localhost:8080/geoserver/rest/
 layers/ne_50m_populated_places'
headers = {'Accept: text/xml'}
resp = requests.get(myUrl, auth=('admin','pwd'),
 headers=headers)
if resp.status_code == 200:
  file = open('ne_50m_populated_places.xml','w')
  file.write(resp.text)
  file.close()
```

3. Open the `ne_50m_populated_places.xml` file; it starts with a styles collection. You need to insert the code for the new style you created. We do not need all the elements returned from GeoServer. Modify the file as shown in the following piece of code. (Note that we inserted the `enabled` element; the default value being `false` for it. If you make a `PUT` request and don't explicitly set it to `true`, your layer will be modified and disabled):

```
<layer>
  <styles class="linked-hash-set">
    <style>
      <name>PopulatedPlacesStroke</name>
    </style>
    <style>
      <name>PopulatedRotateTransparent</name>
    </style>
    <style>
      <name>PopulatedPlacesComplex</name>
    </style>
    <style>
      <name>PopulatedPlacesGraphics</name>
    </style>
    <style>
```

```
    <name>PopulatedPlacesLabeled</name>
  </style>
  <style>
    <name>PopulatedPlacesBlueLabeled</name>
  </style>
 </styles>
</layer>
```

4. Now save the file as `addStyle.xml` and send the `PUT` request to GeoServer, to modify the layer's configuration:

```
$ curl -u admin:pwd -XPUT -H 'Content-type: text/xml'
  -T addStyle.xml http://localhost:8080/geoserver/rest/
  layers/ne_50m_populated_places
```

5. In Python, the code is as follows:

```
import requests
myUrl = 'http://localhost:8080/geoserver/rest/
 layers/ne_50m_populated_places'
file = open(addStyle.xml','r')
payload = file.read()
headers = {'Content-type: text/xml'}
resp = requests.put(myUrl, auth=('admin','pwd'), data=payload,
 headers=headers)
print(resp.status_code)
```

6. Now go to the Layer Preview interface and open the **OpenLayers** preview for the `ne_50m_populated_places` layer; then, open the tools and look at the drop-down list for styles. Is the new one there? Select it and your map should look like the following screenshot:

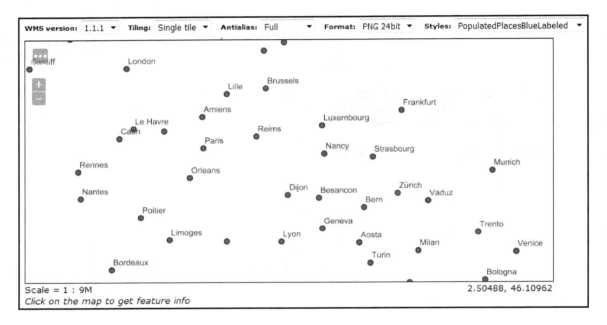

You added a new style to an existing layer. You can also change the default style by just adding the XML code for it to the code sent with the `PUT` request.

Administer GeoServer with REST

In the previous sections, we explored how to work on data configuration. Other than data configuration, REST operations also let you manage general settings for GeoServer. In this last section, we will explore some useful commands.

Managing global settings

We can get a list of global settings and update them using the following entry point:

```
/settings
```

Using `curl`, we can retrieve the settings and save them in an XML file as follows:

```
$ curl -u admin:pwd -XGET -H "Accept: text/xml"
  http://localhost:8080/geoserver/rest/settings
  -o globalSettings.xml
```

Of course, you can update any parameter contained in the file by editing the XML file, or better preparing a new file containing just the changes. Let's try to update the reference information. Prepare a new XML file with information about yourself and your organization:

```
<contact>
  <addressCity>Rome</addressCity>
  <addressCountry>Italy</addressCountry>
  <addressType>Work</addressType>
  <contactEmail>stefano.iacovella@myself.myhome</contactEmail>
  <contactOrganization>Packt</contactOrganization>
  <contactPerson>Stefano Iacovella</contactPerson>
  <contactPosition>Chief Geographer</contactPosition>
</contact>
```

Then send an update request to GeoServer as follows:

```
$ curl -u admin:pwd -XPUT -H "Content-type: text/xml"
  -T contact.xml http://localhost:8080/geoserver/
  rest/settings/contact
```

You can check the result from the web interface:

Primary Contact

Contact

Stefano Iacovella

Organization

Packt

Position

Chief Geographer

Email

stefano.iacovella@myself.myhome

Reloading configuration

As you learned in Chapter 3, *Exploring the Administrative Interface*, you can force GeoServer to reload all configurations from the web interface. In addition, there is a REST operation to do the same. Issue the following command in `curl` and GeoServer will reload all the settings stored in the configuration XML files:

```
$ curl -u admin:pwd -XPUT -H 'Accept: text/xml'
  http://localhost:8080/geoserver/rest/reload
```

Managing services

Managing services' settings with REST is easy; in the following steps, we will deal with WMS. The same operations also apply to WFS and WCS, of course, with appropriate parameters.

The entry point is at the following line:

```
/services/<service>/settings
```

Where the service may assume the `wms`, `wfs`, and `wcs` values.

1. Using `curl`, we can retrieve the settings and save them in an XML file, as follows:

```
$ curl -u admin:pwd -XGET -H 'Accept: text/xml'
  http://localhost:8080/geoserver/rest/services/wms/settings
  -o wmsSetting.xml
```

2. The following script will do the same in Python:

```python
import requests
myUrl = 'http://localhost:8080/geoserver/rest/
 services/wms/settings'
headers = {'Accept: text/xml'}
resp = requests.get(myUrl, auth=('admin','pwd'), headers=headers)
if resp.status_code == 200:
  file = open('wmsSettings.xml','w')
  file.write(resp.text)
  file.close()
```

3. The XML file obtained contains all WMS settings; we want to change some of the following:

```
<wms>
...
  <srs>
    <string>4326</string>
    <string>3857</string>
    <string>4269</string>
  </srs>
  <watermark>
    <enabled>false</enabled>
    <position>BOT_RIGHT</position>
    <transparency>0</transparency>
  </watermark>
  <interpolation>Nearest</interpolation>
...
  <maxRequestMemory>65536</maxRequestMemory>
  <maxRenderingTime>60</maxRenderingTime>
  <maxRenderingErrors>1000</maxRenderingErrors>
</wms>
```

4. So, edit the file and replace the lines you want to update with the following:

```
<srs>
  <string>4326</string>
  <string>3857</string>
  <string>4269</string>
  <string>3003</string>
  <string>3004</string>
</srs>
```

5. Now, issue an update operation with cURL so that the two EPSG codes will be added to the WMS settings:

```
$ curl -u admin:pwd -XPUT -H 'Content-type: text/xml'
-T wmsSettings.xml http://localhost:8080/geoserver/
rest/services/wms/settings
```

6. And, as usual, you can do the same with a Python script:

```
import requests
myUrl = 'http://localhost:8080/geoserver/rest/
 services/wms/settings'
file = open('wmsSettings.xml','r')
payload = file.read()
headers = {'Content-type': 'text/xml'}
```

```
resp = requests.put(myUrl, auth=('admin','pwd'), data=payload,
 headers=headers)
print(resp.status_code)
```

7. Now, go to the web interface, navigate to WMS settings, and check if your update
operation was successful:

We have covered the essential operations you should know to use GeoServer's REST
interface. The online documentation covers all of the allowed operations on each resource.
A good approach, when you are not sure what your XML code should look like to perform
a request, is to check the syntax with a GET request on the same object. When creating your
application, you may want to take a look at the following reference page:
http://docs.geoserver.org/latest/en/user/rest/index.html#rest.

Summary

In this chapter, you learned how to automate configuration tasks. Using the REST interface,
you can publish data from a remote procedure that checks for updates; extracts transforms,
and loads the data on a filesystem or a spatial database; and then sends a request to
GeoServer to configure and publish the data.

In the next chapter, we will explore security--a real issue if you deploying your GeoServer
to the internet.

We will explore how to create a set of users and link them to security policies. Each user can
be profiled to access only a set of data. The most important keywords are users, groups, and
roles. Understanding these topics will enable you to fine tune GeoServer's security system.

10
Securing GeoServer Before Production

In the previous chapters, you've extensively used the web interface. To do this, you always needed a user ID and password. Also, when using the REST interfaces to manage the GeoServer configuration, you had to submit your login credentials. However, you could anonymously access the layers and maps. This is because we used the default settings in the GeoServer security, configured to provide free access to your data for everyone.

While this is quite understandable when you are developing your application, it may not be the best option for a real site.

There could be many different reasons to hide your services, or at least a part of them. Your maps could be a part of a bigger site with a security system requiring your user to log on.

Whenever your data should not be freely available, you need to update the **Security Settings**. Users may be linked to different roles, with some confidential data only visible from a few of them. GeoServer security can help you secure your data, both in simple and complex cases. If you just want to publish your maps, or if you will work with the data of a large corporation, you should read this chapter carefully.

In this chapter, we will cover the following topics:

- Adding strong cryptography support
- Adding users and set their properties
- Defining groups of users
- Defining roles and link them to groups
- Filtering data access with specific roles

Basic Security Settings

You already changed the administrator password from the default of `geoserver` while installing GeoServer; that was the first step to secure your server. Exploring basic **Security Settings** will move you a little further down the path to building a secure site.

From the **Web Administration** interface of GeoServer, select the **Security Settings**. You now have a new panel in the browser window; here you will find a drop-down list showing you the **Active role service**. The first time you have just one choice; we will create more role services when we deal with users and roles.

Note that you may have just one **Active role service**:

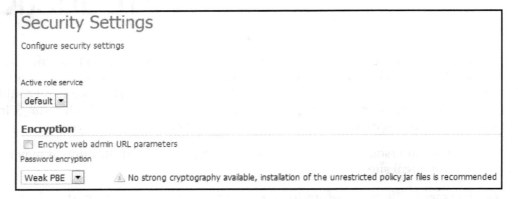

The **Encryption** section lets you hide web admin parameters. Encrypting parameters in a URL is a good idea. If you click on **Web interface** on the **Styles** list and select one, your browser's address bar should contain this URL:

```
http://localhost:8080/geoserver/web/wicket/bookmarkable/
  org.geoserver.wms.web.data.StyleEditPage?
  6&name=PopulatedPlacesBlueLabeled
```

The parameter's names and values are plain text. If you check the flag for encryption and browse to the same page, you should see something similar to the following URL:

```
http://localhost:8080/geoserver/web/u9tP01s6YXd2kNgDUX7woPsSH-
  8zLdrj8a3qeXeHpM1TzzQVhUeLXuhMxdMO7
  3leoMLTKFH2tjzaTo14NSyNWZr5GUz1G1Zk6z
  S5C1v3uedylTqB2J5UDAiKMhEXHBBM/u9taf/KFH7c
```

If there is someone sniffing packets, it is harder to understand the parameters.

Enabling strong encryption

The last setting on the page is about the method of storing passwords. GeoServer can store passwords in plain text or encrypted. You should select one of the two available encryption types from the basic **Security Settings** page. Due to legal considerations, strong encryption is not available with the standard installation. We will enable it by adding a couple of files to our installation. Please refer to the following points:

1. The first step is getting the files you need. Open your browser and point to `http://www.oracle.com/technetwork/java/javase/downloads/jce8-download-2133166.html`.

2. Before you can download the file, you need to accept the license agreement, and then the download link will be available. Save the archive to a convenient folder and unzip it as follows:

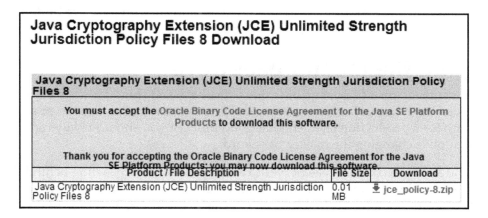

3. There are three files inside the archive. You need to copy the two JAR files to your `<java-home>/lib/security` folder. Then restart Tomcat as follows:

```
$ sudo service tomcat restart Tomcat
```

4. Open the **Security Setting** page in the GeoServer web interface. Now you shouldn't see any warning about **Strong PBE** not being available:

5. Select **Strong PBE** from the drop-down list and click on the **Save** button.

Changing the master password

Passwords are saved on a filesystem or inside a database and should always be encrypted to avoid usage by unauthorized users. A stronger encryption makes GeoServer safer, but it is not enough for a production site. Another good practice you should always adopt on a new installation is changing the master password.

You used the admin account on GeoServer to administer it. Silently acting behind the scenes is another account in GeoServer, called the **root account**. It is the real super user account and it is present for your safety. If you disable the admin account, you may find yourself locked out of GeoServer. In this case, you can use the root account to log in and restore the admin user.

By default, the root password is equal to that of admin, but you will change it as follows:

1. Log in as admin or root. From the **Security** options, select the **Passwords** page:

2. On the top of the page, click on the link to change the master password, as shown in this screenshot:

3. Insert the **Current password** of the master account, which is the same as the admin password, and then a new one. Click on **Change Password**:

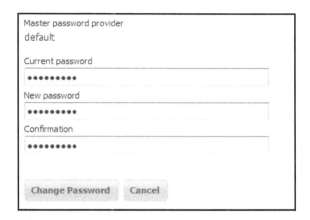

We have changed the master password. If you are in charge of several GeoServer instances and are not the only one performing administrative tasks on them, the master password may help you when in need of a disaster recovery.

Defining users, groups, and roles

To ensure data security, you need to identify who is accessing your layers and your services. When securing your data, the first step is disabling anonymous access.

Security in GeoServer is based on a role system where each role defines a specific set of functions. You can assign roles to users and groups; that is, assign functions to real people using your system.

To organize your real users, GeoServer provides you with the user, group, and role concepts. With the first two, you can insert real people into the GeoServer security subsystem and, with roles, you can grant rights to real users.

User definition

In GeoServer, a user is someone entitled to use the system; it may be another software or a real person. When you add a user to the security system, GeoServer stores a username, uniquely identifying the user, a password, and a set of key/value pairs to store general information about it. You can disable a user at any time, preventing him from using the system.

Group definition

A **group** is a set of users. GeoServer stores a list of usernames belonging to the group and a group name, uniquely identifying the group. A group can be disabled, but note that this only removes the roles deriving from the disabled group and does not disable the users belonging to the group.

The Users/Groups services

Users and groups are stored in a user/group service. This defines the storage medium, the encryption type for passwords, and the password policy. The storage may be one of the following--XML files (default), a JDBC Database, or a LDAP directory. Although you may have more than one user/group service, you will usually be fine with the default one.

Roles definition

GeoServer roles are associated with performing certain tasks or accessing particular resources. Roles are assigned to users and groups, authorizing them to perform the actions associated with the role.

Creating users and groups

In order to fully understand how security works in GeoServer, we will use a typical scenario. Consider an organization working with data in the Packt workspace. We want to restrict access to this data to only the organization's members. Inside the organization, there are a few people editing data to create new data sets or to update existing ones, and many more members who need to read data to compose maps. There is also a need for an administrator to keep it all working. Lastly, we need to consider that our GeoServer site also contains data that should remain freely available. We will now create the security organization from an unsecured GeoServer as follows:

1. We will start creating groups. In the **Security** section of the left pane, select the **Users, Groups, and Roles** link. The following screenshot shows you the **User Group Services** configured. You will find the default service shipped with GeoServer. We already changed it to use **Strong PBE** encryption and that is fine. Click on the **Name** to edit it:

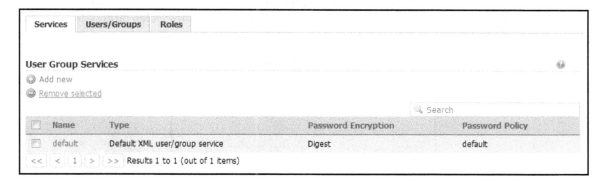

2. Select the **Groups** tab. The list is empty. Click on **Add a new group**:

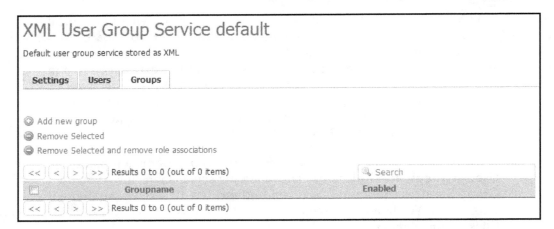

3. Enter `Packt_Publishers` as a group name and leave the group **Enabled**. Do not assign any role to the new group as we will create specific roles later. Click on the **Save** button:

4. Repeat the previous step to create the **Packt_Editors** and **Packt_Admins** groups. Your list should now show the three groups as follows:

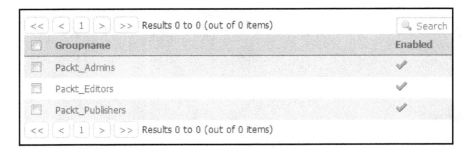

5. Now switch to the **Users** tab. Obviously, it lists the only existing user, that is, **admin**, as shown in the following screenshot:

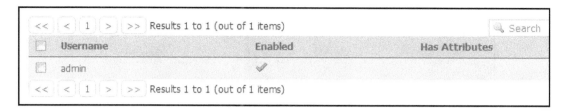

6. I am pleased to introduce you to **Steven Plant**, the Packt Data Administrator. Click on the **Add new user** link, and add him with a password of your choice:

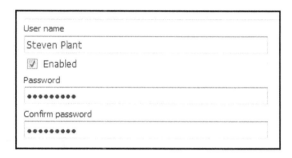

7. Add **Steven** to the **Packt_Admins** group, then click on the **Save** button:

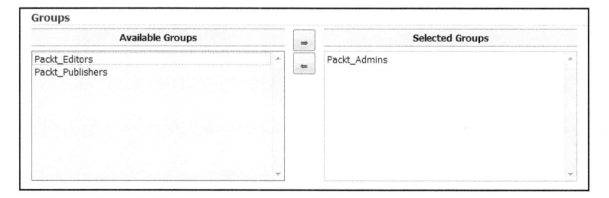

8. Repeat the previous step to create a user, **Michael Ford**, a member of the **Packt_Editors** group, and **John Smith**, a **Packt_Publishers** group member. Your list now shows the three users as follows:

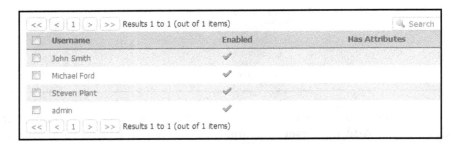

We just created three users for the three groups and this may seem overkill to you. Consider them as templates for the real users. In the real world, we do not want to have too many administrators; we will probably need several Michaels and Johns processing the data. Now, we need to define what they can do on GeoServer.

Defining roles

A user or a group without any role assigned is useless. It is now time to create roles and assign them to our users. Please refer to the following points:

1. From the **User, Groups, and Roles** section, select the **Roles** tab. You will find that two roles already exist. They are the administrative roles assigned to the admin account, and they grant access to all GeoServer configuration. Click on the **Edit** link, as shown in the following screenshot:

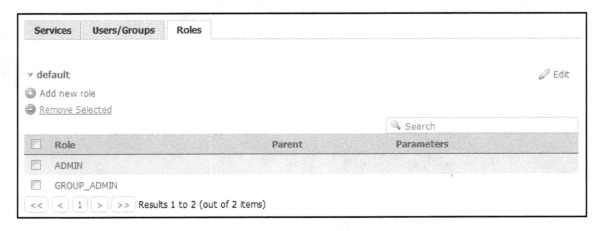

2. You entered the Role service definition. Leave the **Settings** tab untouched and switch to the **Roles** tab. Click on **Add new role**:

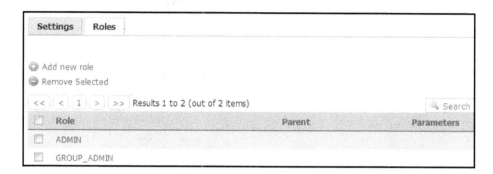

3. Enter PACKT_VIEWER as a new role name. We do not need a **Parent role**. A child role inherits all the grants from the **Parent role**, making it useful when you want to extend a basic role with more grants. Indeed, we will do this in the next step:

4. Click on the **Save** button and then repeat the previous step to create the **PACKT_EDITOR** role. This time, select PACKT_VIEWER as the **Parent role**, as shown in the following screenshot:

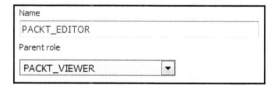

5. Click on the **Save** button and then repeat the previous step to create the **PACKT_ADMIN** role. This time, select `PACKT_EDITOR` as the **Parent role**. Once saved, your role's list should look like the following screenshot:

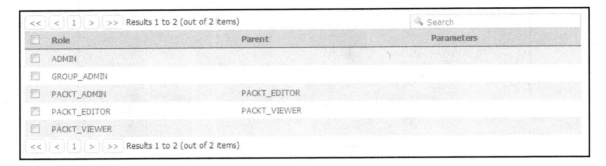

6. The final step is to associate a role to users or groups. Select the **User, Groups, and Roles** page from the left pane, then select the **Groups** list and click on the **Packt_Publishers** group to edit it. Add the **PACKT_VIEWER** role to the group and save it as shown in the following screenshot:

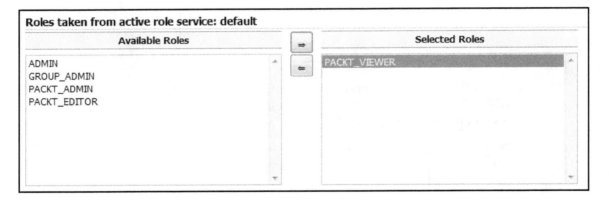

7. Now click on the **Packt_Editors** group and associate it with the **PACKT_EDITOR** role.

8. Finally, associate the **Packt_Admins** group to the **PACKT_ADMIN** role.

By defining roles and associating them to the users, we completed the definition of our organization. Now, we need to explore how data is bound to roles and users.

Accessing data and services

GeoServer supports access and control, both at the service level, allowing for the lockdown of service operations to only authenticated users who have been granted a particular role, and on a per-layer basis.

The two approaches cannot be mixed. If you lock down a service to a role, you cannot grant the access on a specific layer to the same role.

When working with layers, you can define rules that specify what a role can do on any specific layer. The operations controlled are the view, write, and admin access. When granting read access on a layer, you enable a user to add it on a map; while granting write access you enable the user to update, create, and delete features contained in the layer. The admin access level enables the user to update the layer's configuration.

Securing layers

We want to protect the data set contained in the Packt workspace from unauthorized access, while leaving the remaining layers freely available to all users. In this section, we will associate layers and roles:

1. Under the **Security** section on the left pane, select **Data**. The rules list shows the two shipped with the default GeoServer configuration. Click on the **Add new rule** link:

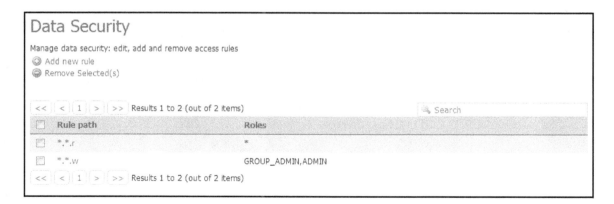

The *.*.r rule is associated with the * roles. This means that every user, including the anonymous one, can access any layer from any workspace configured on GeoServer. The general form of the rule is then as in this code: `workspace.layer.access_mode`.

2. In the rule editing page, select **Packt** as the **Workspace**. Leave * as a **Layer**. Since we want to protect all layers in this workspace, the **Access mode** should be **Read**. Select the **PACKT_READER** role and move it to the right list by clicking on the arrow. Click on the **Save** button to create the reading rule, as shown in the following screenshot:

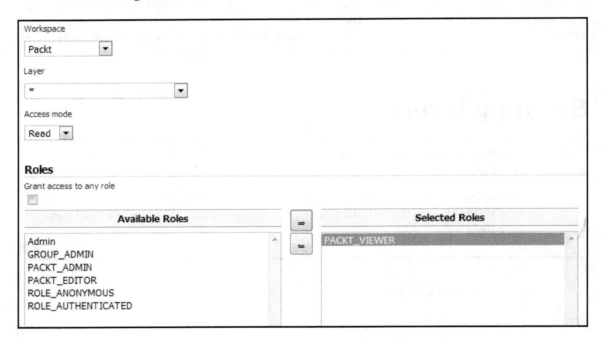

3. Repeat the previous step to create a writing rule. Select **Write** as the access mode and **PACKT_EDITOR** as the role.

4. Then create the administration rule. Select **Admin** as the **Access mode** and **PACKT_ADMIN** as the **Role**. After saving, you will see a rule list like the one displayed in the following screenshot:

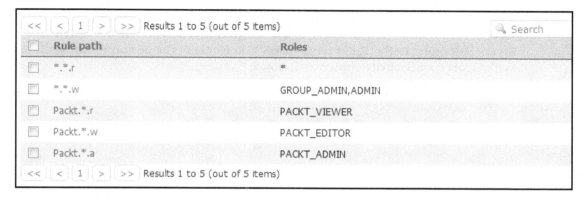

Rule path	Roles
..r	*
..w	GROUP_ADMIN,ADMIN
Packt.*.r	PACKT_VIEWER
Packt.*.w	PACKT_EDITOR
Packt.*.a	PACKT_ADMIN

5. Click on **Save** on the rule list page, and then log off from the GeoServer web interface. If you try to access the layer preview anonymously, you won't see any layers from the Packt workspace while all the others are still listed.

6. Now, log on as `John Smith`, with the password you assigned to him. Going back to the layer preview, you should see the Packt layers listed. Try the Open Layers preview page for the **ne_10m_railroads** layer. It works and you can use the data to compose maps such as the following:

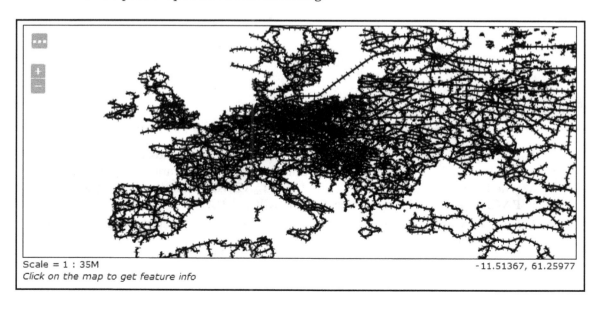

Scale = 1 : 35M
Click on the map to get feature info
-11.51367, 61.25977

7. However, John Smith can't edit the styles associated with the layer or any other property. He would need admin rights granted for it; can you guess who the proper user will be?

8. Log on to GeoServer as `Steven Plant`. Now, the left pane is richer than it was when you were John, but with fewer features than those visible to the GeoServer's default admin role. Click on the **Layer** link; you will see only the layers belonging to the Packt workspace. You can split the admin responsibilities with GeoServer Security shown as follows:

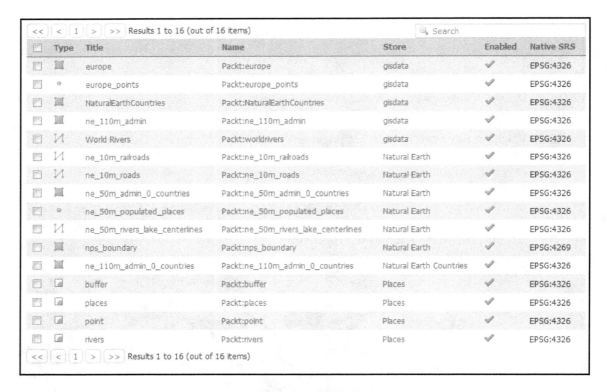

	Type	Title	Name	Store	Enabled	Native SRS
		europe	Packt:europe	gisdata	✓	EPSG:4326
		europe_points	Packt:europe_points	gisdata	✓	EPSG:4326
		NaturalEarthCountries	Packt:NaturalEarthCountries	gisdata	✓	EPSG:4326
		ne_110m_admin	Packt:ne_110m_admin	gisdata	✓	EPSG:4326
		World Rivers	Packt:worldrivers	gisdata	✓	EPSG:4326
		ne_10m_railroads	Packt:ne_10m_railroads	Natural Earth	✓	EPSG:4326
		ne_10m_roads	Packt:ne_10m_roads	Natural Earth	✓	EPSG:4326
		ne_50m_admin_0_countries	Packt:ne_50m_admin_0_countries	Natural Earth	✓	EPSG:4326
		ne_50m_populated_places	Packt:ne_50m_populated_places	Natural Earth	✓	EPSG:4326
		ne_50m_rivers_lake_centerlines	Packt:ne_50m_rivers_lake_centerlines	Natural Earth	✓	EPSG:4326
		nps_boundary	Packt:nps_boundary	Natural Earth	✓	EPSG:4269
		ne_110m_admin_0_countries	Packt:ne_110m_admin_0_countries	Natural Earth Countries	✓	EPSG:4326
		buffer	Packt:buffer	Places	✓	EPSG:4326
		places	Packt:places	Places	✓	EPSG:4326
		point	Packt:point	Places	✓	EPSG:4326
		rivers	Packt:rivers	Places	✓	EPSG:4326

9. If you go on **Layer** preview and select the **ne_10m_railroads** layer again, can you see the map? Of course, you can, because of roles inheritance, which you set when creating the Packt roles. So, **PACKT_ADMIN** inherits all the grants from **PACKT_EDITOR**, and, hence, from **PACKT_VIEWER**.

10. We now want to check if **Michael Ford** can really edit the data. Log out from GeoServer.

11. From the left pane, select the **Demos** link. It gets you to a page containing links to the demos applications. We will use the page to create editing requests in order to test the security:

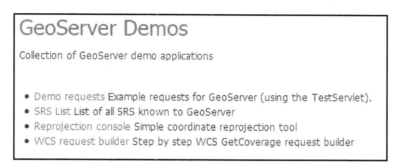

12. In the **Demo requests** page, select the request for a WFS insert.

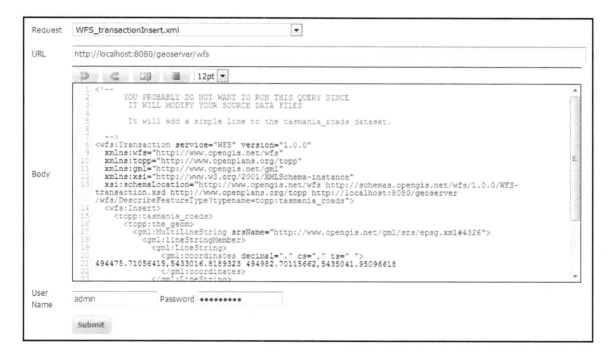

WFS is an OGC standard for services delivering you features instead of their representations, which are maps. **WFS-T** is an extension to add features from the client to the server. This way, you can perform editing, that is, creating, deleting, or updating features. We will cover WFS in `Chapter 12`, *Going Further - Getting Help and Troubleshooting*.

13. Remove the code in the body--it is an XML example for a layer shipped with the GeoServer default configuration--and replace it with the following piece of code. You don't need to fully understand the code; it basically contains a GML fragment defining the feature we want to create:

```xml
<wfs:Transaction service="WFS" version="1.0.0"
xmlns:wfs="http://www.opengis.net/wfs"
xmlns="http://www.opengis.net/ogc"
xmlns:Packt="https://www.packtpub.com/"
xmlns:gml="http://www.opengis.net/gml"
xmlns:xsi="http://www.w3.org/2001/XMLSchema-instance"
xsi:schemaLocation="http://www.opengis.net/wfs
http://schemas.opengis.net/wfs/1.0.0/WFS-transaction.xsd
https://www.packtpub.com/ http://localhost:8080/geoserver/wfs?
request=DescribeFeatureType&amp;service=wfs&amp;
version=1.0.0&amp;typeName=Packt:places">
<wfs:Insert>
<Packt:places>
 <Packt:shape>
   <gml:Point srsName="EPSG:4326">
     <gml:coordinates decimal="." cs="," ts="
     ">115.86,-31.908</gml:coordinates>
     </gml:Point>
 </Packt:shape>
 <Packt:name>Perth</Packt:name>
 <Packt:country>Australia</Packt:country>
</Packt:places>
</wfs:Insert>
</wfs:Transaction>
```

Geography Markup Language (GML) is an OGC standard defining an XML grammar to describe geographical features. It is often used as an interchange format for spatial transactions. For more information, visit the following link: `http://www.opengeospatial.org/standards/gml`.

14. Click on the **Submit** button. A form showing you the result will appear, shown as follows:

```
- <ServiceExceptionReport version="1.2.0"
  xsi:schemaLocation="http://www.opengis.net/ogc http://schemas.opengis.net
  /wfs/1.0.0/OGC-exception.xsd">
  - <ServiceException>
      {https://www.packtpub.com/}places is read-only
    </ServiceException>
  </ServiceExceptionReport>
```

15. The message is not unexpected. We are trying to insert a point in a feature type with anonymous access, while we previously defined a rule granting write access only to the **Packt_Editors** group's members. In the demo request page, enter the proper credentials and try editing again:

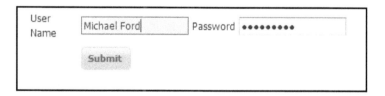

16. This time, the response shows us that GeoServer has accepted our insert request, as shown in the following screenshot:

```
- <wfs:WFS_TransactionResponse version="1.0.0"
  xsi:schemaLocation="http://www.opengis.net/wfs http://localhost:8080/geoserver
  /schemas/wfs/1.0.0/WFS-transaction.xsd">
  - <wfs:InsertResult>
      <ogc:FeatureId fid="new0"/>
    </wfs:InsertResult>
  - <wfs:TransactionResult>
    - <wfs:Status>
        <wfs:SUCCESS/>
      </wfs:Status>
    </wfs:TransactionResult>
  </wfs:WFS_TransactionResponse>
```

17. Repeat the previous step to insert other locations with the following values:

```
Brisbane 153.030 -27.450
Sydney 151.210 -33.868
Melbourne 144.974 -37.812
Darwin 130.839 -12.455
```

18. Now, open the **myLocations** layer's configuration, update its bounding boxes, and set the style to `PopulatedPlacesLabeled`. Then, open the layer preview for it; in the map, you should see the five locations you created, as in the following image:

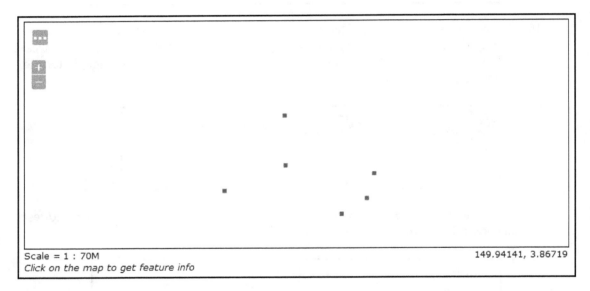

Scale = 1 : 70M
Click on the map to get feature info
149.94141, 3.86719

We have completed the security scenario. By defining rules for data access, we restricted what actions a user can perform on the data and we also tried impersonating the users we created. Unless you know the admin password, there is no way to bypass the security system and access restricted data.

Summary

We took a brief journey through GeoServer security. From the plain installation, which ships with a very low-security level, you learned how to create users and give them grants to access data and perform tasks on GeoServer.

In the next chapter, we will focus on performance, which is a big challenge when you eventually deploy your site in production. Users might wait in anticipation for your maps; however, if it takes too long to download them, they will soon abandon your site.

11
Tuning GeoServer in a Production Environment

Everyone hates slow websites; web maps are no exception. Your users will look for a nice user experience with the map promptly reacting to their input.

Speed is not the only factor you need to take into account. A user will expect the site to be available; frequent downtime will make your users go away to some other website.

In this chapter, we will cover the configuration of GeoServer to optimize its speed and availability. You have already learned how to cache layers to optimize the map speed using GWC. It is a great tool and proper configuration can boost your map's performances. However, caching is not always feasible, such as in cases of frequently changing data; hence, GeoServer offers you other tools to increase performance.

In this chapter, we will cover the following topics in detail:

- Optimizing runtime parameters for JVM
- Improving image manipulation performance using JAI
- Using a proxy
- Creating a GeoServer cluster

Tuning Java

When we installed Tomcat, we did not change any of the JVM settings. Tomcat's startup script is configured for booting quickly, but of course it can't match all the requirements of the application. Tuning your Java runtime parameters can greatly increase performance. There are many runtime parameters you can tune, modifying the startup script for JVM. In the following section, you will set the parameters that are most effective on GeoServer performances. Note that the values may vary according to the hardware configuration on your site.

 Unfortunately, there is no way to cut corners on the path of tuning parameters for a Java application. While the options presented in this chapter have been widely tested on GeoServer and are recommended by core developers, you should note that the best options may vary depending on your scenario. A valuable resource to help you understand how each parameter works can be found at https://docs.oracle.com/javase/9/tools/java.htm#JSWOR624.

Configuring Java runtime parameters

In Chapter 2, *Getting Started with GeoServer*, we created a startup script for an automated startup of GeoServer on Linux. Now you will edit the script and add a few more values for the Java runtime parameters. You will find a brief description of each parameter in the following steps:

1. Open the startup file to edit:

   ```
   $ sudo vi /etc/init.d/tomcat
   ```

    The most famous editor on Linux is probably vi. System administrators and developers often love it for its flexibility and power. On the other hand, it has a steep learning curve, where newcomers may find its command/insert mode's dual nature uncomfortable. On Debian distributions, you may find nano, which is a more user-friendly console editor. And it goes without saying that you can use a powerful IDE such as Gedit or Jedit if you can access a desktop environment.

2. Locate the following line:

   ```
   export JAVA_OPTS="-Djava.awt.headless=true"
   ```

3. Insert a new line just before it. The first parameter that you will tune is the HEAP size. It really depends on the available memory on your system. 2 GB, as indicated, is a good figure. You may want to decrease it if you are hosting it on a tiny cloud machine where the total memory size is limited. Type the following values on a new line:

```
HEAP="-Xms2048m -Xmx2048m"
```

4. Now add a second line and insert the following code. We will enable it using the **Parallel Garbage Collector** which enables multithreaded garbage collection and improves performance if more than two cores are present:

```
PGC="-XX:+UseParallelGC"
```

5. Add another line and increase the lifetime of soft references. GeoServer uses soft references to cache data stores, spatial reference systems, and other data structures. By increasing this value to 36000, which is 36 seconds, these values will stay in memory longer, increasing the effectiveness of the cache. This is shown as follows:

```
SRP="-XX:SoftRefLRUPolicyMSPerMB=36000"
```

6. To set a higher ratio for short-lived objects, insert the following line:

```
SLO="-XX:NewRatio=2"
```

7. The last set is to force the JVM server. On most Linux systems it is the default, but having it explicitly set doesn't cause any harm:

```
SERVER="-server"
```

8. Now go to the line where we started and add all the values you set in the JAVA_OPTS variable. The JVM reads it at startup and will use your values:

```
export JAVA_OPTS="-Djava.awt.headless=true $HEAP $PGC $SRP $SLO $SERVER"
```

9. Save the file and restart your Tomcat.

You customized the Java runtime environment hosting GeoServer. If you are on a Windows machine, you can insert the values in the Tomcat Configuration Console. Go to the **Java** tab and insert each parameter on a new line in the **Java Options** textbox. You can insert the heap size in the textboxes called **Initial memory pool** and **Maximum memory pool**:

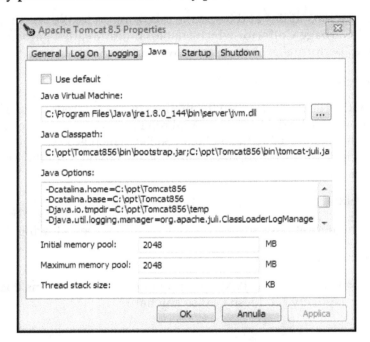

Installing native JAI

Java Advanced Imaging (**JAI**) is a library developed by Oracle for advanced image manipulation. GeoServer can run without it, as it is shipped with a pure Java version of JAI. Installing JAI greatly improves performance when working with images, that is, raster format data. If you don't use spatial raster data, GeoServer works with image formats when you ask for a map, for example, in a WMS GetMap request, so it is really worthwhile to have it on your production site:

1. Download the proper package for your system, Linux or Windows, from `http://download.java.net/media/jai/builds/release/1_1_3/` as follows:

   ```
   $ wget http://download.java.net/media/jai/
   builds/release/1_1_3/jai-1_1_3-lib-linux-amd64.tar.gz
   ```

2. Extract the file into a temporary directory:

   ```
   $ tar xfz jai-1_1_3-lib-linux-amd64.tar.gz
   ```

3. Move JAR files into the `JDK/JRE lib/ext` folder:

   ```
   $ mv ./jai-1_1_3/lib/*.jar $JAVA_HOME/jre/lib/ext/ && \
   ```

4. Move so files into the `JDK/JRE lib/amd64` folder:

   ```
   $ mv ./jai-1_1_3/lib/*.so $JAVA_HOME/jre/lib/amd64/ && \
   ```

5. Now download the JAI Image, `I/O 1.1`:

   ```
   $ wget http://download.java.net/media/jai-
   imageio/builds/release/1.1/
   jai_imageio-1_1-lib-linux-amd64.tar.gz
   ```

6. Extract the file contained in the archive:

   ```
   $ tar xvfz jai_imageio-1_1-lib-linux-amd64.tar.gz
   ```

7. Move JAR files into the `JDK/JRE lib/ext` folder:

   ```
   $ mv ./jai_imageio-1_1/lib/*.jar $JAVA_HOME/jre/lib/ext/ && \
   ```

8. Move so files into the `JDK/JRE lib/amd64` folder:

   ```
   $ mv ./jai_imageio-1_1/lib/*.so $JAVA_HOME/jre/lib/amd64/ && \
   ```

9. You can now remove the two archives you have downloaded, as follows:

   ```
   $ rm jai_imageio-1_1-lib-linux-amd64-jre.bin
   $ rm jai-1_1_3-lib-linux-amd64-jre.bin
   ```

10. Stop your Tomcat service:

    ```
    $ sudo service tomcat stop
    ```

11. Now remove the pure Java version of JAI:

```
$ cd /opt/apache-tomcat-8.0.56/webapps/geoserver/WEB-INF/lib/
$ sudo rm jai_codec-1.1.3.jar
$ sudo rm jai_core-1.1.3.jar
$ sudo rm jai_imageio-1.1.jar
```

12. Restart the Tomcat service as follows:

```
$ sudo service tomcat start
```

13. Open the GeoServer web interface and go to the **Server status** page. You can now see that it is using **Native JAI**:

Native JAI	true	
Native JAI ImageIO	true	
JAI Maximum Memory	181 MB	
JAI Memory Usage	0 KB	Free memory
JAI Memory Threshold	75.0	
Number of JAI Tile Threads	7	
JAI Tile Thread Priority	5	

You installed JAI libraries for advanced imaging manipulation. This will make your GeoServer faster at writing rasters, for example, when preparing a response to a `GetMap` request. Although tuning Java can greatly improve your server performances there is another little step that is often forgotten--removing unneeded features.

Removing unused services

In this book, we have mainly used GeoServer as a **map server**; in fact, GeoServer ships with three OGC services enabled--WMS, WFS, and WCS. If you will only use GeoServer to produce maps, you should disable WCS and WFS, or at least set them to read-only mode. Do you remember when we used WFS-T to edit data in the chapter about security? If your data is static, the most secure way to avoid accidental updating or deleting is disabling WFS-T.

Now, you should turn off WCS and WFS, or only WFS-T, according to your needs:

1. Open the GeoServer web interface. On the left pane, you can see the **Services** category and, under it, a list containing **WMTS**, **WCS**, **WFS**, and **WMS**. Select **WCS**, shown as follows:

2. Remove the flag from the **Enable WCS** checkbox to disable the service and click on the **Submit** button, shown as follows:

3. Now select **WFS** in the **Services** list. If you don't want to deliver features to your users, disable the service as you did for **WCS**:

4. If you do not want to block your user from downloading geometries, leave the service enabled. You can still tune the service parameters. Scroll down until you find the **Maximum number of features** textbox. This value limits the number of records returned on a single `GetFeature` request. Lower the default value to `10000`:

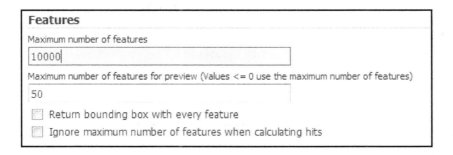

5. In the very next section, set the **Service Level** option. Unless you want your users performing editing on the published data, you should disable WFS-T, that is, the transactional level. Select **Basic** and then click on the **Submit** button:

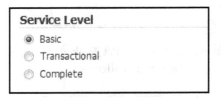

6. Now select **WMS** in the **Services** list. Of course, you do not want to disable the WMS service; this would turn your installation into a useless piece of software, but you can set some values to optimize map rendering.

7. Scroll down to the **Resource consumption limits** section. The three values limit the amount of memory, time, and errors that GeoServer can use while rendering a map. Set the memory to 20480, which is enough for a full-screen map:

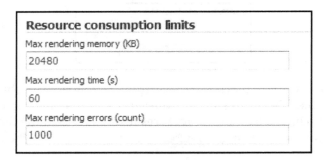

8. Click on the **Submit** button to save your settings.

Disabling unneeded services improves resource usage and helps you avoid out-of-memory errors. The more features you discard from GeoServer, the fewer classes it will need to load in the memory.

Enabling the Marlin rasterizer

You can greatly improve rasterizing performance and scalability while rendering vector data in Java 8 and replacing the default rasterizer in JDK or OpenJDK with the Marlin rasterizer.

1. Download the JAR from
   `https://github.com/bourges1/marlin-renderer/releases`.
2. Save it in the `webapps/geoserver7WEB-INF/lib` folder inside your Tomcat installation.
3. Edit the startup file for Tomcat, adding the following JVM startup options. Replace the `$MARLIN_JAR` variable with the path to the folder where you saved it:

```
-Xbootclasspath/a:$MARLIN_JAR
-Dsun.java2d.renderer=org.marlin.pisces.MarlinRenderingEngine
```

Setting a proxy

Whether you are using GeoServer on Tomcat or you used the Windows installer that incorporates a Jetty instance, it is not a good idea to expose it directly to your users, especially if they are on the internet. A safer option is to use a more stable web server, such as Apache HTTPD--one of the most popular and widely used web servers across the web. To expose GeoServer, or more generally, a Java application from the web server, you need to set a `proxy` on the web server. Users will point to an alias and their requests will be redirected to Tomcat, more safely deployed in a protected LAN.

We will configure the Apache HTTP web server to act as a `proxy` for GeoServer. First of all, we need to get it working; you will learn that, just like many other open source projects, this is surprisingly simple! Perform the following steps:

1. To install Apache on Linux, you can use the distribution repository. At the time of writing, it installs release 2.4.18 for Linux Mint:

   ```
   $ sudo apt-get install apache2
   ```

    You can also download and install a binary package from `http://httpd.apache.org/download.cgi`. This is the easier option if you are on Windows.

2. If your server is not registered on a DNS, you should insert the full hostname inside the site's configuration file. Open the following file:

   ```
   $ sudo vi /etc/apache2/sites-available/default
   ```

3. Insert the following code as the first line of the file:

```
$ ServerName mint18x64vm
```

If you perform a manual installation of Apache, or if you are on a Windows machine, the file and folder locations are different from those shown.

4. Point your browser to http://localhost. If the installation was successful, you should see the following message on the home page of your web server:

> **It works!**

5. The Apache HTTPD default installation does not contain any proxy capabilities. To use these features, you need to enable some optional modules. You can find which modules are available on your system as follows:

```
$ ls /etc/apache2/mods-available | grep proxy
proxy_ajp.load
proxy_balancer.conf
proxy_balancer.load
proxy.conf
proxy_connect.load
proxy_ftp.conf
proxy_ftp.load
proxy_http.load
proxy.load
proxy_scgi.load
```

6. For configuring a proxy, you need the proxy and proxy_ajp modules. Enable them using the a2enmod command-line tool. After that, you need to restart the Apache service as follows:

```
$ sudo a2enmod proxy proxy_ajp
$ sudo service apache2 restart
```

7. Now, you will configure a proxy; edit the http.conf file:

```
$ sudo vi /etc/apache2/httpd.conf
```

8. You have to insert a `ProxyPass` directive in the Apache configuration file. With the following syntax, you are informing the web server that each incoming request for `/geoserver` will be forwarded to your host on port `8009` using the `ajp` protocol:

```
ProxyPass /geoserver ajp://localhost:8009/geoserver
<Location /geoserver>
Order deny,allow
Deny from all
Allow from 127.0.0.1
</Location>
```

9. Now open your browser and point it to `http://localhost/geoserver/web/`:

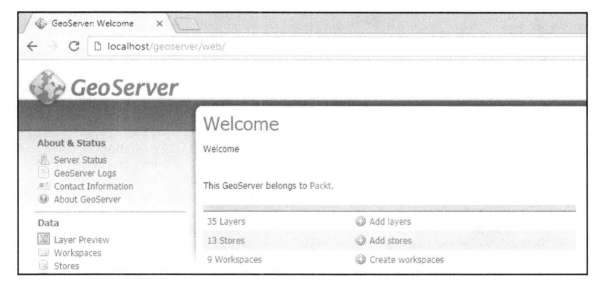

You learned the basic method of configuring Apache to act as a `proxy`. Properly configuring a web server for security is far out of the scope of this book, but you should keep in mind that the HTTP protocol exposed by Tomcat and Jetty is not intended for real internet use. You should always avoid deploying GeoServer in a DMZ (`http://en.wikipedia.org/wiki/DMZ_(computing)`).

Avoiding service faults

GeoServer is a great piece of software, and core developers hit bugs every day, enhancing existing functions and delivering new capabilities. Despite all of this work and the careful configuration of your site, failing is always a risk. It is just a matter of time before you encounter a failure preventing your GeoServer from delivering maps. In the simplest case, it will only affect some specific requests; more often, it will halt it for a while, and, sometimes, you will need to restart it to get it working again.

It happens to almost all software applications that you will have worked with, either proprietary or open source, free of charge or very expensive. Avoiding faults is out of your control, but you should learn how to manage them to avoid service interruptions.

A high availability or fault-tolerant configuration is what you need. Indeed, this is a very common approach in software deployment, and what you will learn here is best practice for any kind of software service, not only for the map services.

So, how do you get a fault-tolerant configuration? It is all about redundancy; if you cannot avoid faults, you can yet eliminate a single point of failure. In fault-tolerant configurations, a single point of failure is a part of both hardware and software that does not have a spare companion to succeed in its job if it fails.

The basic idea is quite simple but very effective. If you have two GeoServers working in parallel, they probably will not break at the same time. So, while you or, even better, an automated procedure work to restore the broken instance, the other GeoServer will continue to process the users' requests. From the users' point of view, there is no fault; they can only experience a slowdown in the response time. Of course, this model can be implemented with far more than just two instances of GeoServer; you may have a lot of them. This model will not only make your system more reliable, but it will also greatly improve your site's performance.

Of course, having two GeoServer instances is not enough. First of all, their configurations need to be synchronized; besides, you need a way to share requests among the instances. Indeed, you need a load balancer to distribute the request load across a pool of servers. Consider the following figure:

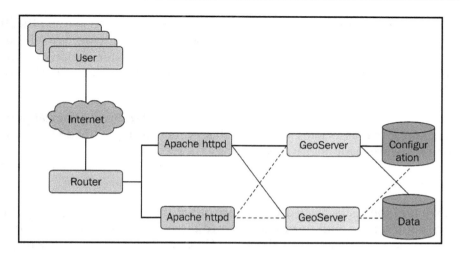

The previous diagram displays all the components of a fault-tolerant configuration. Starting from the right, we find two repositories designed with the symbol usually used for databases--one holds the **Configuration** files and the other stores the **Data**. As you learned in the previous chapters, GeoServer's configuration is contained in a folder. This folder is contained inside war; so, when you deploy it on Tomcat, it is contained in the GeoServer folder. You can put it on an external filesystem to make it accessible by all instances.

To avoid a single point of failure and corruption in access contention, you can't simply copy the configuration folder on a server and have all your GeoServers pointing to it. You need to copy it to a special filesystem thought to be simultaneously mounted on multiple servers; these filesystems are called **Cluster File Systems**. Of course, the same issue applies to data not in an RDBMS, for example, shapefiles. For more information, take a look at
http://en.wikipedia.org/wiki/Clustered_file_system.

The data store may be an RDBMS, for example, a PostGIS server, or a folder containing shapefiles and georeferenced images.

Going leftwards, you will find two GeoServers. Note the lines connecting to both data and configuration. They are differently styled, just to make the connected items clear, but their function is the same. Each GeoServer needs to access the same configuration store and data store to expose exactly the same layers.

On the left of the map servers, there are a couple of web servers. You learned that they act as a `proxy` for GeoServer; here, they also balance the load among them. We will see the configuration's details in the following section configuring a cluster section; for now, you should note that each web server is connected to each GeoServer. This way, if one of them fails, the other will forward requests to the map servers.

In front of the web servers, there is a component called **Router**. From a logical point of view, it is a balancer that associates all your web servers to a single IP address. It may be a hardware or a software component; check out `http://en.wikipedia.org/wiki/Load_balancing(computing)` for a discussion and a list of implementations.

Eventually, we find the users. They are unaware of the architectural complexity; they just have an entry point for the map service to forward the requests. The cluster configuration takes care of the requests, dispatching them to a GeoServer and returning the responses.

There is an important fact to keep in mind. WMS, WFS, and WCS are stateless. There is no session state to maintain across the client requests, so you don't need to synchronize session data among your servers. A user request may be filled by server1 and then dispatched to server2. The request's body contains all the information needed by server2 to process the request. This greatly reduces complexity and you can cluster your configuration just by implementing load balancing and redundancy.

Configuring a cluster

In the configuration schema, we did not mention the hardware. Of course, having software redundancy while deploying all components on a single physical server is not a good idea. You can deploy each component on a separate server (and, in a modern server farm, they will probably be virtual ones), but the basic idea is that you should never have all the instances of a component on a single machine.

For the sake of simplicity, and to save you having to buy a lot of hardware, we will use a single Linux machine in the following section:

1. As a first step, we will relocate the configuration folder out of the GeoServer web archive. Stop the Tomcat service as follows:

   ```
   $ sudo service tomcat stop
   ```

2. Now, move the folder to an external location:

```
$ sudo mv /opt/apache-tomcat-8.0.56/webapps/geoserver/data
/opt/geoserver_config
```

3. Now, you have to edit the web.xml file to make GeoServer aware of the new configuration folder:

```
$ sudo vi /opt/apache-tomcat-8.0.56/webapps/
geoserver/WEB-INF/web.xml
```

4. Locate the following commented code fragment:

```
<!--
<context-param>
  <param-name>GEOSERVER_DATA_DIR</param-name>
   <param-value>C:\eclipse\workspace\geoserver_trunk\
   cite\confCiteWFSPostGIS</param-value>
</context-param>
-->
```

5. Remove the first and last line to uncomment it and insert the location of the new folder in the param-value element:

```
<context-param>
 <param-name>GEOSERVER_DATA_DIR</param-name>
 <param-value>/opt/geoserver_config</param-value>
</context-param>
```

An alternative way to set the path for the GeoServer data directory is using an environment variable. On Windows systems, you can add a system environment variable named GEOSERVER_DATA_DIR and set its value to the desired folder. On Linux systems, you can set the same variable as in the following command line:
```
export GEOSERVER_DATA_DIR = /opt/geoserver_data_dir
```

6. Save the file and then restart the Tomcat service:

```
$ sudo service tomcat start
```

7. Log in to GeoServer and check that the configuration was properly read. Now we need a second Tomcat instance. Again, stop the Tomcat service and copy it to a new location:

```
$ sudo cp -r /opt/apache-tomcat-8.0.56 /opt
/new_apachetomcat-8.0.56
```

8. With two different servers, you could leave the Tomcat configuration untouched and it would work perfectly. However, when you have both on the same machine and you start them, they will try to bind to the same TCP port (for example, `8080` for HTTP protocol), and one of them will fail in doing so. Open the `server.xml` file of the new Tomcat with an editor, as follows:

```
$ sudo vi /opt/new_apache-tomcat-8.0.56/conf/server.xml
```

9. Locate the following code--it is the first uncommented line--and modify the Server port value from `8005` to `8105`:

```
<Server port="8105" shutdown="SHUTDOWN">
```

10. Now, look for the code section where the HTTP connector is configured. Change the connector port from `8080` to `8180`:

```
<Connector port="8180" protocol="HTTP/1.1"
connectionTimeout="20000" redirectPort="8443" />
```

11. Scroll down until you find the code for the AJP connector and modify the port number from `8009` to `8109`:

```
<Connector port="8109" protocol="AJP/1.3"
redirectPort="8443" />
```

12. Save the file and close it. Before starting the two Tomcat servers, we need to add a couple of parameters for JVM, otherwise, the integrated GWC will lock the data folder and only one GeoServer will be able to start:

```
$ sudo vi /etc/init.d/tomcat
```

13. We need to disable the integrated GeoWebCache, as they would conflict. To do this, insert the following code just after the line setting the `-server` parameter:

```
GWC="-DGWC_DISKQUOTA_DISABLED=
true -DGWC_METASTORE_DISABLED=true"
```

14. Add the `GWC` variable in the line setting `JAVA_OPTS`:

```
export JAVA_OPTS="-Djava.awt.headless=
true $HEAP $PGC $SRP $SLO $SERVER $GWC"
```

15. Save the file, then open the startup script for the new Tomcat server:

```
$ sudo vi /opt/new_apache-tomcat-8.0.56/bin/catalina.sh
```

16. Insert a new line, just after the initial comments, and set the same parameters:

```
JAVA_OPTS="-DGWC_DISKQUOTA_DISABLED=
    true -DGWC_METASTORE_DISABLED=true"
```

17. Save the file.

18. Now we can start the two Tomcat servers. You can start the old one with the service command utility. To start the newly created one, you will use the following default startup script:

```
$ sudo /opt/new_apache-tomcat-8.0.56/bin/startup.sh
```

19. Now open your browser and point to http://localhost/geoserver and http://localhost:8180/geoserver. Go to the **Layer Preview** page; now you see the same layers list as expected.

20. Now we need to set a proxy for both the Tomcat servers and add a balancer. This is delivered by the apache mod_proxy_balancer module. Enable it using the following commands:

```
$ sudo a2enmod proxy_balancer
$ sudo service apache 2 restart
```

21. In order to change the proxy configuration, you have to edit the httpd.conf file:

```
$ sudo vi /etc/apache2/httpd.conf
```

22. We need to modify the ProxyPass directive. Comment the lines you inserted previously, by inserting a # character at line start. Then, insert the following code snippet:

```
ProxyPass /geoserver balancer://geoserver
<Proxy balancer://geoserver>
  BalancerMember ajp://localhost:8009/geoserver
  BalancerMember ajp://localhost:8109/geoserver
  Order deny,allow
  Deny from all
  Allow from 127.0.0.1
</Proxy>
```

23. Save the file and restart the Apache service. Now open your browser and go to http://localhost/geoserver. Apache will forward your request to one of the two GeoServers.

24. You may wonder how the balancer works, how it balances requests, and what happens if a server fails. Apache `mod_proxy_balancer` comes with a practical interface to manage and monitor the balancer. You have to explicitly expose it in the `httpd.conf` file:

```
$ sudo vi /etc/apache2/httpd.conf
```

25. Insert the following code snippet:

```
<Location /balancer-manager>
  SetHandler balancer-manager
  Order Deny,Allow
  Deny from all
  Allow from 127.0.0.1
</Location>
```

26. From your browser, open `http://localhost/balancer-manager`:

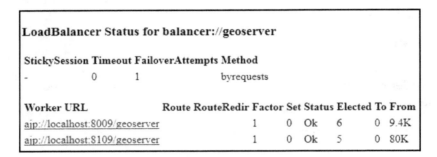

27. From the web interface, you can monitor the main parameters for each node of the configuration. The status tells you if the node is working or if it is down. Right next to it, you can find the number of requests that each node has processed since the service started. The method field shows you how the requests are distributed. The default mode to perform weighted request counting is `byrequests`. You can also modify it to `bytraffic` to perform weighted traffic byte count balancing. By default, each node is assigned an equal load, but you can distribute traffic asymmetrically using the `loadfactor` parameter. Let's change our configuration to split 75 percent of the requests to one node and the remaining 25 percent to the other, as follows:

```
<Proxy balancer://geoserver>
  BalancerMember ajp://localhost:8009/geoserver loadfactor=1
  BalancerMember ajp://localhost:8109/geoserver loadfactor=3
  Order deny,allow
```

```
Deny from all
Allow from 127.0.0.1
</Proxy>
```

28. Restart the Apache service, then open the **GeoServer web** interface, and navigate it to send a few requests. If you now open the **balancer-manager** interface again, the page should look as follows:

LoadBalancer Status for balancer://geoserver

StickySession	Timeout	FailoverAttempts	Method
-	0	1	byrequests

Worker URL	Route	RouteRedir	Factor	Set	Status	Elected	To	From
ajp://localhost:8009/geoserver			1	0	Ok	10	0	14K
ajp://localhost:8109/geoserver			3	0	Ok	31	33	43K

29. You can also set a node as a host standby. The balancer will fetch requests to it in case the node fails. To set a backup, you have to insert the `status=+H` parameter as follows:

```
<Proxy balancer://geoserver>
  BalancerMember ajp://localhost:8009/geoserver status=+H
  BalancerMember ajp://localhost:8109/geoserver
  Order deny,allow
  Deny from all
  Allow from 127.0.0.1
</Proxy>
```

You learned how to configure a simple yet effective high availability configuration. In this section we didn't introduce any routers; this task is usually performed by network engineers, and you are safe knowing that it has to be done.

Summary

In this chapter, we discussed basic considerations to safely deploy the GeoServer in production.

Deploying a successful configuration requires you to take care of several topics. JVM optimization may enhance performance, and a high availability configuration can rock your GeoServer. Although, as a beginner, some of the issues may seem out of your scope for now, it is important to know where to focus your attention when planning a new installation. Most of the time, you will be working with system and network engineers who know very little about map servers. You will be expected to guide them in identifying the critical details in the configuration.

In the next chapter, we will focus on the next steps to take once you are confident with GeoServer, how to get further help, and what else GeoServer can offer you that we did not cover in this book.

12
Going Further - Getting Help and Troubleshooting

Our journey into GeoServer is coming to an end. What you have learned should enable you to create a map service and make your data accessible to everyone on the internet.

GeoServer is far more complex than what we have covered so far. There are lots of advanced features for data sharing and performing spatial analysis.

In this chapter, we will briefly cover some advanced features, for example, other standard protocols supported by GeoServer, how to get help, and how to collaborate with the project. We will cover the following topics in detail:

- **Web Feature Service (WFS)**
- **Web Coverage Service (WCS)**
- Monitoring GeoServer
- Online resources
- Pooling Database Connection

Going beyond maps

We focused on the maps in this book and usually used the WMS protocol in our examples. As you learned in Chapter 1, *GIS Fundamentals*, a map is a representation of data. A map can include vector or raster data, but it always represents them as a raster output, that is, an image. While maps are an easy and useful way to show your data, there are other scenarios where users need not to use a representation, but the original data, for example, to process the data on a client-side task. Here, two other OGC protocols come into use--WFS and WCS.

Delivering vector data

If a user needs to get your vector data, for example the USA railroads, he can use the **Web Feature Service** (**WFS**) protocol. It is a standard protocol defined by OGC that refers to the sending and receiving of geospatial data through HTTP.

When delivering data, the most important thing to define is the data format. Vector data is usually stored in a binary format--think of a shapefile or a PostGIS table--but for practical purposes, we need a more standard approach. Indeed, WFS encodes and transfers information in **Geography Markup Language** (**GML**) based on XML.

There exists a few versions of WFS and GML. The current GeoServer release supports the 1.0.0, 1.1.0, and 2.0.0 WFS versions.

> You can find the full reference for WFS and GML at the OGC repository at `http://www.opengeospatial.org/standards/is`; look for OpenGIS Geography Markup Language (GML) Encoding Standard and OpenGIS Web Feature Service (WFS) Implementation Specification.

WFS defines a set of operations that a user can perform on data. You used transactional operations in `Chapter 10`, *Securing GeoServer Before Production*, for data editing. We will now focus on retrieving data.

Retrieving vector data

We will use WFS to get vector data encoded in GML. In case you disabled it, as we did in `Chapter 11`, *Tuning GeoServer in a Production Environment*, you will need to enable the WFS in GeoServer. Open your command-line console; we will use curl to send requests:

1. The first operation that we will use is `GetCapabilities`. It describes which feature types and operations are available on the server:

```
$ curl -XGET "http://localhost/geoserver/wfs?
service=wfs&version=1.0.0&request=GetCapabilities"
-o getCapabilities.xml
```

2. The XML returned is quite huge; apart from a standard part describing the WFS service and the supported operation, it contains a description for any `FeatureType` configured on GeoServer. The total length of the file depends on the `FeatureTypes` number. The following lines show you the brief description for a `FeatureType` element:

```
<FeatureType>
  <Name>Packt:ne_10m_railroads</Name>
  <Title>ne_10m_railroads</Title>
  <Abstract/>
  <Keywords>features, ne_10m_railroads</Keywords>
  <SRS>EPSG:4326</SRS>
  <LatLongBoundingBox minx="-150.11222194444446"
    miny="-51.89527777777778" maxx="179.35777833333333"
    maxy="69.60437472222222"/>
</FeatureType>
```

3. Before using a `FeatureType` element, for example, railroads, it is a good idea to take a look at its full description. You can get it using the `DescribeFeatureType` operation, which returns an XML code containing a description for the `FeatureType` element you requested. Note that you can omit the `TypeName` parameter; in this case, you get the full list for the `FeatureType` element, ordered by workspace:

```
$ curl -XGET "http://localhost/geoserver/wfs?
  service=wfs&version=1.0.0&request=DescribeFeatureType
  &TypeName=Packt:ne_10m_railroads" -o railroads.xml
```

4. Let's analyze the description contained in the XML response. You can find the name and type of each attribute:

```
<?xml version="1.0" encoding="UTF-8"?>
...
<xsd:complexType name="ne_10m_railroadsType">
  <xsd:complexContent>
    <xsd:extension base="gml:AbstractFeatureType">
    <xsd:sequence>
      <xsd:element maxOccurs="1" minOccurs="0" name="the_geom"
      nillable="true" type="gml:MultiLineStringPropertyType"/>
      <xsd:element maxOccurs="1" minOccurs="0" name="rwdb_rr_id"
      nillable="true" type="xsd:int"/>
      <xsd:element maxOccurs="1" minOccurs="0" name="mult_track"
      nillable="true" type="xsd:int"/>
      <xsd:element maxOccurs="1" minOccurs="0" name="electric"
      nillable="true" type="xsd:int"/>
      ...
```

```
      </xsd:sequence>
     </xsd:extension>
   </xsd:complexContent>
  </xsd:complexType>
  <xsd:element name="ne_10m_railroads"
   substitutionGroup="gml:_Feature"
   type="Packt:ne_10m_railroadsType"/>
</xsd:schema>
```

5. Once you have understood the properties of the `FeatureType` element, it is time to get the features. The `GetFeature` operation retrieves them from the GeoServer. To avoid getting a huge number of features, you can limit the number of elements returned with the `maxFeatures` parameter:

```
$ curl -XGET "http://localhost/geoserver/wfs?
service=wfs&version=1.1.0&request=GetFeature
&TypeName=Packt:ne_10m_railroads&maxFeatures=1"
-o getFeature.xml
```

6. The XML code returned contains the GML for the single feature that we specified. In this case, we have a single `lineString` element with a lot of vertices listed in the `gml:coordinates` element:

```
<gml:featureMembers>
<Packt:ne_10m_railroads gml:id="ne_10m_railroads.1">
  <Packt:the_geom>
    <gml:MultiLineString srsName="urn:x-ogc:def:crs:EPSG:4326"
    srsDimension="2">
      <gml:lineStringMember>
        <gml:LineString>
          <gml:posList>69.46111083 30.78250167 69.45611083
            30.77138944 69.45305556 30.75555667
            69.45246639 30.75275472 69.4497225
            30.73972111 69.44805444 30.73027528
          </gml:posList>
        </gml:LineString>
      </gml:lineStringMember>
    </gml:MultiLineString>
  </Packt:the_geom>
<Packt:rwdb_rr_id>1</Packt:rwdb_rr_id>
<Packt:mult_track>1</Packt:mult_track>
<Packt:electric>1</Packt:electric>
<Packt:other_code>1</Packt:other_code>
<Packt:category>1</Packt:category>
<Packt:disp_scale>1:3m</Packt:disp_scale>
<Packt:add>0</Packt:add>
<Packt:featurecla>Railroad</Packt:featurecla>
```

```
<Packt:scalerank>10</Packt:scalerank>
<Packt:natlscale>1.0</Packt:natlscale>
<Packt:part>ne_global_not_north_america</Packt:part>
<Packt:continent>Europe</Packt:continent>
</Packt:ne_10m_railroads>
</gml:featureMembers>
```

7. Limiting the elements returned with `maxFeatures` is OK for a sample request. In general, you want to have more control over the numbers and types of features you want to extract. Indeed, you can filter them with a spatial operator or with alphanumerical filtering on attributes. In the following sample, we use the `bbox` operator to filter the railroad elements that intersect to an extent:

```
$ curl -XGET "http://localhost/geoserver/wfs?
  service=wfs&version=1.0.0&request=GetFeature
  &TypeName=Packt:ne_10m_railroads
  &bbox=-116.68,36.29,-111.36,39.90"
  -o getBboxFeature.xml
```

8. This time, the request returns more than a feature; indeed, the root element is `FeatureCollection`. If you try to extend the extent of the area requested, increasing the values in the `bbox element`, more features will be listed inside it:

```
<wfs:FeatureCollection ... >
...
  <gml:featureMember>
    <Packt:ne_10m_railroads fid="ne_10m_railroads.19711">
      <Packt:the_geom>
        <gml:MultiLineString
         srsName="http://www.opengis.net/gml/srs/epsg.xml#4326">
...
      </Packt:the_geom>
      <Packt:rwdb_rr_id>19711</Packt:rwdb_rr_id>
      <Packt:mult_track>0</Packt:mult_track>
      <Packt:electric>0</Packt:electric>
      <Packt:other_code>1</Packt:other_code>
      <Packt:category>2</Packt:category>
...
    </Packt:ne_10m_railroads>
  </gml:featureMember>
  <gml:featureMember>
    <Packt:ne_10m_railroads fid="ne_10m_railroads.20462">
      <Packt:the_geom>
        <gml:MultiLineString
         srsName="http://www.opengis.net/gml/srs/epsg.xml#4326">
...
      </Packt:the_geom>
```

```
        <Packt:rwdb_rr_id>20462</Packt:rwdb_rr_id>
        <Packt:mult_track>0</Packt:mult_track>
        <Packt:electric>0</Packt:electric>
        <Packt:other_code>1</Packt:other_code>
        <Packt:category>2</Packt:category>
...
        </Packt:ne_10m_railroads>
    </gml:featureMember>
</wfs:FeatureCollection>
```

9. In the previous examples, we used the GET method to send our requests.
   Although this is possible when using filters, a more proper method to use is
   POST. In fact, when using the POST method, we use an XML file to save the filter.
   Using an external file, let's create more complicated filters than including it in the
   URL. For example, we can use the same BBOX filter by saving the following piece
   of code in a file:

```
<wfs:GetFeature service="WFS" version="1.0.0" outputFormat="GML2"
  xmlns:Packt="https://www.packtpub.com/"
  xmlns:wfs="http://www.opengis.net/wfs"
  xmlns:ogc="http://www.opengis.net/ogc"
  xmlns:gml="http://www.opengis.net/gml"
  xmlns:xsi="http://www.w3.org/2001/XMLSchema-instance"
  xsi:schemaLocation="http://www.opengis.net/wfs
  http://schemas.opengis.net/wfs/1.0.0/WFS-basic.xsd">
    <wfs:Query typeName="Packt:ne_10m_railroads">
      <ogc:Filter>
        <ogc:Intersects>
          <ogc:PropertyName>the_geom</ogc:PropertyName>
          <gml:Box srsName="EPSG:4326">
            <gml:coord>
              <gml:X>-116.68</gml:X>
              <gml:Y>36.29</gml:Y>
            </gml:coord>
            <gml:coord>
              <gml:X>-111.36</gml:X>
              <gml:Y>39.90</gml:Y>
            </gml:coord>
          </gml:Box>
        </ogc:Intersects>
      </ogc:Filter>
    </wfs:Query>
</wfs:GetFeature>
```

10. Now send the request with `curl`; the result will be exactly the same as before:

```
$ curl -XPOST -H "Content-type: text/xml"
-d @propertyFilter.xml http://localhost/geoserver/wfs
-o output.xml
```

11. We can also include an alphanumerical condition in filters. The following code block uses an equality condition on an attribute of the `NaturalEarthCountries` feature type:

```
<wfs:GetFeature service="WFS" version="1.0.0"
  outputFormat="GML2"
  xmlns:Packt="https://www.packtpub.com/"
  xmlns:wfs="http://www.opengis.net/wfs"
  xmlns:ogc="http://www.opengis.net/ogc"
  xmlns:gml="http://www.opengis.net/gml"
  xmlns:xsi="http://www.w3.org/2001/XMLSchema-instance"
  xsi:schemaLocation="http://www.opengis.net/wfs
   http://schemas.opengis.net/wfs/1.0.0/WFS-basic.xsd">
  <wfs:Query typeName="Packt:NaturalEarthCountries">
    <ogc:Filter>
      <ogc:PropertyIsEqualTo>
        <ogc:PropertyName>subregion</ogc:PropertyName>
        <ogc:Literal>Western Europe</ogc:Literal>
      </ogc:PropertyIsEqualTo>
    </ogc:Filter>
  </wfs:Query>
</wfs:GetFeature>
```

12. The result is a collection of features:

```
<wfs:FeatureCollection
...
>
...
  <gml:featureMember>
    <Packt:NaturalEarthCountries fid="NaturalEarthCountries.17">
...
      <Packt:sovereignt>Austria</Packt:sovereignt>
...
    </Packt:NaturalEarthCountries>
  </gml:featureMember>
  <gml:featureMember>
    <Packt:NaturalEarthCountries fid="NaturalEarthCountries.20">
...
      <Packt:sovereignt>Belgium</Packt:sovereignt>
...
```

```
        </Packt:NaturalEarthCountries>
      </gml:featureMember>
  ...
    </wfs:FeatureCollection>
```

You learned how to use WFS to retrieve data with all the geometrical and alphanumerical details. Combining the retrieval with the capabilities to insert or update data (WFS-T), you can build an online editing system for vector data.

Delivering raster data

When it comes to raster data, **Web Coverage Service** (**WCS**) is the equivalent of WFS for delivering original data. Like vector data, raster data may be rendered in a proper way on a map, and you will get the result with WMS and a `GetMap` request. WCS is intended to get a raster dataset or its subset in its original form, without any rendering or other processing and data transformation.

With WCS, you don't have a standard format for data delivery; it depends on the original format of your data.

The current release of GeoServer supports the 1.0.0, 1.1.0, 1.1.1, and 2.0.1 WCS versions.

 As with WFS, you can find the full reference for WCS at the OGC repository (`http://www.opengeospatial.org/standards/is`); look for OpenGIS **Web Coverage Service** (**WCS**) Implementation Specification.

Retrieving raster data

We will use WCS to get raster data by using the sample data shipped with GeoServer. In case you disabled it, as we did in `Chapter 11`, *Tuning GeoServer in a Production Environment*, you will need to enable the WCS in GeoServer. Like in the WFS examples, we will use `Curl` for sending requests:

1. As with WFS, the first operation we will use is `GetCapabilities`. It returns a list of available `coveragetype` and operations:

   ```
   $ curl -XGET "http://localhost/geoserver/wcs?
     service=wcs&version=1.0.0&request=GetCapabilities"
     -o getCapabilities.xml
   ```

2. The following lines show you the brief description for a coverage, extracted from the list returned:

```
<wcs:CoverageOfferingBrief>
  <wcs:description>A very rough imagery of North
  America</wcs:description>
  <wcs:name>nurc:Img_Sample</wcs:name>
  <wcs:label>North America sample imagery</wcs:label>
  <wcs:lonLatEnvelope srsName="urn:ogc:def:crs:OGC:1.3:CRS84">
    <gml:pos>-130.85168 20.7052</gml:pos>
    <gml:pos>-62.0054 54.1141</gml:pos>
  </wcs:lonLatEnvelope>
  <wcs:keywords>
    <wcs:keyword>WCS</wcs:keyword>
    <wcs:keyword>worldImageSample</wcs:keyword>
    <wcs:keyword>worldImageSample_Coverage</wcs:keyword>
  </wcs:keywords>
</wcs:CoverageOfferingBrief>
```

3. The `DescribeCoverage` operation lets you get a full description of it:

```
$ curl -XGET "http://localhost/geoserver/wcs?
service=wcs&version=1.0.0&request=DescribeCoverage
&Coverage=nurc:Img_Sample" -o describeCoverage.xml
```

4. Inside the description, the returned code contains a list of the supported data formats for the output:

```
<wcs:supportedFormats nativeFormat="WorldImage">
<wcs:formats>GeoTIFF</wcs:formats>
<wcs:formats>GIF</wcs:formats>
<wcs:formats>PNG</wcs:formats>
<wcs:formats>TIFF</wcs:formats>
</wcs:supportedFormats>
```

5. Now, we will retrieve the coverage. The `GetCoverage` operation retrieves it from GeoServer. Unlike the `GetFeatures` operation in WFS, a few parameters are mandatory. You have to specify the bounding box (`bbox`) and the `width` and `height` parameters. The `bbox` operator defines the geometrical extent you want to extract, while `width` and `height` define the image size:

```
$ curl -XGET "http://localhost/geoserver/wcs?
service=wcs&version=1.0.0&request=GetCoverage
&coverage=nurc:Img_Sample
&crs=EPSG:4326&bbox=-130.85168,20.7052,-62.0054,54.1141
```

```
&width=982&height=597&format=geotiff&bands=1"
-o coverage.tiff
```

6. If you open the `coverage.tiff` file with a picture viewer, you will see that it contains the same data as the original coverage:

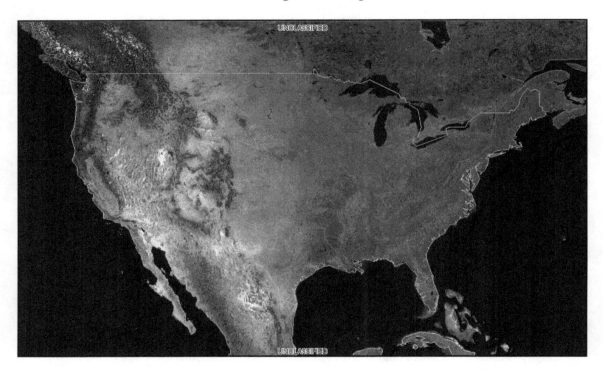

You learned the basics of retrieving raster data. If your project needs to process the raster data on the client side, it is very important that they are not transformed by the map server, as with WMS.

Advanced configuration - Database connection pooling

When discussing the data storage in `Chapter 4`, *Adding Your Data*, we explored several options. One of the best choices was using an RDBMS, in fact, PostgreSQL, with the PostGIS spatial extension.

Configuring spatial data from an RDBMS in your GeoServer requires you to create a connection setting for several parameters from the admin web interface. In fact, we did it when we loaded some data in PostGIS. Whatever database you are using, it may be useful to configure the connection using the **Java Naming and Directory Interface (JNDI)** standard.

For more information about JNDI, refer to the following websites:

http://en.wikipedia.org/wiki/Java_Naming_and_Directory_Interface

http://tomcat.apache.org/tomcat-8.5-doc/jndi-resources-howto.html

http://docs.oracle.com/javase/jndi/tutorial/

JNDI allows GeoServer and any Java application, in general, to access data just by using a predefined name.

In the following section, you will use JNDI to retrieve information about a JDBC data source from the servlet container.

Using JNDI, you can store all configuration information in the container, and also, the connections are not replicated. This can prove very useful when you have multiple instances on GeoServer in the same container, or when GeoServer is deployed along with other applications that need to access the database. In this case, all the database connections are instantiated and managed by Tomcat to avoid any component allocating resources connecting to the data.

Creating a connection pool

We are now going to create and configure a JNDI connection pool in Tomcat. It requires a few easy steps. Get your keyboard and follow the instructions:

1. Stop Tomcat using the following command:

```
$ sudo service tomcat stop
```

2. Move the JDBC PostgreSQL driver into the lib folder of Tomcat:

```
$ cd /opt/apache-tomcat-8.0.56/webapps/geoserver/WEB-INF/lib
$ sudo mv postgresql-9.4.1211.jar /opt/apache-tomcat-8.0.56/lib/.
```

3. Now, edit the Tomcat configuration file in order to set up the connection pool:

```
$ sudo vi /opt/apache-tomcat-8.0.56/conf/context.xml
```

4. Insert a new resource inside the `<Context>` tag:

```
<Context>
  <Resource
    name="jdbc/postgis"
    auth="Container"
    type="javax.sql.DataSource"
    driverClassName="org.postgresql.Driver"
    url="jdbc:postgresql://127.0.0.1:5432/gisdata"
    username="postgres"
    password="postgres"
    maxActive="20"
    maxIdle="10"
    maxWait="-1"/>
</Context>
```

5. Now, edit the GeoServer `web.xml` file:

```
$ sudo vi /opt/apache-tomcat-8.0.56/webapps/
  geoserver/WEB-INF/web.xml
```

6. Insert a new reference into the JNDI resource, paste the following code snippet at the end of the file inside the `<web-app>` tag, and then save and close the `web.xml` file:

```
<resource-ref>
  <description>PostGIS Datasource</description>
  <res-ref-name>jdbc/postgis</res-ref-name>
  <res-type>javax.sql.DataSource</res-type>
  <res-auth>Container</res-auth>
</resource-ref>
```

7. Start Tomcat.

8. Log in to the GeoServer web interface and create a new data store, select the
    PostGIS (JNDI) type, and populate the parameters according to the following
    screenshot. The most important value is the JNDI path to the database that lets
    the GeoServer identify the pool you want to use. This is the value you insert in
    the **jndiReferenceName** textbox:

Edit Vector Data Source

Edit an existing vector data source

PostGIS (JNDI)
PostGIS Database (JNDI)

Basic Store Info
Workspace *

Packt ▾

Data Source Name *

PostGISJNDI

Description

☑ Enabled

Connection Parameters
dbtype *

postgis

jndiReferenceName *

java:comp/env/jdbc/postgis

schema

Namespace *
https://www.packtpub.com/

---

9. Leave the other parameters unchanged and then click on the **Save** button. You will be presented with a list of spatial tables stored in the database for publishing them on the GeoServer:

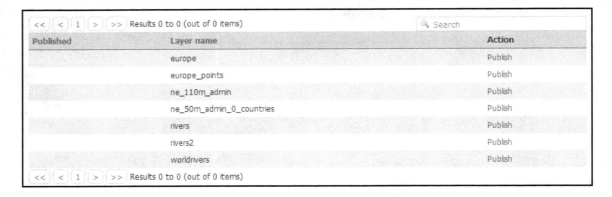

Advanced configuration - Monitoring GeoServer

In order to enhance the performance of your GeoServer, you may consider monitoring usage. Monitoring lets you know what the most used services and datasets are.

A low-level approach, and the simplest possible is to analyze the GeoServer logs and the web server logs. All requests are, in some way, tracked there, so it is just a matter of how to find a convenient way to extract and organize them in a structured data model.

Analyzing the logs may be quite challenging. Besides, according to the detail level, you may find too much information or totally miss the piece you are looking for.

Luckily, GeoServer developers have been working on a clever extension that helps you to analyze what requests GeoServer has been receiving. Unsurprisingly, it is called the Monitor Extension.

Installing and configuring the monitoring extension

Installing the monitoring extension is easy. You need to download two different packages. In the following steps, we will get them and install them on GeoServer. As usual, the installation process is the same on Windows or Linux, just modify the folder path according to your system. Let's do it:

1. Open your browser and point it to `http://geoserver.org/release/stable/`. In the miscellaneous section, you will find two packages; you need to download both the core and hibernate archive:

> **Miscellaneous**
>
> - Chart Symbolizer
> - Control Flow
> - Cross Layer Filtering
> - CSS Styling
> - CAS
> - Monitor (Core, Hibernate)
> - Importer (Core, BDB Backend)
> - INSPIRE
> - Printing
> - YSLD Styling

2. Download the two ZIP archives. Verify that the version number in the filenames is the same as the GeoServer WAR file you installed.

 If you do not remember your GeoServer release, you can look for it in the web admin interface at `http://localhost/geoserver/web/wicket/bookmarkable/org.ge oserver.web.AboutGeoServerPage`.

3. Stop your Tomcat instance, and then extract the contents of the ZIP archives into the `/WEB-INF/lib/` directory in the GeoServer `webapps` folder. For example, if you have deployed the GeoServer WAR file, you should place the control flow module's JAR file in `CATALINA_HOME/webapps/geoserver/WEB-INF/lib/`.

4. After extracting the extension, restart Tomcat in order for the changes to take effect. Open the GeoServer web interface and log in as the administrator. On the left panel, you will see a new section, as shown in the following screenshot:

5. Click on the Activity link; you will see a panel with four tabs. Now, all of them are empty, as you just installed the extension and there are no records in the monitor database:

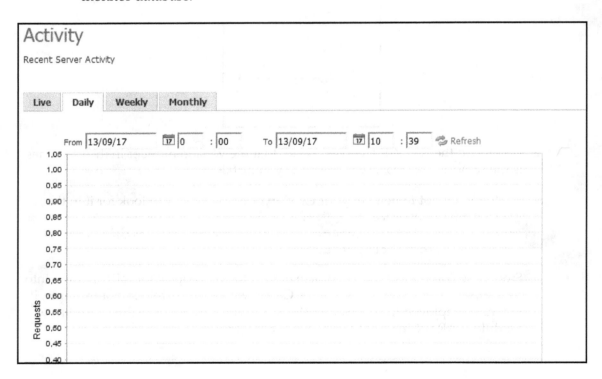

6. Open the GeoServer web interface and go to the **Layer Preview** section. Open the **OpenLayers** preview for some of the configured layers and browse the maps by panning and zooming.

7. After a while, turn back to the GeoServer web interface and go to the monitor section. Open the **Activity** link, click on the **Daily** tab, and you should see a graph of requests, as shown in the following screenshot:

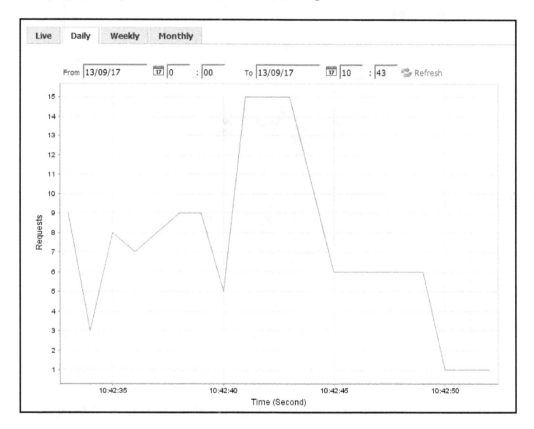

8. From the GeoServer web interface, go to the **Monitor** section on the left panel and click on the **Reports** link. Click on the **OWS Request Summary** link to open the preconfigured charts and go to the WMS tab. Here, you will find a chart that represents a proportion of each WMS operation, as shown in the following screenshot:

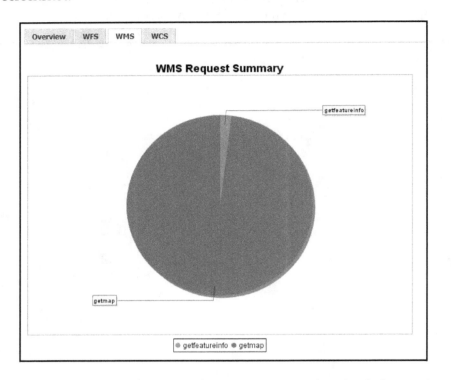

These simple reports are built using the information persisted; indeed, the services and operations are among the saved details.

A full reference of the captured information is available in the GeoServer official documentation at
`http://docs.geoserver.org/latest/en/user/extensions/monitoring/index.html`.

This is a good starting point if you plan to analyze the monitoring data using external tools and build your own stats and charts.

Getting help

Throughout this book, you have learned a lot about web mapping and GeoServer; however, being an ultimate reference is far outside of this book's scope.

When you are in trouble or simply curious about the new features, there are a lot of online resources that can help you. The project site (`http://geoserver.org`) contains a lot of information about GeoServer. Besides the basic features, you can find descriptions of the community modules which are plugins developed by the contributors to address specific requirements. Maybe you will find something really useful to you.

The project blog `http://blog.geoserver.org` announces new releases, ideas, and contributions. Your RSS feed reader can't miss it!

There are two mailing lists, one user-oriented and the other for developers, that are hosted on `sourceforge.net`. Information and links to the subscription point are at `http://geoserver.org/comm/`.

Another relevant source of information and help is at `http://gis.stackexchange.com`, although it is not GeoServer specific. You can find a large community of users and power users on StackExchange willing to help you. Several core developers also read the forum and often help to solve the users problems.

On both, you can ask for information about the software in general and about specific issues. Many core developers read both lists and you can get an answer that can save you from wasting your time. As with any other mailing list, some of the following rules may increase your chances of getting a solution to your problem:

- **Be specific**: If you write an email stating GeoServer does not seem to work, you can be sure that nobody will reply to you. You should describe a clear sequence to replicate your issue, also giving details about your configuration.
- **Be polite**: People on the lists are there to help you but are not at your service. Most of the time, they will do their best to find a solution for your issue, but, sometimes this cannot be done. It could be that nobody knows how to solve your issue or it is too complicated to be solved. If your issue requires a lot of coding, you cannot expect that someone will start working on it as soon as you post it on the lists.
- **Be collaborative**: If you have coding capabilities, you might try to build a patch for the issue and submit it to the source code repository. It will be checked and, hopefully, committed.

To report an issue, you should use the issue tracker at `http://geoserver.org/issues/`.

You need to register. It is free and you only have to insert a valid email address, and then you can report a new issue. Browsing for the current status is allowed for both registered and anonymous users.

Summary

In this final chapter, we gave a brief description of WFS and WCS--two different ways to serve spatial data on the Web. However, there is much more than this to the GeoServer project.

We will just mention the main features we did not cover in this book, such as the **Web Processing Service** (**WPS**), which is a standard protocol to invoke the geospatial processing services and time support for vector and raster data.

Whatever your needs in serving spatial data, GeoServer has an answer, or will have it soon!

Index

L

labels
    adding 186
    lines, labeling 188, 191
    points, labeling 186, 188
    polygons, labeling 191
latitude 9
layer group 201
layers
    grouping 201
    managing 292
    securing 311, 318
    seeding 260
    working with 291
Leaflet
    exploring 228
    map, creating 228, 231
    URL 127, 209
lines
    labeling 188, 191
LineString symbols
    about 170
    border, adding 171
    centerline, adding 171
    dashed lines, using 175
    dashing lines, mixing 177
    hatching, using 173
    markers, mixing 177
    simple line style, creating 170
Linux Mint
    Tomcat, configuring as service 45
longitude 9

M

map server 326
maps
    about 341
    choropleth maps 24
    colors, adding 24
    overview 31
    proportional maps 26
    thematic map, creating 27
Marlin rasterizer
    enabling 328

N

namespaces
    working with 269
national park boundaries, United States
    URL 248
native JAI
    installing 324, 325, 326
Natural Earth
    references 157
    URL 100, 116
Notepad++
    URL 66, 151

O

OGC Standards
    reference link 342
    URL 17
ogr2ogr tool
    URL 124
Open Geospatial Consortium (OGC) 14, 123
OpenLayers library 237
OpenLayers
    about 127
    GeoServer, integrating 217, 220
    KML, preview 73
    options, exploring 128
    parameters 127
    preview 71
    references 73
    tiled WMS, using 221
    tiles, using 255
    URL 209
    using 217
    WMS, mixing with WFS 223, 227
OpenStreetMap
    exploring 21, 23
    URL 21
Oracle Express Edition
    URL 120
Oracle JDBC
    URL 121
Oracle
    data, loading 123
    support, adding in GeoServer 120